JESUS

and the

MIRACLE

TRADITION

¶JESUS

and the

MIRACLE

TRADITION

Paul J. Achtemeier

CASCADE *Books* · Eugene, Oregon

JESUS AND THE MIRACLE TRADITION

Cascade Books
A Division of Wipf and Stock Publishers
199 W. 8th Ave., Suite 3
Eugene, OR 97401

ISBN 13: 978-1-59752-364-6

Cataloging-in-Publication data:

Achtemeier, Paul J.
Jesus and the miracle tradition / by Paul J. Achtemeier.

xviii + 256 p.; 23 cm.

ISBN 13: 978-1-59752-364-6

1. Bible. N.T. Gospels—Criticism, interpretation, etc. 2. Jesus Christ. 3. Miracles.
4. Apocryphal Gospels—Criticism, interpretation, etc. I. Title.

BS2555.2 A24 2008

Manufactured in the U.S.A.

To my colleagues in the guild
who have aided and encouraged me along the way

Contents

Preface

¶ WITH THE EXCEPTION OF THE FINAL ESSAY IN THIS VOLUME ("Miracles in the New Testament and in the Greco-Roman World"), the other essays have appeared in a variety of publications and periodicals. I am grateful to the editors of those publications for their permission to reproduce them here. While the essays appear substantially in the form in which they were originally published, the first essay ("Jesus and the Storm-Tossed Sea") has been significantly augmented with the addition of Ugaritic materials to supplement the original evidence drawn from the Babylonian Enuma Elish. This material was supplied by Dr. K. C. Hanson, and strengthens the argument made in this article, and for that help I am grateful. I am also indebted to Dr. Hanson who, as editor in chief of Wipf and Stock, proposed the present volume, and has been a steady and encouraging presence as the volume was assembled and edited. Thanks are also due Dr. Sandra M. Levy, both for encouragement, and help in the editing.

I must also express my thanks to my fellow scholars in the Society of Biblical Literature, who, early in my career, provided stimulus and support for my work in this area, and arranged an early outlet for publication with the appearance of the articles on the pre-Markan miracle catenae in the Journal of Biblical Literature. James M. Robinson and Robert W. Funk were particularly helpful in this regard, and I want to acknowledge my debt to them. The same point needs to be made about my colleagues in the Catholic Biblical Association, who similarly have offered encouragement and support over the years. Here, among many others, I must single out Raymond E. Brown and Joseph A. Fitzmyer, who have given friendship and scholarly guidance and inspiration through the years of our association. All scholars profit from such association with peers and superiors, and I am certainly among that group.

Introduction

¶ THE PROBLEM ADDRESSED IN THESE ARTICLES—HOW TO UNDER-
stand the miracle traditions of Jesus—remains timely. The reports of
Jesus' mighty acts continue to cause concern to preachers and scholars
alike, not only in terms of their possible historicity, but also in terms of
the meaning they had for those who handed them on and wrote them
down in the canonical Gospels.

While the historical question remains of interest to the articles in
this volume, sometimes more evident than at other times, the principle
task underlying the articles in this book is the attempt to determine the
meaning the miracles recorded of Jesus had for the earliest Christian
traditions, both in their canonical and pre-canonical forms, where
these latter can be recovered. Such a task requires understanding not
only the broad outlines of the theological traditions embodied in the
canonical Gospels, but also how the reports of the activity of other
miracle-workers were understood in the surrounding cultural milieu.

In order to understand the significance the reports of the mighty
acts of Jesus had for the early Christian tradents, literary-critical methods must be employed to isolate pre-canonical traditions concerning
the mighty acts of Jesus, both in their individual form, and, where that
seems indicated, in their pre-canonical collections. If we can detect a
development within these traditions from their pre-canonical to their
canonical form, we can gain insight both into the way those early traditions dealt with the miracle stories, as well as how those stories were
incorporated into the proclamation of the words and deeds of Jesus as
they are found in the canonical Gospels.

The essays included in this volume were selected as examples
of some specific problems faced in considering these early Christian
miracle traditions, rather than for any attempt at a complete survey of
the canonical materials dealing with Jesus' mighty acts. Analyses of in-

dividual miracle stories, for example, are drawn exclusively from Mark, while a broader consideration of the use of such traditions within a Gospel is limited to Mark and Luke. These limitations are partly due to the prevailing scholarly situation—at the time they were written, the miracle traditions contained in Matthew had been more adequately covered than those found in Mark and Luke—and partly to my view that Mark, as the earliest of the Gospels, gives most promise of gaining perspective on the possible form miracle stories assumed prior to their later form found in the canonical Gospels.

With respect to the essays that deal with three individual miracle stories in Mark, the first ("Jesus and the Storm-Tossed Sea") indicates some of the theological background to the report of Jesus' miracles furnished by the pre-Christian traditions as mediated through Hebrew Scripture—in this instance particularly Genesis, Job, Psalms, and Isaiah. The use of ancient Semitic and other near-eastern materials shows how the narration of Jesus' stilling the stormy sea reflects traditions associated with the divine creation of the world and the redemption of Israel, indicating the theological framework within which this particular mighty event of Jesus is to be understood. The essays on Miracles and Discipleship (7) and Miracles and the historical Jesus (6) attempt to isolate the pre-canonical form of these two stories (Mark 9:14–29 and 10:46–52), in an effort to determine how a story of a mighty act of Jesus was employed in the tradition to make a theological point (7), and how such a story must be dealt with if it is to furnish reliable historical evidence concerning Jesus of Nazareth (6).

Three further essays examine the way the miracle traditions are employed in a given canonical Gospel, in this instance Luke and Mark, to determine how they aid in gaining perspective on the broader theological outlook of the Gospel author. The essay concerning the Lukan Perspective on the Miracles of Jesus (2) seeks to show how the framework Luke provided for the miracle stories he reports, affects the way they are to be understood within the larger portrait of Jesus' mission. Surprising is the fact that such an adaptation of miracle reports seems not to reflect the broader Lukan theological themes as they have been developed by Hans Conzelmann and others. The two essays on the Markan use of miracle traditions propose a possible pre-Markan collection of miracle stories (4: "Toward the Isolation of Pre-Markan Miracle Catenae"), the use of which then illustrates some of the theological points the author of the canonical Gospel sought to make (5: "The Origin and Function of the Pre-Markan Miracle Catenae").

The three remaining essays consider the way in which miracle traditions were conveyed and dealt with in the non-Christian milieu within which the Gospel miracle traditions developed. In the examination of the Gospel Miracle Tradition and the Divine Man (3), the cultural setting of the stories of Jesus' mighty acts is examined, as well as the fate of miracle stories about Jesus and the apostles in non-Gospel literature, canonical and post-canonical. Remarkably, while miracles reported of Jesus' followers proliferated, miracles told of Jesus did not. This same phenomenon is then examined in more detail in the apocryphal New Testament (8: "Jesus and the Disciples as Miracle-workers in the Apocryphal New Testament") with the same results, which call into question the widely accepted conclusion that miracle reports were late in entering the tradition, but then proliferated as the tradition developed. If miracles of Jesus did not proliferate in the post-canonical tradition, and if the later canonical Gospels have proportionately less space devoted to such miracle stories than do the earlier ones, one must then reckon not with a later entry, and proliferation, but with an early entry into the tradition, and a reticence to increase emphasis on such stories. The implications for the historical Jesus as wonder-worker are evident from such a trend within the tradition.

The final article, appearing here for the first time in print, surveys literature dealing with wondrous acts in the New Testament as well as the Greco-Roman world (9), indicating the form such accounts assumed in Jewish, and in secular accounts. It is clear from such a comparison that the form the stories assumed in the canonical tradition is much closer to the Greco-Roman than to the Jewish form.

The evidence assembled in these essays, and conclusions drawn from that evidence indicates that stories of the mighty acts of Jesus of Nazareth may have played a larger role in the earliest traditions assembled concerning him than often assumed, and that Jesus as worker of miracles may need to be reconsidered in any attempt at a historical portrait. The Jesus of the earliest tradition was clearly much more than simply inspired storyteller and inspiring teacher. What he did may have been as important to the early tradition as what he said for understanding the theological meaning of his career.

Abbreviations

Ancient

'Abod. Zar.	*'Abodah Zarah*
Acts Andr.	*Acts of Andrew*
Acts Andr. Mth.	*Acts of Andrew and Matthias*
Acts Barn.	*Acts of Barnabas*
Acts John	*Acts of John*
Acts Paul	*Acts of Paul and Thecla*
Acts Pet.	*Acts of Peter*
Acts of Pet. Paul	*Acts of Peter and Paul*
Acts Pil.	*Acts of Pilate*
Acts Thad.	*Acts of Thaddaeus*
Acts Thom.	*Acts of Thomas*
Actus Ver.	*Actus Vercellenses*
Ant.	Josephus, *Antiquitates judaicae* (Antiquities of the Judeans)
1 Apol.	Justin, *First Apology*
2 Apol.	Justin, *Second Apology*
(Arab.) Gos. Inf.	*Arabic Gospel of the Infancy*
b.	Babylonian Talmud (*Babli*)
B. Bat.	*Baba Batra*
Ber.	*Berakot*
B. Meṣiʿa	*Baba Meṣiʿa*
B. Qam.	*Baba Qamma*
Cels.	Origen, *Contra Celsum* (Against Celsus)
Clem. Hom.	*Clementine Homilies*
D	Codex Bezae (Cantabrigiensis)
Dial.	Justin, *Dialogus cum Tryphone* (Dialog with Trypho)
Ep. Apos.	*Epistula Apostolorum*
Ep. Barn.	*Epistle of Barnabas*
'Erub.	*'Erubin*
Giṭ.	*Giṭṭin*
Gos. Bart.	*Gospel of Bartholomew*
Gos. Eb.	*Gospel of the Ebionites*
Gos. Eg.	*Gospel of the Egyptians*
Gos. Heb.	*Gospel of the Hebrews*

Gos. Nic.	*Gospel of Nicodemus*
Gos. Phil.	*Gospel of Philip*
Gos. Thom.	*Gospel of Thomas*
Gos. Truth	*Gospel of Truth*
Haer.	Irenaeus, *Adversus haereses* (Against Heresies)
Hist.	Tacitus, *Historiae* (Histories)
Hist. eccl.	Eusebius, *Historia ecclesiastica* (Ecclesiastical History)
Incar.	Athanasius, *De incarnatione* (On the Incarnation)
Inf. Gos. Thom.	*Infancy Gospel of Thomas*
Life	Philostratus, *Life of Apollonius*
Lives	Suetonius, *The Lives of the Caesars*
LXX	Septuagint
m.	Mishnah
Meʿil.	*Meʿilah*
Metam.	Apuleius, *Metamorphoses* (The Golden Ass)
Metam.	Ovid, *Metamorphoses*
Nat. hist.	Pliny, *Naturalis historia* (Natural History)
NT	New Testament
OT	Old Testament
Peregr.	Lucian, *De morte Peregrini* (The Death of Peregrinus)
Pesah.	*Pesaḥim*
P. Heid.	Papyrus Heidelberg
Philops.	Lucian, *Philopseudas*
P. Oxy.	Oxyrhynchus Papyri
Qidd.	*Qiddushin*
1QSa	*Rule of the Congregation* (Appendix a to 1QS)
R.	rabbi
Recog. Clem.	*Recognitions of Clement*
Sanh.	*Sanhedrin*
Shabb.	*Shabbat*
Sib. Or.	*Sibylline Oracles*
Taʿan.	*Taʿanit*
War	Josephus, *Bellum judaicum* (Judean War)
Yebam.	*Yebamot*

Modern

ANF	Ante-Nicene Fathers
ANT	*Apocryphal New Testament: A Collection of Apocryphal Christian Literature in an English Translation.* Edited by J. K. Elliott. Oxford: Clarendon, 1993
BHT	Beiträge zur historischen Theologie
BibSt	Biblische Studien
BWANT	Beiträge zur Wissenschaft vom Alten und Neuen Testament
CBQ	*Catholic Biblical Quarterly*
CQ	*Congregational Quarterly*
ETL	*Ephemerides theologicae lovanienses*

ExpTim	*Expository Times*
FoiVie	*Foi et Vie*
HTR	*Harvard Theological Review*
Int	*Interpretation*
JBL	*Journal of Biblical Literature*
JJS	*Journal of Jewish Studies*
LCL	Loeb Classical Library
LS	*Louvain Studies*
NovTSup	Novum Testamentum Supplements
NTA	*New Testament Apocrypha*. Rev. ed. Edited by Wilhelm Schneemelcher. 2 vols. Louisville: Westminster John Knox, 1991–92
NTAbh	Neutestamentliche Abhandlung
NTD	Das Neue Testament Deutsch
NTL	New Testament Library
NTS	*New Testament Studies*
PW	A. F. Pauly and G. Wissowa, editors. *Real-Encyclopädie der classischen Altertumswissenschaft*
RGG[1]	*Die Religion in Geschichte und Gegenwart*. Edited by Hermann Gunkel and Otto Scheel. 5 vols. Tübingen: Mohr/Siebeck, 1909–1913
RGG[2]	*Die Religion in Geschichte und Gegenwart*. Edited by Alfred Bertholet et al. 5 vols. Tübingen: Mohr/Siebeck, 1927–1931
RGG[3]	*Die Religion in Geschichte und Gegenwart*. Edited by Kurt Galling. 7b vols. Tübingen: Mohr/Siebeck, 1957–1965
SBLMS	Society of Biblical Literature Monograph Series
SBT	Studies in Biblical Theology
SE	*Studia Evangelica*
SJT	*Scottish Journal of Theology*
SNTSMS	Society for New Testament Study Monograph Series
SO	Symbolae osloenses
ST	*Studia Theologica*
THNT	Theologischer Handkommentar zum Neuen Testament
TUGAL	*Texte und Untersuchungen zur Geschichte der altchristlichen Literatur*
WMANT	Wissenschaftliche Monographien zum Alten und Neuen Testament
ZNW	*Zeitschrift für die neutestamentliche Wissenschaft*
ZTK	*Zeitschrift für Theologie und Kirche*

Jesus *and the* Storm-Tossed Sea   1

❡ THE PRESENCE OF MIRACLE STORIES IN THE GOSPEL TRADITIONS has, on occasion, been the source of some embarrassment for New Testament students. Various attempts have been made, some more, some less successful, to explain them or explain them away. Some argue that these stories arose late, and thus may safely be disregarded. Others give the impression, tacitly, at least, that such stories contribute little to our understanding of the mission and message of Jesus that we cannot gain, perhaps even in a less distorted form, from the other traditions about him. Yet even a hasty reading of the Gospels indicates that miracle stories do play an important role in these writings. In Mark, the earliest Gospel, for example, about one-third of the material concerns itself with the miraculous. In the first ten chapters, where the bulk of the account of Jesus' activity is reported (apart from the last week), almost one-half of the material is devoted to accounts of, or allusions to, miracles (about 200 of the approximately 425 verses). In short, the miracles of Jesus cannot be dismissed as something peripheral to the Gospel traditions. The early Christians who put together our Gospels apparently shared with the traditions with which they worked the conviction that miracle stories were essential to any account of the career of Jesus of Nazareth.

While much can and has been said with respect to the significance of miracle stories in the Gospel traditions, let two observations suffice for the present. First, it must be pointed out that the fact that miracles are recorded of Jesus in no way makes him unique for his age. The fact that Jesus performed miracles, or that miracles could be reported of him, does not in itself prove his uniqueness. Similarly miraculous acts are reported of many of his contemporaries, Jewish and Gentile alike. Rudolf Bultmann, in his work on form criticism, has assembled a large amount of material that indicates the relative commonness of miracle-stories in Jesus' time.[1] Thus, whatever miracles as such would prove about Jesus, they would also prove about a number of his contemporaries.

Secondly, one cannot avoid the impression that the Gospel traditions themselves understood the basically neutral character of the miraculous. That is to say, witnessing a miracle performed by Jesus would not convince a person that Jesus unquestionably was the Son of God. Quite the contrary. In one instance at least, a miracle of Jesus proved to his contemporaries that he was working, not at the behest of God, but of the Devil (Mark 3:22)! The fact of miracles as such, then, does not make Jesus unique for his age, nor does it constitute irrefutable proof that he was God's Son.

This, in turn, means that we must look elsewhere to find the significance that the miracles had for the Gospel traditions. A careful study of the miracles will indicate that the significance lies, not in the acts themselves but in the *person* who performs them. Therefore, Jesus does not draw significance from the fact that he performs miracles; rather, the miracles are significant because they are performed by Jesus, who is the Son of God. This is illustrated in the account of Jesus stilling the storm (Mark 4:35–41). The reaction of the disciples to this miracle—"Who then is this?"—indicates that it was the person of Jesus which holds the significance.

To understand the kind of significance his person holds, however, it is necessary to see this pericope in the light of the OT and the Semitic mentality. That this is the case is indicated by the story itself. It is apparent, as Ernst Lohmeyer has suggested,[2] that the language of this pericope has a Semitic coloring. This is shown both in the idiomatic structure of the language used ("feared with a great fear," v. 41, is a Semitic form), and by the fact that vv. 37b–41 can be arranged in the kind of parallel forms that are characteristic of Semitic poetry. Again, the fact that the disciples' astonishment is based on their observation that "even *wind and sea* obey him" points again to the OT, and the sig-

---

1. Bultmann, *History*, 231–38.
2. Lohmeyer, *Markus*, 89.

nificance played in it by such concepts as "sea," "the deeps," the "many waters," and the like.[3]

In fact, the sea had a religious significance that spread far beyond the borders of ancient Israel. We have abundant evidence to conclude that Israel shared many of these ideas about the sea with the religious traditions of her neighbors, and especially the Babylonians and people of Ugarit. Thus, before we can understand the significance of the sea in the OT, it is necessary to look briefly at two forms of this tradition, the form it takes in a Babylonian epic, *Enuma Elish,* and in the Ugaritic Baal cycle of stories.

This Babylonian epic contains accounts of the origins of the Babylonian gods, and along with them, an account of the creation of the world. The hero of this epic is Marduk, who becomes involved in a desperate battle on behalf of some of the gods, with a dragon named Tiamat, the goddess of the sea.

> . . . valiant Marduk
>
> Strengthened his hold on the vanquished gods,
>
> And turned back to Tiamat whom he had bound.
>
> The lord trod on the legs of Tiamat,
>
> With his unsparing mace he crushed her skull.
>
> . . .
>
> Then the lord paused to view her dead body,
>
> That he might divide the monster and do artful works.
>
> He split her like a shellfish into two parts:
>
> Half of her he set up and ceiled it as sky,
>
> Pulled down the bar and posted guards. (IV:126–39)[4]

Half of this dragon he causes to form an arch, which becomes the sky, holding back the primeval waters from above; the other half, stretched out beneath the arch, he makes into the land. In this way, he creates an open space in the midst of the primeval waters. At the proper places, he sets up guards to insure that the sea does not escape its newly-prescribed bounds.

For the Babylonians, then, creation results from the victory of their chief god over the sea dragon, who is the personification of the

3. See Malina, "Assessing."

4. Speiser in *ANET,* 67.

chaotic primeval sea. Creation is achieved by the overcoming of the forces of chaos. Along with virtually all the people of the ancient Near East, therefore, the Babylonians felt that the world exists in the midst of these chaotic waters, which surround the cosmos above and below. Within this vast, chaotic water-mass, the world represents almost a bubble, suspended in the midst.

At Ugarit, Baal is the storm god who also creates the earth. He does this by defeating his foe, the god of the sea, Prince Sea (*Yamm*)—also called Judge River (*Nahar*). After Kothar-wa-Ḥassis, the craftsman of the gods, makes him war clubs, Baal attacks his enemy:

> The club swoops in the hand of Baal,
>> Like an eagle between his fingers;
> It strikes the pate of Prince [Yamm],
>> Between the eyes of Judge Nahar.
> Yamm collapses,
>> He falls to the ground;
> His joints bend,
>> His frame breaks.
> Baal would rend, would smash Yamm,
>> Would annihilate Judge Nahar. (UT 68:24–28)[5]

In *Enuma Elish* Tiamat is split in two, and in the Baal cycle Yamm is torn apart. This is the general view of cosmology found in the OT. For the OT, as for the ancient Near East, the cosmos is surrounded by the waters of the primeval sea, in the midst of which there is a place for dry land. There is water above the firmament, as there is beneath the earth. Thus, when the author of Genesis describes the flood, he reports that God simply let the water come down from above and up from below. In Gen 7:11, describing this, he affirms that "on that day all the fountains of the great deep burst forth [that is, coming up from underneath] and the windows of the heavens were opened [that is, to let it come down from above]." When the flood is over (Gen 8:2), God seals up the fountains and closes the windows of heaven. That is to say, when God wants to destroy the earth, he simply ceases to restrain the chaotic waters. He lets the earth return to its watery chaos, a sort of creation in reverse. That is why the flood is such a terrible thing: it is

---

5. Ginsburg in *ANET,* 131.

God's renunciation of the work of creation by ceasing to withhold the forces of chaos. For that reason, God's promise (covenant) to Noah never again to flood the earth is so important: it represents his promise not again to let chaos reinvade the earth. This same cosmology—water above and below—is behind the phrase "the waters under the earth" (Exod 20:4), and informs a number of the Psalms (74:13; 104:5–6; and others).

The OT reflects more than simply the general cosmological picture found in the Babylonian traditions, however. The forms by which creation is described in the OT also bear no little resemblance to those traditions.

Philological evidence in Gen 1:2 points in this direction as well, as scholars have long recognized. This verse reads: "And the earth was waste and void [וֹהבוּ וֹהת; *tohu wabohu*], and darkness was upon the face of the deep [תְהוֹם; *tehom*]." The key words in this verse are the words that describe this primeval chaos out of which the earth was formed. The words designating waste and void (*tohu* and *bohu*) show by their form that they belong to the "old vocabulary of the language."[6] While the derivation of these words is uncertain (*tohu* from *tehom*? *bohu* from the Babylonian god Bau or Phoenecian Baau?), in the light of the Babylonian epic it is not impossible that these words derive from the names of certain chaos minor deities in Tiamat's army, although this remains, until future confirmation from sources, pure speculation.[7]

These two words (*tohu* and *bohu*) are used in Gen 1:2 with the word *tehom* (deep). This word is quite apparently directly related to the name of the Babylonian goddess of chaos, Tiamat (through the similarity of consonants, the basic letters of Semitic languages). As scholars have long suggested, there seems little question that in this verse of the creation story, there is reference to that ancient Babylonian legend, now totally reshaped into a doctrine of creation by the word of Yahweh.

In addition to philological relationships, the OT also reflects these ancient Akkadian-Babylonian and Ugaritic traditions in its picture of creation seen in terms of God's conquest of the primeval chaos-dragon (*tiamat—tehom*; also reflected, if indirectly, in Gen 1:2). Isaiah, for example, indicates this:

6. Dillmann, *Genesis*, 1:57.

7. See Gunkel, *Genesis*, 104–5; idem, *Creation and Chaos*, 6–7.

> Awake, awake, put on strength,
>> arm of the LORD!
> Awake, as in the days of old,
>> the generations of long ago.
> Was it not thou that didst cut Rahab[8] in pieces,
>> that didst pierce the dragon? (Isa 51:9)

One is reminded here of the fact that Marduk cut Tiamat into pieces and Baal cut Yamm at the time of creation. Again, Ps 74, in discussing creation, proclaims,

> You divided the sea by your might;
>> you broke the heads of the dragons in the waters.
> You crushed the heads of Leviathan.[9] (Ps 74:13–14a)

One is again reminded of the fact that Marduk, in his battle with Tiamat, crushes her skull (IV:130). Psalm 89, in the context of God's creation of the world from chaotic waters, announces, "You crushed Rahab like a carcass" (v. 10a). Job also reflects this legend. Job 9:8 can read that God "alone stretched out the heavens, and trampled the back of the sea dragon (margin)." And in Job 26:12–13, the author refers, again in the context of creation from chaotic waters, to God smiting Rahab, and to God's hand piercing the fleeing serpent. Thus, in the OT, the chaos out of which God brought the order of the world is at times spoken of in terms of a chaos-dragon, which represents the primeval, chaotic waters.

Again, the act of setting limits beyond which the waters cannot pass, present in the Babylonian epic, is also reflected in the OT. Here again it is Yahweh who prescribed the limits for the chaos-sea, limits beyond which it dare not go. Thus, Job can complain to an over-watchful God that he, Job, is not "the sea, or a sea monster," needing such continual watching (7:12). The Psalms also contain such allusions. Psalm 33:7 declares that at the time of creation, God "gathered the waters of the sea [הַיָּם; ha-yam] as in a bottle; he put the deeps [תְּהוֹמוֹת; tehomoth] in storehouses." Again, Ps 104:9 says that "you set a bound that they [viz. the seas] should not pass, so that they might not again

---

8. Rahab is another OT name for the sea-dragon; see Spronk, "Rahab."

9. Leviathan is another name for the chaos-dragon; see Uehlinger, "Leviathan."

cover the earth." The same concepts are also reflected in Prov 8:28 and Job 38:9–11, to mention but two more.

It is clear, therefore, that one of the ways in which the OT understood creation—indeed, it would seem the dominant way—was in terms of God's conquest of chaos, pictured in terms of overcoming a chaos-dragon. By conquering this chaos-dragon, God first brought forth the orderly world out of the primeval chaotic seas.[10]

Therefore, it is no accident that in the book where the final end is described, the Book of Revelation in the New Testament, the enemy of God, and thus of his Son, is a dragon! It is further small wonder that this dragon (δράκων) arises out of the sea (13:1–10; cf. also 12:7–17). That which threatens the work of God's Son, and the existence of his faithful people, is pictured in the form of a monstrous serpent. These are not accidental details. The author knows and understands the tradition within which he stands. The author of Revelation understood, as did the author of Daniel (7:1–9), that creation means God's triumph over chaos, and he understood that this chaos, pictured in the form of dragons that arise from the sea, is God's ultimate enemy. The final end cannot come, creation is not finally safe from the threat of chaos, until that chaos-dragon, that last enemy, is defeated.[11]

It is further significant that in that great vision of the new heaven and new earth, which come down only after the dragon is finally vanquished, the sea is once again mentioned. "Then I saw a new heaven and a new earth; for the first heaven and the first earth had passed away, and the sea [θάλασσα] was no more" (Rev 21:1). No more sea, no more chaos, no more threat to God's orderly world! And this can happen only when the sea dragon, the chaos-monster, whom Revelation names Satan, the Devil—only when that one is finally and completely conquered. "And the sea was no more"—the threat of chaos is banished, the redeemed creation rests secure.

In the light of this brief discussion of the significance of the sea in the OT, it is instructive to look again at the account of Jesus stilling the sea. In the light of this OT background, there are at least three points at which one can perhaps begin to see the deep significance this pericope apparently had for the Gospel traditions.

---

10. See Fisher, "Chaos."

11. See Gunkel, *Creation and Chaos*, 115–250.

The first point must center on Jesus' act in this pericope: stilling a storm-tossed sea. Jesus, in this account, is doing what, in the OT, God alone can do. Consider Ps 107:28–29:

> Then they [sailors in a stormy sea] cried to the LORD in their
>   trouble,
>   and he delivered them from their distress;
> he made the storm be still,
>   and the waves of the sea were hushed.

The similarity to the account in Mark is striking: men in trouble on a stormy sea cry to their Lord, who stills the sea and thus delivers them. But in the Psalm, it is *God* who does this! Similarly Ps 89:9:

> You rule the raging of the sea;
>   when its waves rise, thou stillest them.

Here again, it is God who stills the raging sea. Small wonder, then, that the disciples were astonished: Jesus in this pericope is doing what in the OT God alone can do. Small wonder that they ask who this man is, whom wind and sea obey, for this man is doing what only God can do: he stills chaotic waters.

Secondly, it is of no small significance that the sea in the OT represents the powers of chaos. God's creative power is seen in his stilling of the primeval, chaotic sea. Is it not significant that, in a similar way, with a word (!) Jesus here stills a chaotic sea? God, says the OT, created the world by overcoming the chaotic sea; Jesus in this pericope rescues his disciples by similarly stilling the raging sea. This understanding is reinforced when one considers the fact that, in the OT, God's work of creation and his work of redemption are so closely linked. Consider again Ps 74, where God is described as dividing the sea, and as breaking the head of the dragons in that act of creation (vv. 13–14). That section begins with praise of God as the worker of *salvation!*

> Yet God my King is from of old,
>   working salvation in the midst of the earth.
> You divided the sea by your might;
>   you broke the heads of the dragons in the waters.
> You crushed the heads of Leviathan;
>   you gave him as food for the creatures of the earth.
> (Ps 74:12–14)

In an Ugaritic text, the goddess Anat claims she crushed "Shalyat, the seven-headed serpent" (UT V AB D:38–39).

And in what is perhaps the most interesting example of all, Isa 51:9–10, the author identifies the act of dividing the waters at the time of creation with the act of dividing the waters to redeem his people from bondage in Egypt:

> Was it not thou that didst cut Rahab in pieces,
>> that didst pierce the dragon?
> Was it not thou that didst dry up the sea,
>> the waters of the great deep [*tehom!*]?

Up to this point, the author rather clearly has described the act of creation, but in the verse following, he moves, without indication, into a description of God's saving act at the time of the Exodus: "that didst make the depths of the sea *a way for the redeemed to pass over?*" Here the decisive act of creation—overcoming chaos—is linked to what the OT sees as the decisive act of redemption—the deliverance from Egypt. Here, clearly, redemption and creation are seen in the same light. In fact, as Exod 15:8 and Isa 63:12–13 indicate, Israel understood its redemption in terms of a creative act that was paralleled only by God's original act of creation, when he overcame the primeval chaos.

Similarly, with the appearance of the new heaven and new earth in Revelation, chaos is utterly defeated; but that defeat grows directly out of Christ's redemptive act on the cross. Not until that redemptive act has been completed can creation finally be secured against its arch-enemy, chaos. Therefore, is it not possible that in this story of the stilling of the storm, the early tradition saw that Christ, by his redemptive presence, secures God's creation from its arch foe, chaos? Just as God defeated chaos in his act of creation, an act paralleled by his redemption of Israel, so here Jesus also defeats that symbol of chaos, the stormy sea, in the course of his redemptive life. Jesus is continuing that careful watch over the threat of chaos to which Job referred (7:12)! Finally, it is interesting to note that Mark uses the same word to describe the calming of the storm (ἐκόπασεν, 4:39) that the Septuagint uses to describe the calming of the chaotic flood waters (Gen 8:1).

Thirdly, this miracle demonstrates that in the presence of Jesus, the demonic is defeated. This is indicated, as many commentators have noted, by the words Jesus uses to still the storm. In Mark 4:39, Jesus "rebuked" the storm and told it to "be still." These are the same words that Jesus employed to cast out a demon in Capernaum (Mark 1:25). There is, apparently, no difference in the way Jesus deals with a demon causing illness and the way he deals with the storm. Both are dealt with in the same way because, it would appear, both are caused by the same element: the enemy of God and Christ, the demonic. It is instructive in this light to recall how closely the forces of chaos are linked in the OT to the dragon that God overcame, and then to recall that in Revelation, the dragon, the chaos-monster rising from the sea, is given the name "Satan," the prince of demons. In short, Jesus is combating and defeating the demonic powers when he stills the storm just as he does when he exorcises a demon. In both instances, he is overcoming the demonic element it was his purpose to destroy, because that element is at enmity with God, and therefore with God's creature, man. This the demons recognize, and they often give voice to this recognition with the question: Have you come now to destroy us? Or with the cry that Jesus has come to torment them (Mark 1:24; 5:7). The demons know that with the presence of Jesus, their defeat is near, a defeat mirrored as surely by the stilling of a storm as by their being cast out of a man.

Thus, with the presence of Jesus, the final victory of God over the powers of darkness is, in fact, present; with him the victory of God over evil and its prince, begun with the creation, is about to be consummated. With the coming of Jesus, the powers of darkness have received their death blow, and can only beg to inhabit pigs where once they could inhabit man himself. Thus, the miracle of the stilling of the storm indicates in part what the cross, with the resurrection, indicates supremely: in Jesus, the power of God can and does conquer the powers of darkness arrayed against him. The same power of God at work in the resurrection was also at work in the wondrous deeds of the earthly Jesus. The demonic is defeated as surely in these events as in its self-betrayal in the crucifixion of Jesus (1 Cor 2:8).

Small wonder then, that the disciples in that storm-tossed boat, suddenly becalmed, reacted as they did: "Who then is this, that even wind and sea obey him?" (Mark 4:41). Who is this man, that in him even the primeval forces of demonic chaos find their master?

The Lukan Perspective
on the Miracles *of* Jesus 2

¶ THE PROBLEM OF THE WAY LUKE VIEWED AND USED THE MIRACLES of Jesus is a subject that has remained remarkably innocent of systematic treatment in recent biblical scholarship. Conzelmann, in his epoch-making redaction-critical study, devoted only three pages to this problem, and although Held does on occasion refer to the Lukan miracles, it is only to gain a clearer perspective on the way Matthew employed the traditions about Jesus' miracles, his actual theme.[1] Periodical literature has been equally sparse. The few articles that have been written deal primarily with the way in which miracles function within the narrative of Acts.[2] There is, in short, no serious redaction-critical study of the Lukan miracle-stories of which I am aware, and it is at that point that this preliminary sketch finds its place.

As the title indicates, the emphasis will fall on the miracles of Jesus, and since none are reported in Acts (they are referred to only twice, 2:22 and 10:38), material from that second volume of Luke's "History of Primitive Christianity" will be used only occasionally. We shall consider, first, the methods to be used in this kind of study, and shall then proceed to outline the results of the application of such methods. A brief summary of our conclusions will then be appended.

METHODS OF APPROACH

As far as the number of miracles reported of Jesus is concerned, both Luke and Matthew have proportionately fewer than Mark. By my count,

1. Conzelmann, *Mitte*, 165–67. Held, "Matthew as Interpreter."
2. E.g., Fenton, "Order of the Miracles"; Ferguson, "Thoughts on Acts"; Harden, "Miracle Narratives." There are, of course, remarks on Jesus' miracles in the commentaries on Luke, but not in the context of any systematic attempt at a redaction-critical judgment.

Mark has 18 miracle-stories and 4 summaries of miraculous activity, Luke has 20 stories and 3 summaries, and Matthew has 19 stories and 4 summaries. But since Mark is only about 57% of the length of Luke, and 63% the length of Matthew, it is apparent that miracles occupy a larger proportion of the total narrative in Mark than in either of the other two.

	Miracle Stories	Miracle Summaries
Mark	18	4
Matthew	19	4
Luke	20	3

Luke has also been selective in his use of Mark's miracle-narratives, having omitted six of them (Mark 6:45–52; 7:24–30; 7:31–37; 8:1–10; 8:22–26 and 11:12–14, 20) and adding eight of his own (5:1–11; 7:1–10; 7:11–17; 11:14; 17:11–19; 22:50–51; two others, while vaguely reminiscent of Mark 3:1–6, are sufficiently different, in my judgment, to be considered independent stories: 13:10–17; 14:1–6). Five of the six miracles which Luke has omitted occur in the "Great Omission" (Mark 6:45—8:26),[3] and the sixth is the cursing of the fig tree.[4] Luke is thus no more bound to the Markan miracle-traditions than he is to the other Markan materials and is as free in adding miracle-stories as he is in adding parables.

One of the miracles that Luke adds came from "Q" (7:1–10), although, as we shall see, the emphasis is different from that of the story in Matthew. Others may also have come from "Q" but since none are included in Matthew, we have no way of learning which, if any, did. Two of the stories are more concerned with the correct interpretation of the law than with the miracle (13:10–17; 14:1–6), and another wants to contrast the Jews' lack of faith with that of non-Jews (17:11–19; in

3. The reasons for this omission have long puzzled scholars. I have suggested elsewhere that Luke, perhaps aware of the two miracle-catenae that Mark had incorporated into his gospel, simply omitted the second catena, the contents of which roughly parallel Luke's omitted Markan material (see chapter 4: "Isolation").

4. Luke may have thought it unworthy of Jesus, although he is not averse in principle to punitive miracles; cf. Acts 5:1–10; 13:8–12. In that same section, he also omits mention of Jesus leaving Jerusalem after the temple-cleansing (cf. Mark 11:19; Matt 21:17), although he knows that is what Jesus did (Luke 21:37).

this case a Samaritan), a point made in other stories in the Gospel (e.g., 10:30–35) and in Acts (13:36; 18:6; 19:8–9; 28:28). The call of Peter is set around a miracle in Luke (5:1–11), perhaps to emphasize that his preeminence came from being first to be called, as well as first to see the risen Lord (24:34), since the story bears similarities to a Johannine story of an appearance of the risen Lord (John 21:4–8). Another miracle is used to introduce the account of a controversy over miracles (11:14), characteristic of Luke, who likes to report miracles performed when miracles are discussed (see 7:21); and still another is so obvious (22:51, the healing of the ear of the high-priest's servant) that one wonders how the other evangelists could have avoided it. The final story to be mentioned concerns Jesus' raising of a dead youth (7:11–17), an activity known both to Mark (5:35, 42) and "Q" (Matt 11:5), and hence not in itself an unusual story.[5]

One way of getting at the Lukan perspective on Jesus' miracles is thus to compare what he includes as miracle stories with those included in one of his sources, viz., Mark. Another method of learning how Luke understood and used miracle-stories of Jesus is to compare what he did with the stories that he took from the source we have, again, Mark. A careful comparison will show, for example, that Luke attempts to remove ambiguities in the Markan narrative. For example, in his treatment of Mark 1:21–28, Luke makes it clear that the adverbial phrase κατ᾽ ἐξουσίαν (with authority) is related to ἐπιτάσσει (commands), eliminating the alternative possibility in Mark that it is related to διδαχὴ καινή ([a new teaching] Mark 1:27). Again, Luke clears up the question inherent in Mark 1:45 (Who couldn't enter cities? Jesus? The healed leper?), by making it clear that Jesus remained in the wilderness (5:16). Again, Luke will smooth out a story by rearranging details (cf. Luke 8:40–42a, 49–55 with Mark 5:22–24, 35–43), or even by omitting them (cf. Luke 9:37–43 with Mark 9:14–29). Again, Luke will change the emphasis in a story, as in 4:31–37 (cf. Mark 1:21–28), where Jesus' mighty act and his teaching are paralleled, rather than having the miracle subordinated to Jesus' "new teaching," as in the Markan form of the story![6]

5. There is a story told of Apollonius of Tyana that has some parallels; for a treatment of them, cf. Petzke, "Historizität."

6. Such changes are, of course, not unique to the miracle-stories. The fact that Luke exercises the same freedom in shaping the miracle-stories as he does in shaping

Such a comparison also indicates that Luke can adapt a miracle in such a way that interest is pointed away from the recipient of the miracle and toward Jesus, e.g., 18:35–43, where many details about the blind man (Bartimaeus in Mark 10:46–52; Luke does not name him) are omitted, thus lessening our interest in him; or 8:42–48, where details about the woman with the flow of blood are similarly omitted. On the other hand, details about the one who requests the miracle can be added, thus heightening our interest in someone other than Jesus (cf. Luke 7:1–10 with Matt 8:5–13, and the added details about the kind of man the centurion was).[7]

A third way of approaching the Lukan miracle stories is by way of formal analysis, i.e., to see at what points the stories no longer fit the typical form of a gospel miracle-story, which in turn may give us clues about the point Luke wants to make. To take Luke 7:1–10 again as an example, our analysis of the form will show that the "solution" has, in fact, been omitted. That is, we are never told how, or even that, Jesus healed the boy (that the story once contained such a solution can be seen in Matt 8:13). The major point has thus become the fact that the centurion was worthy to receive the requested miracle (v. 4), a point confirmed by his own humility (v. 7; both points are absent in Matthew). Thus, while Matthew's point concerns the power of faith in healing,[8] Luke emphasizes the worthiness of a non-Jew to receive the benefits of Jesus' power. Formal analysis also indicates Luke's predilection for adding a reaction of the crowd, usually to praise God for what they have seen, an emphasis to which we will return in another context.

A fourth way of discerning Luke's intention in his use of miracle-stories told of Jesus is to note their placement in his narrative. Thus, for example, instead of placing the sending out of the twelve after Jesus'

---

the other traditions he receives, however, will become important when we consider some changes that Luke might have made in these miracle-traditions, but did not. His reticence there will have nothing to do with an unwillingness to modify such traditions in other ways; it is simply that point that we want to make here.

7. Luke occasionally adds details that make the story, more colorful, e.g., a child healed becomes for Luke an only child (7:12; 8:42; 9:38; the latter two Luke himself has changed from his sources); a sick youth is "valued" (7:2); a man's crippled hand is his right one (6:6). Such details have little apparent theological significance, except perhaps to make the stories more gripping, and thus more memorable.

8. So Held, "Matthew as Interpreter," 196, 274.

rejection in Nazareth (implying that he is now free to turn to others), as in Mark, or instead of introducing it with a statement on the need for harvesters (implying that the leaderless people need to hear Jesus' message), as in Matthew, Luke has it follow immediately on a series of four miracles, thus strengthening the impression that such activity was an important part of their mission. Again, Luke postpones the calling of disciples until after miracles are performed, both implied (4:23b) and discussed (4:25–27), and then presents the call of Peter (and, almost as an afterthought, James and John: 5:10a) in the context of a miracle of which Peter is a witness, hinting at the view that Luke held of the relationship between miracles and discipleship.

In such ways, then, it is possible to gain some insight into Luke's perspective on the significance and meaning of the miracles of Jesus. Let us turn now to consider some of the points that emerge when these ways of examining the miracle-accounts in the Third Gospel are undertaken.

APPLICATIONS OF METHODS OF STUDY

A clue to the importance Luke finds in the miraculous activity of Jesus can be seen in the way in which he, in several instances, attempts to balance Jesus' miraculous activity and his teaching in such a way as to give them equal weight. An indication of this balancing can be seen, in the fact that Jesus' first sermon (4:23–27) has as its contents a justification of Jesus' activity as miracle-worker (4:23–27) as well as references to his activity as proclaimer (4:18–22). The programmatic nature of that sermon has long been recognized by commentators.

Such balancing is also indicated in the manner in which Luke reproduces the first miracle story in Mark (Mark 1:21–28). In its Markan form, the account clearly brackets the miracle with references to Jesus' teaching (1:21–22, 27), thus subordinating Jesus' miracle-working to his teaching.[9] In Luke (4:31–37), on the other hand, the teaching

---

9. I am impressed by the evidence that indicates that Mark is responsible for giving the story this framework in vv. 21–22, 27–28, and should argue that such a way of presenting Jesus' first miracle in his Gospel is programmatic for the way he understood Jesus' activity as miracle-worker. Matthew seems to do the same by presenting first (chs. 5–7) an example of Jesus' teaching, and only then (chs. 8–9) an example of his miracle working. Unfortunately, a detailed justification of such assertions is not possible within the limits of this study.

is limited to the opening verses (31–32), after which the healing is recited. In that way, Luke transforms the reaction of the crowd (vv. 36–37) into a reaction to the miracle alone, and not to Jesus' teaching. And both teaching (v. 32) and miracle-working (v. 36) are examples of Jesus' activity ἐν ἐξουσίᾳ (with authority). In its Lukan form, then, the story tells first of Jesus' teaching, and then of his miracle, thus balancing them, rather than subordinating the one to the other.

In a similar way, when Luke (5:12–16) gives the Markan account of the healing of the leper (Mark 1:40–45), he concludes it by noting that the great crowds who came to Jesus as a result of the news of that healing, came to hear and to be healed of their diseases (5:17). Again, both characterize the activity of Jesus. Further evidence of such balance is also to be found in the way Luke has arranged his Gospel in chs. 6–7. Luke has followed Mark closely, beginning with the account of the healing at Capernaum (Mark 1:21; Luke 4:31) through the healing of the withered hand on the Sabbath (Mark 3:6; Luke 6:11—Luke's one deviation was to insert 5:1–11). But he then inverts Mark's order (Mark 3:7–19), placing first the choosing of the Twelve, then a summary of miracles (Luke 6:12–19), and then the "Sermon on the Plain." That "Sermon" is then immediately followed by a series of miracles (7:1–17). In this way, Luke has bracketed his long teaching-session of Jesus (6:20–49) with Jesus' activity as miracle-worker (6:17b–19; 7:1–17), being unwilling, apparently, to emphasize the one at the expense of the other.[10]

Within that section of Mark that Luke followed, he has also made some changes in source that further reflect a balancing of proclamation and miracle-working. In the account of the man with the withered hand (Mark 3:1–6), Luke begins by adding specific mention of the fact that Jesus taught in the synagogue before the healing occurred (6:6), something Mark did not do. In giving the Markan summary of healings (Mark 3:7–12), Luke makes a subtle change to introduce the element of teaching by changing the Markan reference to the crowds coming because they heard what Jesus did (i.e., miracles, Mark 3:8), to an indication that they came "in order to hear him and be healed of

10. Matthew has the same general order; but, in his arrangement, specific miracle stories come only after the long discourse, indicating, I think, their subordinate importance. Note also the inversion of Matt 4:24 (healings) and 4:25 (crowds) in Luke: to 6:17 (crowds) and 6:18–19 (healings).

their diseases" (Luke 6:18). Thus Luke again balances the two activities by introducing the one (in this case, teaching) into an account of
the other (miracles). Again, in Luke's only account of the feeding of
the multitudes, he adds to the Markan mention that Jesus taught the
crowds (Mark 6:34) reference to the fact that Jesus also healed those
who needed it (Luke 9:11).[11] In these ways, then, it would appear, Luke
has balanced Jesus' teaching and his miraculous acts by carefully men-
tioning the other when his source contained only one.

A second result that emerges from a study of the miracle-stories
in Luke centers on the importance of Jesus. Such importance is evident
in the fact that Luke will frequently change a detail in a miracle-story to
show that Jesus must not be disobeyed. For example, in Mark's account
of the cleansing of the leper (1:40–45), although the leper is sternly
warned not to speak to anyone of his cure (v. 43), he does so anyway
(v. 45). In Luke's version (5:12–16), the "report" of the event simply
"goes out" (v. 15a), thus lifting responsibility for disobedience from the
leper. Again, when Luke (5:17–26) takes over from Mark (2:1–12) the
story of the paralytic let down through the roof, he specifically adds the
detail that the cured man did, in fact, return to his own home (v. 25b),
as Jesus had commanded him (v. 24b). Mark may have understood
such compliance as implied in his phrasing of 2:12a, but Luke makes
it specific. This carries through even to so small a point as the fact
that the man with the withered hand, commanded to stand up, does
so (Luke 6:8), while in Mark, compliance with Jesus' command to the
man to "come here" is never indicated (3:3). Similarly, in the story of
the demoniac in the Capernaum synagogue, Luke displaces the detail
of the loud cry from the exiting demon (Mark 1:26) to the demon's
initial remarks (Luke 4:33), in that way making the demon obedient to
Jesus' command to him to be silent (Luke 4:35). In the Markan account,
that final cry comes after Jesus' command to silence (Mark 1:25–26).
In a somewhat similar way, Jesus' importance is indicated in two short
notices Luke has placed at the beginning and the end of Jesus' public
career. In 4:30, Jesus simply "passes through the midst" of a murderous
lynch mob; and in 22:51, the presence of a similar mob does not deter

11. Luke is obviously drawing on Mark 6:34 at this point, because in the second
account of the feeding in Mark (8:1–10), there is no mention in the introduction of
any activity of Jesus that would have delayed the crowds. In Matthew's account of the
first feeding (14:13–21), he mentions only healing, not teaching (14:14).

him from an act of compassion: he heals the wounded ear of a member of that mob. In both acts, Jesus, despite the threatening circumstances, shows he is in complete control of the situation, thus pointing to his importance; whatever the situation, he remains in control. The elimination of detail about other characters in two miracle-stories that Luke got from Mark (8:42b–48; 9:37–43) similarly points to the importance of Jesus in the Lukan narrative.

More importantly, however, Luke's treatment of Jesus' miracles shows the importance of Jesus in the fact that miracles have the capacity to validate Jesus. This is most clearly seen precisely in the passage where Jesus is, in fact, asked to validate himself: the question posed to him by John the Baptist (7:18–23; Matt 11:2–6 "Q"). In Matthew, although the question is raised because John hears about "the deeds" of Jesus, the immediate context is the missionary activity of the disciples, indicating this as the cause of John's question. In Luke, on the other hand, the immediate context is two miracle-stories (7:1–17), indicating that "all the things" John heard about were miracles. Thus, the question of Jesus' validity is posed, in Luke, by miracles. Luke then also understands that they will answer the question. Between the question and Jesus' answer, Luke inserts the information that "in that hour" Jesus performed a variety of miracles and then told John's disciples to report on what they had seen and heard (in Matthew, on what they "hear and see!"). Clearly, miracles will answer the question of who Jesus is, and hence they have the power of validating his claims about himself.

That validating power is also indicated in the typically Lukan response to a miracle of Jesus, viz., praising God, indicating the source of Jesus' power. For example, Mark's ambiguous *kyrios* in Jesus' statement in 5:19 ("tell them how much ὁ κύριος [the Lord] has done for you"—Jesus? God?), identified in v. 20 by the healed demoniac as Jesus, is changed in Luke 8:39 to "God" ("declare how much ὁ θεός [God] has done for you"), thus making explicit Jesus' identification of the power by which he performs such acts. This is also very likely the intention of the puzzling phrase at the end of Luke 5:17 ("and the power of the Lord was with him to heal"—the Greek is not entirely clear). It is to identify by what power Jesus performed such acts.

If, then, Luke understood the miracles to have the capacity to validate Jesus, and show the source of his power, two questions immediately follow. If miracles validate Jesus, do they also validate faith in him? And, secondly, if God is the source of Jesus' power, to what extent is Luke influenced in his understanding of Jesus' miracles by views of magic and magicians that saturated the Hellenistic world? Let us consider them in that order.

First, then, the question of miracles and faith: Can Jesus' miraculous activity serve as the basis of faith? It would be surprising, given the way in which Acts is written, if the answer were to be negative. It is rather clear in Acts that miracles were an effective device for turning people to faith. Peter healed a paralytic, "and all the residents of Lydda and Sharon saw him, and they turned to the Lord" (Acts 9:35). Peter raised Tabitha from the dead, "and it became known throughout all Joppa, and many believed in the Lord" (9:42). When Sergius Paulus saw Elymas the magician blinded by Paul's curse, he "believed" (ἐπίστευσεν; 13:12). The jailer, upon observing the earthquake that broke open the prison for Paul and Silas, asks about faith and is then baptized (16:30, 33). When the seven sons of the Jewish high priest Sceva were routed by demons as they attempted an unbelieving use of Jesus' name, that very name was "extolled" (19:17). Harden has shown rather convincingly that in the narrative in Acts, "at every point where the Gospel was first established among a certain people, the foundation was made in a miraculous context, with manifest showing of signs and powers worked by the hands of the Apostles."[12] The many references to "signs and wonders" performed by the apostles (2:43; 5:12; 6:8; 8:6; 14:3; 15:12) make clear Luke's view in this matter. In fact, even a non-Christian could gain a hearing for himself through such acts (Simon, 8:9–11).[13]

Although the evidence for the fact that miracles can be the basis of belief in God is not so massive in Luke's treatment of the miracles of Jesus as it is in Acts, it is nevertheless also present. This can perhaps be most clearly seen in the way Luke characteristically concludes such narratives. For example, there are regular references to the praise of God by those who witness the miracle of Jesus, or by the one who benefited from it (5:25; 7:16; 9:43; 13:13; 17:15; 18:43), and in one instance,

12. See "Miracle Narratives," esp. his discussion beginning on 310; the quotation is from 311.

13. This point becomes the basis for the contest of miracles (and, therefore, of faith) in the *Actus Ver.* §32 between Peter and Simon. Peter wins the contest, and therefore the people specifically believe in Peter and his God, not in Simon and his.

such a reaction is specified by Jesus as the proper response (17:18). While fear is a usual reaction in Luke to manifestations of the divine (e.g., 1:12; 1:65; 2:9; cf. 1:30, where it is implied), Luke also connected it with faith (e.g., Acts 2:43 in its context). Such fear is, then, also a characteristic reaction in Luke's telling of the miracle-stories (5:26; 7:16; 8:35, 37; cf. also 24:5). Thus, in Luke, the reaction to miracles is to see God behind the activity of Jesus, thus acknowledging Jesus to be the one whom God has chosen to do his work. Such an identification of Jesus surely belongs to Luke's understanding of faith (see, e.g., Acts 2:22–23, 36; 1:13; 4:27; 10:38).

The idea that the miracles lead legitimately to faith in Jesus is also shown in some more subtle ways in Luke's narrative. There is, for example, an emphasis on "seeing" that is not found in his sources. For example, in 10:23–24 (par. Matt 13:16–17 "Q"), Luke does not balance the first sentence ("Blessed are the eyes which see what you see") with any reference to "ears" or "hearing," as does Matthew. If that balance was in the "Q" source, Luke chose to alter it; if it was not in the source, Luke did not feel compelled, as did Matthew, to balance "seeing" with "hearing." In either case, the emphasis on "seeing" is clear. Again, in his account of the triumphal entry, Luke gives as the reason for the crowds' praise of Jesus the "mighty works which they had seen" (19:37), an emphasis on "seeing," indeed on the importance of miracles, for the confession of Jesus as the one who comes in the Lord's name, found in neither of the other synoptic gospels. In the account of the response to the Baptist's question, Luke, unlike Matthew (11:4), refers to what John's disciples have first "seen," and then "heard." In the same way, Cleopas' response about Jesus puts "deed" before "word," again giving pride of place to Jesus' mighty acts. Perhaps the same emphasis can be seen in the fact that the content of Jesus' first sermon in Luke (4:16–30) is Jesus' miracles, not the kingdom of God (contrast Mark 1:14–15).

Luke's view that faith legitimately follows miracles also underlies the difficulties in the narrative of the healing of the ten lepers (17:11–19). The conclusion, "Rise and go your way; your faith has made you well" (v. 19), spoken to the Samaritan who returned, implies that his return was a manifestation of the faith that healed him. But that does not comport well with the earlier statement that he, along with his nine companions, had already been healed (v. 14b), or that the nine who showed no such faith were healed despite that fact. But if the order of events in the story is confused, the conclusion is not: Praise of God and gratitude to Jesus (= faith) are the proper response to a miracle of Jesus. That, it appears, is the point Luke wanted to make, and he was so intent on making it that he either wittingly, or unwittingly, distorted the story itself in order to make it. The context confirms that such was Luke's intention: 17:1–19 is organized around the question: "What is faith?" (it forgives, vv. 1–4; it can do all things, vv. 5–6; it is humble, vv. 7–10, and grateful, vv. 11–19). The point of the "miracle-story," therefore, is faith, and the story is reshaped to make that point. That a miracle-story suggested itself to Luke as a vehicle to illustrate the nature of faith is significant for his view of the relationship between the two.

All of this is not to say that Luke had no indication in his sources that miracles could and should lead to a faithful response to Jesus. "Q," for example, holds that those who have not responded correctly to Jesus' miracles (by repentance) are culpable (10:13–14; par. Matt 11:21–23). Similarly, the saying about the relationship of miracles and the kingdom of God (11:20; par. Matt 12:28) gives the basis for a faithful response to miracles: Jesus' mighty acts are done by God's own power. It acknowledges what is the proper response to the miracles. Such a view of miracles was apparently so widespread in the primitive church that Paul took it for granted when he defended the legitimacy of his apostleship (see 1 Cor 2:4; Rom 15:18–20). But Luke, more than any other gospel writer, has developed this idea in his two-volume work.[14]

A clear and supportive corollary to this emphasis on faith legitimately growing out of the observation of miracles, rests in the fact that for Luke, miracles are clearly the basis for discipleship. This is most evident in the way Luke has narrated the call of the first disciples, Peter, James, and John. Luke's source, Mark, placed the calling of the first disciples after a summary of Jesus' proclamation (1:14–15) and before there was any hint of Jesus' wondrous power. In Luke, on the other hand, Jesus' ability to perform miracles has been amply demonstrated (4:31–41) and reported (4:23) before there is any mention of calling disciples. Further, the story within which the call of the first disciples is placed (5:1–11) leaves little room for doubt that they followed Jesus because of his wondrous power. Only after Peter, James' and John see the

---

14. John also knows this kind of tradition (cf. 2:11; 4:53; 6:14; 11:15); but he has included counter-emphases (e.g., 20:29), which I do not find in Luke.

miraculous catch of fish, are they summoned to follow Jesus. In fact, the implication is clear that it was seeing that miracle that prepared Peter to see in Jesus one who ought to be followed. Luke has further altered the Markan order so that even before his call, Peter had seen Jesus heal his mother-in-law. Thus Peter (but not James and John, in Luke) had known of Jesus' wondrous powers some time prior to his call.

Similarly, the second account of the calling of a disciple in Luke (Levi, 5:27) follows immediately after a miracle, identified as such by a technical term (παράδοξος, v. 26). Again, Luke has modified his source. In Mark, there is interposed between the healing of the paralytic and the call of Levi the statement that Jesus taught the crowd (Mark 2:13). Luke has omitted this reference, thus clearly implying that, again, a disciple followed Jesus because of a miracle.[15]

Again, Luke is the only evangelist who mentions that the women who followed Jesus were women whom Jesus had cured, specifically Mary Magdalene, from whom Jesus had expelled seven demons (8:2–3). The fact that they are identified both as followers, and as recipients of wondrous acts from Jesus, adds further evidence that Luke understood discipleship as intimately connected to knowledge of Jesus' ability to perform mighty acts. Even the sending out of the Twelve has been arranged in such a way by Luke that it follows immediately on a series of four miracles, showing again the close connection between discipleship and Jesus' mighty power.

Clearly, then, for Luke, knowledge of Jesus' miracles is a legitimate cause for faith in him. This was true not only for the disciples whom Jesus himself called, but also for the followers later won by apostolic activity. In Luke as in Acts, acceptance of the call to follow Jesus, whether as a disciple or in faith, is intimately connected with the miraculous activity of Jesus.

---

15. It may well be that Luke intends ch. 5 to show correct and incorrect responses to Jesus and his miraculous power. The response of Peter, James, John, and Levi is the correct response. The response of the Pharisees, on the other hand, who also saw Jesus' miraculous power (cf. v. 17 with v. 26; Luke has added the information that Pharisees and teachers of the law came from the whole Jewish homeland in v. 17, thus generalizing their response) is incorrect; they carp at him (vv. 30–33). Verse 39 is then an explanatory summary of the chapter: the unaccountable refusal of Pharisees to accept Jesus is due to their clinging to the old Law (v. 39: "And no one, after drinking old wine, desires new; for he says, 'the old is good'"). They are nonetheless culpable, because they have also seen Jesus' wondrous power (cf. 6:11).

We must turn now to consider the extent to which magical beliefs, so prevalent in the Hellenistic world, influenced the way in which Luke understood and presented the miracles of Jesus. Hull, in his book *Hellenistic Magic and the Synoptic Tradition,* has argued strongly that of all the gospels, Luke was most strongly influenced by such magical belief. "Luke wrote about magic because he saw and believed."[16] I find his argument unconvincing, partly because some evidence cited is speculative, partly because it could be cited of other gospels as well, and partly because some distinctions he makes are without difference.

For example, Hull assumes that "the mature Christ experienced fluctuations in the activity of his power"[17] (an idea long since proposed by Eitrem,[18] to whom Hull does not refer), without providing any supportive evidence. In fact, that supposition rests on a view of the historical validity of individual stories and their arrangement in the gospels which form- and redaction-critical studies have simply rendered outmoded.

Again, when Hull argues that to regard objects as an effective means of cure, because they come from the person of the "divine king" (e.g., clothing, spittle), he is referring to a belief that pervades all four gospels, and it can hardly be said to be Luke's special emphasis, Acts 19:11–12 to the contrary notwithstanding (see Mark 5:25–34; 8:22–26; Matt 9:20–22; John 9:1–7). Further, I find pointless Hull's repeated assertion that Luke's addition of the word "power" to the "authority" that Jesus granted the disciples in Matthew and Mark (Luke 9:1; Matt 10:1; Mark 3:15) somehow gives them greater control over the demonic, thus further showing Luke's magical views.[19] It is clear that Matthew and Mark mean as surely as Luke that Jesus' disciples were given power as well as authority over the demonic (cf. Matt 10:1, where "authority" clearly includes power to cast them out). And Mark is just as sure that Jesus cast out the demon when people remarked on his authority (1:27) as is Luke when he has them note Jesus' authority and power (4:36).

All of this is not to say that all such emphasis on "magic" is absent from Luke's accounts of Jesus' miracles. Luke makes explicit why people

16. Hull, *Hellenistic Magic,* 86. See the whole of his ch. 6: "Luke, the Tradition Penetrated by Magic."

17. Ibid., 106.

18. Eitrem, *Some Notes.*

19. Hull, *Hellenistic Magic,* 107, 115.

wanted to touch him: because when they did, power went forth from
Jesus to heal them (cf. Luke 6:19 with Mark 3:10—Mark also knows
they sought to touch him, but Luke makes the reason explicit). That
"power" is here thought of as objective—to touch Jesus is to contact
that power and thus be healed (cf. Acts 5:15; 19:11–12). In the story
of the woman with the flow of blood, Luke puts into direct speech the
remark that Jesus felt power go forth from him, perhaps showing the
same tendency (cf. Luke 8:46 with Mark 5:30). That Luke also thought
in such objective terms is shown also in his treatment of the feeding
of the multitudes, where he adds αὐτοὺς (them) after εὐλόγησεν ([he
blessed] 9:16), thus making bread the object of the blessing, rather than
understanding it as the Jewish blessing of God before eating (ברוך
אתה אדני אל הנו... [Blessed are you, O Lord our God ...]). Perhaps
Luke thinks that Jesus' blessing on the bread caused it to multiply.

If, however, Luke does contain some indication of an increasingly
magical view of Jesus' miracles, it also contains indications that point
in the opposite direction, viz., that Luke pictures Jesus' miracles in less
magical ways than his sources. For example, in the story of the raising
of Jairus' daughter (8:40–42a, 49–55), Luke omits the foreign phrase
(Mark 5:41), a device that was part of the repertoire of every magician,[20] and Luke strengthens the impression, by his phrasing of v. 50 (to
"only believe," he adds the phrase "and she shall be saved") that Jairus'
faith is an important element in the cure. Again, unlike Hellenistic magicians, Jesus performs his cures openly and allows bystanders to hear
what he says in the course of the wondrous act. In raising the young
man of Nain (7:11–17), for example, his words to the dead youth are
clearly heard. Contrast with that a similar story told of Apollonius of
Tyana (Philostratus, *Life* 4.45) in which he raises a girl by means of
a formula whispered "in secret" (ἀφανῶς). Luke also omits from the
story of the "epileptic" boy (9:37–43) all advice on how to cast out
especially difficult demons (cf. Mark 9:29), thus discouraging "do-it-
yourself" exorcists from the thought that with some magic formula
they could reproduce the act. And, unlike the similarity to sympathetic
magic by which Jesus in Mark raises Peter's mother-in-law (he causes

20. Too much weight cannot be put on this point, however, since Luke omits all
foreign phrases in his account of Jesus; cf. Luke's record of the last words of Jesus in
ch. 23. Yet a "tradition penetrated by magic" would hardly follow such a practice of
eliminating recitation of powerful magic formulae.

her to assume the position of one who is well by pulling her up bodily), in Luke the act is accomplished merely by a word.

Another aspect to which Hull points as evidence of the penetration of magic into Luke's understanding of Jesus is the realm of demons. Arguing that, while magic does not necessarily presume demons, presentation of the demonic almost inevitably includes magic, Hull concludes that Luke has a special emphasis on the demonic. To be sure, Luke does picture the healing of Peter's mother-in-law, contrary to his source, as an exorcism (cf. Luke 4:38–39 with Mark 1:30–31), yet in another instance, Luke omits the words from Mark that imply that the stilling of the storm was an exorcism (cf. Mark 4:39 and 1:25 with Luke 8:24). It is of further interest to note that the one additional story Luke has about demonic possession—the crippled woman, 13:10–13—is presented in a framework (vv. 14–17) that makes it clear that the interest of that tradition is not in demonic possession, but in the contradiction between Pharisaic belief about the law and their own practices. Jesus' words about the law put his adversaries to shame and caused the people to rejoice, not specifically the exorcism. Similarly in 14:1–6, we have here a miracle-story that has been adapted to make another point altogether, and thus, for all practical purposes, it no longer functions within the tradition as a miracle-story. It now concerns primarily Jesus' dispute about the true intention of the Jewish law.

There can be no question that Luke does understand Jesus' ministry as a successful battle against Satan (cf. 10:18). The way Luke phrases 11:21–22 (cf. Matt 12:29) as the interpretation of v. 20 makes it clear that with the appearance of Jesus as the stronger one, Satan's "goods," i.e., those he possesses, are in fact being despoiled, a despoliation that continues in the work of the apostles (cf. Acts 16:16–18). But it is also clear that Luke is by no means preoccupied with Jesus' battle with the demonic, and in his telling, the exorcisms have lost the technical vocabulary of Hellenistic demon-exorcism by means of which Mark, for example, has described them.[21] Thus, the adjuration of the demon against Jesus by means of a phrase similar to that used in Hellenistic accounts (Mark 5:7) has become, in Luke 8:28, simply a plea to Jesus.

In sum, there is as much evidence that Luke has toned down the magical aspects of Jesus' miracles, as there is that he presents such sto-

---

21. This point is convincingly made in Bauernfeind, *Worte,* 100–101.

ries under the particular influence of the Hellenistic understanding of magic. In fact, the Jesus of Luke appears less influenced by magical practices than the Jesus in Mark. That Luke is writing for people who understood, and perhaps even credited, magical practices could hardly be denied; but he does more, I would argue, to combat such belief than he does, if only inadvertently, to foster it (cf. Acts 13:6–11; 19:18–19). His presentation of the miracles of Jesus, in any case, can hardly be described as "traditions penetrated by magic" (Hull's phrase).

There is, on the other hand, no question that Luke does put a certain emphasis on the wondrous aspects of Jesus' career. Of all the gospels, for example, Luke begins his narrative more massively with the miraculous, not only in the first two chapters, but also in the accounts of Jesus himself. After the programmatic first sermon in ch. 4, whose content, as we have frequently noted, concerns Jesus' miracles, Jesus does little preaching (4:31–32; 5:1; 5:17 refer to it), but many miracles. Luke is, to be sure, following Mark's outline.

Yet although Mark has miracles in the first three chapters before he gives the content of a session of teaching (ch. 4), Mark places all of Jesus' activities under the rubric of proclamation (1:14–15), and, as we have seen, places his first programmatic miracle within the framework of Jesus' power as teacher (1:21–28). Luke follows this order, but with some significant changes. He omits Mark 1:14–15 altogether, he lessens the stress on teaching in Mark's first miracle, and he displaces until later, and then subordinates to miraculous deeds the call of the disciples.

Again, there are hints in the body of Luke's gospel that, in his understanding, Jesus can summarize his own career in terms of his mighty acts. His reaction to the Baptist's question, a reaction that involves the added performance of miracles, is an example. Again, when threatened by Herod, Jesus sums up his career with the words: "Behold, I cast out demons and perform cures" (13:32). The implication of the whole passage (vv. 31–33) seems to be that such activity on the part of Jesus ultimately causes his death (v. 33); nevertheless, Jesus must finish his predestined course. And Luke alone records that in the midst of his fatal crisis, Jesus continues to function as a wondrous healer (22:50–51—this event seems to serve the same function as Matt 26:53: Jesus' power remains intact but he chooses not to use it to save himself).

Along the same line, Luke understands that Jesus' fame is based more on his mighty acts than on his teaching. The spread of Jesus' fame in Luke 4:37, for example, omits the Markan emphasis on Jesus' teaching (Mark 1:28). Similarly, the report in Luke 5:15 is no longer due to the leper's spreading the word, as in Mark 1:45. Rather, the report about Jesus simply goes forth, clearly based on the wondrous act. A third such summary (7:17) has been added by Luke, as the conclusion of Jesus' raising of the youth of Nain. As a result of his view, it is quite in keeping that Luke would understand Herod to have known of Jesus chiefly as a wonder-worker (23:8). The prominence of mighty acts for Luke's understanding of the origins of the faith is also clear in the uniquely Lukan account of the sending out of the Seventy. Given the power to heal (10:9), they single it out at their return as the most impressive characteristic of their mission (v. 17), and v. 19 confirms the miraculous nature of the power Jesus has given them. The results of such power then are evident in the narrative in Acts, with its regular and frequent mention of the miraculous acts of the disciples, both in general and in specific cases.[22]

Conclusions

With the conclusion of our rapid survey of the Lukan perspective on Jesus' miracles, we may underline one or two points that have emerged. Perhaps most important is the impression that of all the gospels, Luke appears to have a more unambiguous reliance on the possibility that miracles, and thus miracle-stories, can serve as the basis for faith in Jesus. They also serve more clearly in Luke to validate Jesus as the one sent by God. To be sure, such conclusions are a matter of degree. Obviously, all gospel authors thought miracle-stories important for faith and for understanding Jesus or they would not have included them in their accounts of his career. The apocryphal gospels show clearly enough that religious tracts about Jesus could be written with no reference to Jesus' miracles at all (e.g., *Gospel of Thomas, Gospel of Truth,* etc.). Yet of the

22. The extent of miracles reported or mentioned in Acts is indicated in the following survey: miracles generally mentioned of apostles and disciples: 2:43; 4:30; 5:12; 5:16; miracles attributed to specific people: Jesus: 2:22; 10:38; Peter: 3:2–8; 5:9–11; 5:15; 9:32–34; 9:36–41; Stephen: 6:8; Philip: 8:6; 8:13; 8:39; Paul: 13:9–11; 14:9–10; 16:16–18; 19:11–12; 20:9–10; 28:3–6; 28:8; 28:9; Paul and Barnabas: 14:3; 15:12. In addition, there are three miraculous releases from bondage: 5:19; 12:6–10; 16:25–26.

canonical gospels, Luke seems to view the miracles with a less critical eye,[23] according them, in a number of subtle ways, a more important role in his account of Jesus. A glance at Acts confirms that impression and shows the extent to which Luke understood the miraculous to play an important, if not, indeed, a central role, in the origins of the Christian church.

Luke has done this, I would argue, in full awareness of the magical views and practices that pervaded the Hellenistic world. Indeed, no author of that period, it would seem, could have been unaware of them. Yet Luke has not subordinated his presentation of Jesus to a magical worldview. If he shares to a greater extent than the other gospel authors the importance that his Hellenistic contemporaries accorded to such phenomena, he has not, to the extent Hull has proposed, allowed the traditions of the faith to be penetrated by magic. Perhaps, in the end, the author of the Third Gospel is, of all evangelists, most closely attuned to the Hellenistic world for which he writes, and his perspective on the miracles of Jesus has been shaped accordingly.

In fact, Luke's accounts of the miracles of Jesus are remarkable for the extent to which they have remained unaffected by any attempt to link them to the thought-world of the OT. In light of some explicit statements to the effect that in Jesus, prophecies are fulfilled (e.g., Luke 24:27, 44; Acts 10:32–33; cf. also 2:25–31; 3:22–26; 13:32–37—all in speeches in Acts), and in light of the way Luke introduces Jesus' ministry in 4:16–30, one would expect some indication that Jesus' miracles, as narrated in Luke, did in fact perform that function. This is made all the more likely by the fact that in that introduction to Jesus' public ministry, Jesus, immediately after claiming that he is the fulfillment of prophecy (Luke 4:18–20), relates in his own defense two miracles, one

---

23. A good perspective on the more critical use that Matthew makes of the miracle-tradition can be seen in the way he has adapted the miracle-stories to other points; cf. the essay by Held (see n. 1 above). I would urge that the miracle with which Matthew chose to conclude his collection of miracles, 9:32–34, indicates that he saw them as essentially ambiguous in their witness to Jesus, being open to widely differing interpretations. Even the greatest of all wondrous acts, the resurrection, is open to ambiguity; note the second phrase of 28:17. We have already mentioned John 20:26–29 as an indication of the Johannine critique of a faith based on miracles. I have attempted to show the critical handling that the miracle traditions received in Mark's hands in my work on pre-Markan miracle-catenae (see ch. 4: "Isolation"; ch. 5: "Origin and Function").

of Elijah and one of Elisha. If one is not thus to expect Jesus' miracles to resemble specifically those of Elijah and Elisha, at the least one would expect them to fulfill OT prophetic motifs. Yet strangely, Luke has not shaped the miracle-stories of Jesus in that direction, neither those he got from Mark, nor those from "Q," nor those from his special source. In the one story (Luke 7:11–17) that quotes a phrase from a miracle of Elijah (Luke 17:15b = 1 Kgs [3 Kgdms] 17:23 LXX), the story is so close to a similar one told of Apollonius of Tyana by Philostratus (*Life*, 4.45) that the question of a common source could be raised.[24] While the typically Lukan ending of a miracle of Jesus (glorifying God) may imply fulfillment of prophecy (e.g., 7:16), it need not (e.g., 5:26). That is, in the Lukan ending, "glorifying God" does not equal fulfillment of OT prophecy, or fulfillment of God's prophetic word. That miracles point to God is clear in Luke, but that in itself is not sufficient to affirm that Luke shapes the miracles of Jesus to serve the theological motif of fulfillment of prophecy. That Luke would find precedents for Jesus' miracles in the OT could hardly be denied, but he shares that insight with the entire synoptic tradition. We are concerned here with special Lukan emphases, and fulfillment of prophecy by the miracles of Jesus does not seem to be one of them.

A second possible way Luke could have attempted to link Jesus to the OT may be mentioned, viz., by designating Jesus as "prophet" in order to tie him to OT traditions. Indeed, the only miracle-workers available for such linking to the OT were prophets (Moses, Elijah, and Elisha). Did Luke identify Jesus as a miracle-worker because such activity was expected of a prophet? The evidence does not appear to support such a suggestion.[25]

Of seven references to Jesus as "prophet" in Luke, two have as their focus the knowledge that Jesus, as a prophet, ought to have (7:39; 22:64), two give identifications of Jesus by the people (9:8, 19), one is a self-

24. For a more detailed exposition of this question, see Petzke, "Historizität," 371–78.

25. While Jesus does seem to refer to himself as prophet in Luke (13:33), the reference has to do more with Jesus' impending death than with his miracles (cf. 11:49–50; 13:34), even though it appears in a context in which miracles are mentioned (13:32). There is another possible such self-designation in 4:24; but, again, although in a context in which miracles are mentioned, the emphasis in this saying on prophet is not on miracles. It is perhaps worth noting that John the Baptist is also called "prophet" in Luke's gospel (1:76; 7:26; 20:6), in one instance by Jesus himself (7:26).

designation (13:33), and two, from special Lukan sources, refer to miracles (7:16, crowd reaction; 24:19, identification of Jesus by Cleopas and his companion).[26] One could also cite the fact that in the programmatic opening sermon in Nazareth, Jesus compares himself to the miracle-working Elijah (4:25–26) and Elisha (4:27). Such hints are not, however, carried through in any systematic, or even perfunctory, way, when Luke makes use of his miracle traditions. That is to say, while Luke is quite willing to change and adapt the miracle-stories he receives, he does not adapt them to make the point that when Jesus does such things, he is acting as one would expect a prophet to act. The one observable addition to a received tradition, where Luke identifies Jesus as prophet, occurs in the form of a hostile remark on Jesus' lack of appropriate knowledge (7:39; cf. Mark 14:4–5). If Luke did think of Jesus as prophet because he did the things a prophet was to do, Luke did not in any consistent way adapt the miracles-stories of Jesus to make that point.

It is perhaps worth noting, in conclusion, that few if any of the themes normally identified as characteristically Lukan emerge from Luke's telling of the miracles. This is all the more strange in the light of Luke's apparent willingness to adapt the miracle-stories in Acts to such theological motifs. It is clear that Luke is quite willing to adapt and change accounts of the miracles of Jesus. It is not clear why he has not adapted them in ways one would have expected him to, given his theological outlook. The answer to that problem must await further reflection in this particular area of NT scholarship.

26. I remain unpersuaded by the efforts of Miller ("Character of Miracles") to demonstrate Luke's attempt to shape miracles in terms of the OT. He has allowed the accounts in Acts to influence excessively what he sees in the Gospel and is able to find allusions to the OT where I am not, on occasion even in "unquoted portions" of an OT text (e.g., 162). The work also suffers from a lack of clarity in distinguishing between what is characteristic of synoptic miracles in general, and what is uniquely Lukan.

Gospel Miracle Tradition
and the Divine Man

3

¶ INTEREST IN, AND CONCERN FOR, THE SIGNIFICANCE OF MIRACLE stories for the development of the early traditions about Jesus has seen an upsurge in the past few years. Research into the possibility of pre-Markan and pre-Johannine sources has led a number of scholars to a reexamination of the miracle traditions in those gospels.[1] In a similar way, interest in the theology, and more especially in the Christology, of the Gospel writers has led to a redaction-critical examination of miracles and the way they are interpreted by the various evangelists.[2] All of this has called attention anew to the problem of the relationship of these traditions to similar or dissimilar traditions current in the Hellenistic world within which, and for which, the New Testament documents as we have them were developed. Discussion of miracle stories as they circulated in the Hellenistic world inevitably brings with it the problem of the title "divine man" (θεῖος ἀνήρ) and its use in that world, along with the question of whether or not that category played a part in the interpretation of Jesus that was carried on by the primitive church as it developed its traditions about him. It is the purpose of this article to review selected evidence from the Hellenistic world that is relevant to the problem of the place and meaning of miracles in the Jesus-tradition and in that connection, to examine the title "divine man" as it bears on the formation of the traditions contained in our canonical Gospels. While no claim to completeness can be raised, either with regard to the evidence discussed or the conclusions reviewed, it is the intention of these pages to inform the reader on some of the major aspects currently surfacing in this particular New Testament problem.

1. For Mark, see ch. 4: "Isolation"; Koester, "One Jesus"; Keck, "Mark 3:7–12." For John, see Becker, "Wunder"; Fortna, *Gospel of Signs.*

2. See Becker, "Wunder"; Betz, "Jesus as Divine Man"; Held, "Matthew."

Our first task (I) will be a review of two different types of miracle stories current in the Hellenistic world during the period within which our New Testament was being written. These two types are the Jewish as recorded in the Talmud and the secular or Hellenistic type, although we must remain clear on the fact that both types belonged to the same Hellenistic world and that, as we shall see, they may not be considered as having existed in total isolation from each other. When we have gotten an impression of those two kinds of stories and have seen the way in which miracle themes and stories tended to become common property throughout the Hellenistic world, we must raise the question (II) of the interpretation of the New Testament miracle stories and the way in which they fit into their world. This in turn will force us to raise the issue of how miracles were interpreted in that world and whether this throws light on the way New Testament miracles were interpreted. After seeing how the post-canonical traditions dealt with the New Testament material (III), we will be in a position to make a brief evaluation of the evidence and of some possible solutions (IV).

I. MIRACLES IN THE NEW TESTAMENT WORLD

In light of the many wondrous acts associated with various figures in the OT narratives—Moses, who worked (according to Jewish traditions) the ten plagues as miracles; Elijah, with the cycle of mighty acts recorded in First and Second Kings; Elisha, who because of the double portion of the Spirit he received (2 Kgs 2:7–12) was regarded by later Jewish tradition as having worked twice as many miracles as Elijah—it is little wonder that such mighty acts would also continue to be part of Jewish traditions in the Hellenistic period. There is indirect evidence of this in the influence exercised on common magical practices in this period by various Jewish magical formulae and phrases,[3] but there is also direct evidence in the traditions contained in the Talmud.[4]

In the Talmudic accounts, the means by which miracles are brought about is most frequently prayer. For example, there is the following story:

---

3. I owe this observation to Georgi, *Gegner* 115 = *Opponents,* 102.

4. Unless otherwise noted, this material is drawn from the Eng. trans. of the *Babylonian Talmud,* by Epstein. Page numbers in the following footnotes refer to this edition.

> R. Ḥiyya ben Luliani overhearing the clouds saying to one
> another, Come, let us take water to Ammon and Moab, ex-
> claimed: Master of the Universe! When Thou art about to give
> the Law to Thy people Israel Thou didst offer it around amongst
> all the nations of the world but they would not accept it, and
> now Thou wouldst give them rain; let them (the clouds) empty
> their waters here; and they emptied their waters on the spot. (*b.
> Ta'an.* 25a; p. 131)

On another occasion, such a miracle with respect to rainfall occurs
simply to prevent discomfort to a rabbi:

> R. Ḥanina b. Dosa was journeying on the road when it began to
> rain. He exclaimed: Master of the Universe, the whole world is
> at ease, but Ḥanina is in distress; the rain then ceased. When he
> reached home he exclaimed: Master of the Universe, the whole
> world is in distress and Ḥanina is at ease; whereupon rain fell.
> (*b. Ta'an.* 24b; p. 127)

Another account tells at some length of how Ḥoni the Circle Drawer
prayed in vain for rain, whereupon he drew a circle on the ground
and threatened not to move from it until God provided rain. When
rain merely dripped, he asked for more rain (so successfully that floods
threatened) and Ḥoni had to pray for it to abate into a rain of "benevo-
lence, blessing and bounty." Finally, Ḥoni had to pray for it to cease
altogether lest everything be washed away, the final prayer being accompanied by a bullock as thanksgiving offering to God (*b. Ta'an.* 23a;
pp. 116–17). Similar stories concerning the miraculous provision of
rain as the result of prayers are told of R. Johan who would go to a low-
lying spot to pray for rain, in accordance with Ps 130:1, and of Ḥanan
ha-Nehba, the grandson of Ḥoni the Circle Drawer (*b. Ta'an.* 23b; pp.
120–21).

The kind of miracles brought about by the prayer of various rabbis is not limited to provision of rain, however. Ḥanina ben Dosa, re-
nowned for his poverty, and urged by his wife to alleviate it, prayed
"that something may be given" to him, whereupon a hand appeared
giving him a golden table leg. When he saw in a dream, however, that
the other pious men would eat at three-legged golden tables while his
had only two legs, he prayed that the leg be taken away, which also happened (*b. Ta'an.* 25a; pp. 128–29). Also Ḥanina's prayers had the power

to heal. At the request of R. Gamaliel, Ḥanina, by his prayer, caused the fever to leave the afflicted son of Gamaliel, and at the request of R. Johanan ben Zakkai (with whom Ḥanina studied the law) Ḥanina's prayer, uttered while his head was placed between his knees, healed Johanan's son as well (b. Ber. 34b; pp. 215–16).[5]

This kind of story has led Schmithals to observe that rabbinic miracles are done through the power of prayer to God rather than because the rabbi himself has the power to perform such acts.[6] Yet such an observation needs to be qualified in a twofold way. First, as Bammel has observed, any rabbi who can "force God to do certain things" is himself a miracle-worker even if the method of performance be prayer.[7] Secondly, there seems to be evidence from the Jewish traditions themselves of miracles performed without the use of prayer. For example, R. Isaac B. Eliashab caused the in-laws of R. Mani, at his request, to become poor and then rich and Mani's wife to become beautiful and then ugly again, simply by exclaiming "Let them become rich," "May Hannah become beautiful!" and the like (b. Taʿan. 23b; p. 121). Similarly, Ḥanina b. Dosa caused beams that were too short to bridge the roof of a house being built to extend themselves so that they served that purpose by exclaiming to the woman whose house it was: "May your beams reach!" (b. Taʿan. 25a; p. 129). And by his command he limited the range of Maḥalath, queen of demons, to the nights of Wednesdays and Sabbaths (b. Pesaḥ. 112b; pp. 579–80).[8] In some cases miracles simply occur in order to benefit some (usually famous) rabbi. Thus, although the wife of Ḥanina ben Dosa had nothing to bake, she would light the oven each Friday to cover the shame of such poverty; when a prying neighbor entered their house to unmask such deception, "a miracle happened, and (she) saw the oven filled with loaves of bread and the kneading trough full of dough" (b. Taʿan. 24b–25a; p. 128). Again, R. Mani, the son of R. Johan, being annoyed by certain people, "prostrated himself on the grave of his father and exclaimed: Father, father, these people persecute me. Once as they were passing (the grave) the knees of their horses became stiff (and remained so)

5. On Ḥanina, see Vermes, "Ḥanina ben Dosa"; and Freyne, "Ḥanina ben Dosa."

6. Schmithals, Wunder und Glaube, 20.

7. Bammel, "John Did No Miracle," 283 n. 1.

8. Josephus also has an account of Eleazar who cured one possessed by a demon (Ant. 8.42), but it is clearly cast in the Hellenistic, rather than the Talmudic, form.

until they undertook not to persecute him any longer" (*b. Ta'an.* 23b; p. 121). A final example: Ḥanina, having been bitten by a lizard suffered no ill effects, but the lizard died because the first to reach water after such an attack survived, and a spring of water miraculously appeared at the feet of Ḥanina. Thus, the lizard's fate was sealed (*b. Ber.* 33a; p. 204).[9]

An analysis of this kind of story can be undertaken here only briefly, yet several things of importance need to be noted. While there is a certain interest in the miraculous as such manifested in these stories, it is also true that they can be used for purely didactic purposes. There is a story, for example, of Abba Ḥilqiah (another grandson of Ḥoni the Circle Drawer) who, when asked to repeat his previously successful prayers for rain, went through a variety of acts totally unrelated to that request: he ignored the petitioners in his field; he walked barefoot until he reached a stream, whereupon he donned his shoes; his wife met him "well bedecked"; she entered the house before him. Each of these acts was then the basis for teaching on the part of Ḥilqiah, and the fact that rain came at his prayer is a minor detail in the story (*b. Ta'an.* 23a–23b; pp. 118–20). Here, clearly, a "miracle story" is told for another point altogether. The same is true of the story told of Ḥanan ha-Nehba in which we are never told whether his prayer for rain is answered; the point is the content of his prayer (*b. Ta'an.* 23b; p. 120). But perhaps most importantly, despite the existence of some stories in which prayer is not expressly mentioned as the means whereby the miracle is brought about, the framework of the story will assume or imply it. When Ḥanina stretched the timbers, the comment assumes it was by his prayer;[10] when he met Maḥalath she informed him he was protected (she had been warned of him in heaven), apparently because of his piety. Even the story of Ḥanina and the lizard is used for Ḥanina's instruction: "it is not the lizard that kills, but sin that kills." In short, religious instruction appears to be the point for which most of the stories have been told, and the usual method of miracle working is

9. The detail of the spring, and the information about reaching water first comes from the Jerusalem Talmud; cf. p. 204 n. 3.

10. Similarly, in the account of the in-laws made rich and then poor, and the wife made beautiful and then ugly, the language implies at least that prayer is the means (R. b. Eliashab "exclaims"; the same word used to introduce a prayer to God that some action occur).

through prayer. To be sure exceptions exist so that one must speak of a tendency, rather than a regular characteristic, but the thrust of the stories clearly indicates that it is God who performed these acts at the request of his holy and pious rabbis.[11]

The non-Jewish Hellenistic world was also familiar with miracle-workers and magicians who could perform all manner of astonishing acts. One of the central figures in this whole area was Asclepius, a son by Apollo of a human mother, who performed a number of wondrous acts during his life—twice he cured blindness, once he cured insanity, he cured a hip wound Hercules received in one of his adventures—but was killed by a Jovian thunderbolt when he raised Hippolytus from the dead.[12] He belongs therefore to the age of gods and mythical heroes, but his power continued after his death and countless cures were attributed to him when the afflicted found themselves cured after spending a night in his temple. In many instances these healings occurred during sleep in which Asclepius appeared to the afflicted in a dream, as in the following instance:

> Pandarus, a Thessalian, who had marks on his forehead. He saw a vision as he slept. It seemed to him that the god bound the marks round with a headband and enjoined him to remove the band when he left the Abaton and dedicated it as an offering to the Temple. When day came he got up and took off the band and saw his face free of the marks; and he dedicated to the Temple the band with the signs which had been on his forehead.[13]

Other such accounts tell of a woman who after a five-year pregnancy delivered a child who immediately walked about; of people whose sight was restored though they had lost even their eyeballs, of paralyzed limbs cured, of the dumb having their power of speech restored, of the lame walking, and of the dead rising; all accomplished by the power of the god.[14] In one instance, admittedly late, a young girl is healed

11. It is clear that despite the qualifications noted above I would agree in substance with Schmithals' observation; see n. 5 above.

12. These acts are listed and described by Pietschmann, "Asklepios," 1653–54.

13. This is taken from Stele I, found at Epidaurus; the translation is found in Edelstein and Edelstein, *Asclepius,* 1:231 §6. Another story tells of a mother who saw her daughter cured in a dream and on awakening found it to be true (1.233 §21).

14. See ibid., 34, 160, 229ff.

when a man prays for her to Asclepius.[15] Rescue from danger at sea was another act ascribed to Asclepius, as it was also to Serapis.[16]

In addition to gods who through dreams or oracles could perform such wonders the Hellenistic world knew of men who could do similar things. These men accomplished such acts by a variety of means. An eyewitness tells of seeing a man cured of a viper bite by a Babylonian who drew out the poison with a spell and cured the already mordant leg by touching it with a fragment of a virgin's tombstone.[17] Apollonius of Tyana cured a boy bitten by a mad dog by forcing the dog to lick the wound and then cured the dog as well "after offering a prayer to the river" (on the other side of which the dog stood) (Philostratus, *Life*, 6:43). He also cured a woman, who had undergone labor seven times, by having her husband walk around her bed holding a live hare, which was then to be released (Philostratus, *Life*, 3:39). An Egyptian brought a corpse temporarily back to life by placing herbs on its mouth and breast and praying to the sun (Apuleius, *Metam.* 2:28–29).[18]

One of the favorite techniques in the magician's collection was the incantation. The ancient magical papyri are full of incantations for the most varied of purposes, and when they contained foreign words or phrases they were the more potent.[19] So effective were they, that apparently they could be effective even in written form: an Indian sage gave a woman a letter containing threats to a demon, assuring her that they would be effective in the case of her possessed son (Philostratus, *Life* 3:38). But oral speech is the more normal mode of expelling demons. Apollonius compelled a demon to leave a young man by ordering it to do so, and the demon knocked over a statue on the way out to prove it had gone (Philostratus, *Life* 4:20). In one story the teller saw

15. Ibid., 323; it comes from some time in the fifth century AD.

16. On Asclepius, see Pietschmann, "Asklepios," 1655; Weinreich, *Heilungswunder*, 14; on Serapis, see Kertelge, *Wunder*, 97 n. 353.

17. Told by Lucian in *Philopseudas*. The intent of this writing is of course satire, but in this case at least, the satire is conveyed not in the story itself but in Lucian's sarcastic response. When Lucian is fabricating he tells the reader as much, as in the introduction to his "True Histories"; see Harmon, trans., *Lucian*, 3:321–81, sec. 11–12.

18. There is also a legend that Asclepius was able to work his wonders, before his translation into heaven, by means of the Gorgon's blood that Athena had given him; see Edelstein and Edelstein, *Asclepius*, 1:8–9.

19. See the reference to imprecations against a specter, spoken in the "Egyptian language" in *Lucian* 31.

the demon emerging, "black and smoky in color," after narrating how a "Syrian from Palestine" commanded it to come out (*Lucian* 16).[20]

In some cases stories are told where one is not sure whether it was thought a miracle had been performed: A lame man walked without a limp when he had his injured hip massaged, and a girl being carried to her burial was raised; but the reader is not sure whether it was a miracle or whether Apollonius detected a spark of life remaining in the girl.[21] Such stories may simply confirm love of the miraculous in the Hellenistic age, since the hearers of such a story may hold it to have been a miracle if they so desire.

Any analysis of these stories, of which just a small sampling has been cited, can again be done only in summary fashion, yet one or two points stand out. While some of these acts are attributed to the gods, even through the prayer of others, at least as many are performed by men who possess some mysterious power or are able, by incantation and formula, to compel gods and demons to do their bidding. However one may want to judge a rabbi whose prayer is granted by God, he surely differs from the magician who by the force of his formula can compel action; in the latter case the power depends on the words themselves, not on the one or ones being addressed. Moreover, many of the wondrous acts reported in the ancient world are done to enrich the magician or to allow the supplicant to receive his heart's desire that custom and morality would otherwise deny him.[22] The power, in short, resides within the wonder-worker, and it is his to use as he sees fit.

It is evident from all of this that in the Hellenistic age there was quite an interest in stories of the miraculous, whatever the theological framework (or lack of it) in which they were cast. So popular were such stories, in fact, that they tend to "wander," that is, similar stories crop up

20. I am borrowing the language of Harmon.

21. On the lame man, see Philostratus, *Life* 3:39; in the same place, a paralyzed man is cured and a blind man restored without mention of any miracle, but the fact that the man had had both eyes put out leaves little doubt as to the miraculous nature of at least that restoration. On the dead girl, see *Life* 4:45. In all, Philostratus reports some twenty-one events in his account of Apollonius that could be considered, in some measure at least, miraculous.

22. Lucian tells of a young man in love with another man's wife, who achieves his desired goal by purchasing the services of a Hyperborean magician, *Lucian* 14. Eusebius also noted this about magicians; he is noted in this regard by G. W. H. Lampe, "Miracles and Early Christian Apologetic," in Moule, *Miracles*, p. 253.

in different places or different times. That often happens within a body of literature. Ḥanina b. Dosa's wondrous knowledge of the condition of a girl who had fallen into a cistern is told in *b. Yebam.* 121b and in *b. B. Qam.* 50a. Such wandering stories are not confined to the boundaries of a piece of literature, however, or even to the boundaries of a culture. Common miracle themes crop up throughout the Hellenistic world. Someone who sleeps a wondrous length of time, for example, is known both to Jews and Greeks.[23] Stories of poisonous serpents that are helpless against a wonder-worker are also widespread and familiar: sometimes the bite does not affect the wonder-worker, sometimes the one bitten is saved by a miracle; and in some instances, the serpent is forced to suck the poison from the wound and then, as a result, dies.[24] Another such story concerns the ability to stretch a piece of wood that is too short for the task at hand (*b. Ta'an.*, 25a; *Inf. Gos. Thom.* 13 [Latin text 11]).

Given that fact, it should not be too surprising that such popular motifs have also found their way into the stories about Jesus. One such motif is the exorcism of demons, which played a central part in the activity of many a wonder-worker of this period. A common element within the story concerns discussions between demon and exorcist with the demon sometimes pleading for mitigation of banishment. Again, on occasion, some event occurs at the time of expulsion to prove the demon has really left the person.[25] In other instances the power of a wonder-worker is demonstrated when he is able to heal someone physically removed from him, so that his power is not even dependent on his own personal presence or his contact with the afflicted one (*b. Ber.* 34b; John 4:46–54; Matt 8:5–13 and par.).[26] Raising the dead is another way by which the wonder-worker proves his power, whether the dead man be restored for only a short time (Apuleius, *Metam.* 2:28–29) or for an

23. A Cretan priest, Epimenedes, slept 40 years (see Harmon, 3:361 n. 1); Ḥoni the Circle Drawer slept 70 years (*b. Ta'an.* 23a).

24. Bite does not affect wonder-worker: *b. Ber.* 33a; Acts 28:3–6; man bitten saved: *Inf. Gos. Thom.* 16 (Latin text 14); *Lucian*, 11—the man then picks up his litter and carries it off; serpent withdraws its own poison: *Acts Thom.* 33; *(Arabic) Gos. Inf.* 42.

25. Pleading of demon: *Pesaḥ.* 112b; perhaps *Lucian* 16; proof of demon leaving: ibid.; Philosatratus, *Life* 4:20; Josephus, *Ant.* 8:42; both elements are present in Mark 5:1–20.

26. See also Marinus, *Vita Procli* in Edelstein and Edelstein, *Asclepius*, 1:323.

indefinite period (Philostratus, *Life* 4:45; Mark 5:35–43 and par.; Luke 7:11–17; John 11:38–44). And if the person is dead for some length of time, the question of putrifaction is, understandably enough, raised as an issue (*Lucian* 26; John 11:39). We have already mentioned rescue from stormy seas as another familiar act of the wonder-worker.[27] Even summaries of miracle activity are a common editorial device used by an author who wants to convey an impression of the wide-ranging and extensive character of the activity of his subject.[28]

If the content of such miracle stories is not limited to a particular cultural or religious milieu, neither is the form in which the stories are cast, although that form has at some times been regarded as more fixed than an examination of the material itself indicates. Miracle stories tend to begin the same way. Few if any accounts of such activity give any sure indication of the precise point at which they occurred, either in time or place, and very often the introduction of the afflicted person is quite general in its description.[29] That the problem is discussed and the cure is reported is hardly surprising; there is really no other way to report such material, as even modern patent medicine advertisements make clear. There seems to be some tendency to include a number of details in the story to heighten interest, but that is hardly a general characteristic. A number of stories are quite bare of such detail.[30] It is at the conclusion that this kind of story shows the greatest variation. A number of such stories, for instance, omit any indication of the result of the miracle; that is left to the imagination of the reader (Philostratus, *Life* 3:38).[31] And only very rarely is any response on the

27. See n. 15 above.

28. *Lucian* 13: "I saw him soar through the air in broad daylight and walk on the water and go through fire slowly on foot" (trans. Harmon, 3:339); cf. also, in the same writing 13–14; Aristedes (concerning Asclepius): "From many pains and sufferings and distresses, by day and by night, he has delivered many people" (Edelstein and Edelstein, *Asclepius*, 1:161); Mark 1:32–34, 3:10–12, 6:54–56; Matt 9:35; Acts 19:11–12.

29. This is true of many reports of healing attributed to Asclepius: see Pietschmann, "Asklepios," 1687; Mark 1:23, 40; 3:1, etc.

30. For detail see Philostratus, *Life* 4:20; Mark 9: 17–29; for stories with little detail, see Philostratus, *Life* 39 for three such stories; Luke 6:6–11, Mark 1:30–31.

31. The story ends with the mode of the cure, in this case, a letter. *Life* 3:39, where the cure is noted at the beginning of the account. *b. Ta'an.* 19a, where the results of Honi's prayer that the rain cease are not given.

part of bystanders to the miracle recorded. When it is, it may also occur within the story rather than as its conclusion.[32] In this respect the
final acclamation seems to be much more characteristic of the Gospel
miracle accounts than of the non-Christian miracle stories.[33]

It is clear, then, that the miracle accounts we have in the New
Testament belong, in content and style, to the age in which they originated. Yet despite a degree of commonality of type and content, we did
see certain differences between rabbinic and other Hellenistic miracle
stories. We must therefore ask the question: To which of these types
does the New Testament miracle story bear closer resemblance?

It ought to be fairly clear that Jesus was not pictured in the terms
with which the rabbinic wonder-worker was described. Jesus' miracles
do not characteristically occur as the answer to his prayer, and if some
rabbinic miracles do not seem to presume prayer, we must also note
that none of Jesus' miracles do.[34] Nor do miracles occur to benefit Jesus
or those around him, apart from any request by him or word or gesture
from him, as they do for some rabbis. None of the Gospel miracles
have such "accidental" qualities about them. Clearly, the person of
Jesus carries far more authority in the Gospels than does that of any
rabbi of whom the Talmud reports miracles.

On the other hand, there is much that would identify Jesus as
a more or less conventional Hellenistic wonder-worker. Some of the
language used to describe his conduct in the Gospels is rather clearly
of the same order as that used in the narration of non-Christian miracles.[35] Indeed, Duprez argues that the more we learn of the Hellenistic

32. Tagawa, *Miracles*, 93, n. 2, correctly observes that only in *Lucian* 12 is there
mention of crowd reaction at the end of an account, and that none is to be found in
Life of Apollonius. The only crowd reaction in the latter occurred in the midst of the
story when the statue fell, Philostratus, *Life* 4:20. Crowd reaction is also absent in
Apuleius when a corpse was revivified (Apuleius, *Metam.* 2:28–29).

33. It is interesting to note that when Bultmann discussed crowd reaction, his
primary evidence was drawn exclusively from the NT (*Geschichte*, 241 = *History*,
225–26). Yet the closing acclamation continues to be cited as typical of the Hellenistic
miracle story; see Duprez, "Guérisons," 14, for a recent example.

34. So also Becker, "Wunder," 138; Schmithals, *Wunder*, 20. This is true despite the
advice that some miracles only respond to prayer in Mark 9:29. The prayer in John
11:41–42 is not a typical prayer for God to perform the miracle; Jesus himself does
that in v. 43.

35. Bonner, "Traces," 174; Pesch, *Jesu Ureigene Taten?* 62–67; Smith, "Prolegomena,"
176; Held, "Matthew," 207.

age the more clear it becomes that Jesus must have been understood by both crowds and rabbis as a wonder-working healer.[36]

To be sure certain qualifications must be entered into any such judgment about Jesus and the Hellenistic wonder-worker.[37] There are very few traces of magical practices in the activity of Jesus, and one of the favorite devices of the Hellenistic wonder-worker, the magical incantation, is virtually absent from the report of Jesus' miracles. But perhaps the clearest difference is the eschatological interpretation and the subservience of miracle account to proclamation in the Gospel accounts of Jesus. His authority, within that frame of reference, is quite different from that of the ordinary exorcist.[38]

Despite such qualification, it is clear that the miracle accounts in the Gospels are more closely related to the Hellenistic than to the rabbinic types. That point, of course, was not lost on the Hellenistic world, and the comparison of Jesus with Asclepius, for example, shows the way the Gospels tended to be understood (Justin, *1 Apol.* 22:6; 54:10; *Acts Pil.* 1).[39] There is another point that shows the direction in which the interpretation of Jesus' miracles was moving. The inclusion of the Aramaic phrases in two miracle stories of Jesus (Mark 5:41; 7:34) has often been cited as an indication of the Hellenistic love for foreign phrases in incantations. Yet if (as seems highly likely) Jesus spoke Aramaic, then in Jesus' mouth they were not "foreign incantations." They became that only when the story was told in Greek, indicating the direction, I think, in which the interpretation of at least these two stories was moving. The inclusion of those foreign phrases shows that in these cases, at least, the interpretation was carried on by the use of a device familiar to the Hellenistic world.

This point, of course, raises a key question: How was the miracle-worker interpreted in the Hellenistic world? And a further question: Is there any indication that Jesus was also understood in that way by the developing tradition? In raising these questions, we come to the main issue of this article.

36. Duprez, "Guérisons," 22.

37. Cf. Glasswell, "Use," 22.

38. Cf. Pesch, *Jesu Ureigene Taten?* 24–25, 135, 147, 150, 157; Eitrem, *Some Notes,* 30, 40.

39. That Jesus' miracles are of the Hellenistic type, cf. Schmithals, *Wunder,* 20; Tagawa, *Miracles,* 101.

II. Divine Man and Early Christian Tradition

There is neither the space nor the need at this point to rehearse the development of Greek religion, nor to demonstrate the ease with which the divine passed into human form and became involved in the affairs of men (and of women!). By the time of the period in which we are interested, the number of gods was multiplying at an alarming rate,[40] and we have examples of men who in one way or another attempted to bring about their own apotheosis.[41] This simply meant that the Hellenistic world was convinced that contemporary men, like the heroes of old, could be and were endowed with divine powers and ultimately could themselves become gods.[42] The descriptive title for such a man was simply "divine man," (θεῖος ἀνήρ).[43] In such a person the characteristics of the gods were evident, such as, foreknowledge, persuasive speech, the ability to heal and to perform miracles; and in addition they were frequently set apart by an extraordinary birth and death. The divine man thus tended to become anyone who excelled in some desirable capacity, and the term passed into common parlance.[44]

While sages and prophets thus were identified as divine men, there was an increasing tendency to identify the ability to work miracles as the sine qua non; a tendency at work to such an extent that miracles came to be reported of and expected from even the traveling philosophers who crowded the Hellenistic world.[45] In short, a person

40. Lucian, in his *The Parliament of the Gods*, has Momus complain to Zeus about the large number of gods, foreign and peculiar, that have been allowed into heaven (esp. 8–10). A similar point is made in the *Recog. Clem.* 10:25.

41. E.g., Peregrinus Proteus, who cast himself onto a pyre at Olympia at the conclusion of the games; Lucian takes a typically jaundiced view of the whole event (*Peregrinus*).

42. When Apollonius removes his leg from its fetters and then replaces it, with no prayer or any other incantation, it proves to his companion, Damis, that Apollonius' nature is "divine, and greater than that of a man" (VII, 38).

43. On this title, see L. Bieler, ΘΕΙΟΣ ΑΝΗΡ; Hadas and Smith, *Heroes and Gods*. The description of "hero" in Eitrem, *Some Notes*, "Heros," in Pietschmann "Asklepios," esp. 8:1114–15, shows how closely related the divine man was to the hero.

44. Cf. Smith, "Prolegomena," 184–86.

45. Cf. Georgi, *Gegner*, 196 = *Opponents*, 157; Bammel, "John Did No Miracle," 181; any cultic deity worth his salt could also boast a string of miracles, as the votive inscriptions to Asclepius at Epidaurus, and other places, show; cf. Georgi, *Gegner*, 204 = *Opponents*, 161–62, for other examples.

who could do wondrous works in the Hellenistic world tended to be interpreted as a divine man; it was a broad category, but served as a rather widespread interpretative tool.

The manner in which Hellenistic Judaism began to interpret its own religious history bears out the statement that for a religion to be understood in that milieu, it had to make use of the interpretative device of divine man. Thus in the Hellenistic-Jewish religious propaganda designed for that world, the inspired figures of Jewish history came to be described as, and on occasion identified as, divine men (θεῖοι ἄνδρες).[46] Abraham, Moses, Elijah, Solomon, and many others, came to be identified in these terms.[47] Thus Solomon, according to Josephus, was the originator of the magical devices and incantations by means of which demons could be exorcised and his inheritance was, Josephus tells us, still used effectively, as he himself had once observed (*Ant.* 8:42).[48] But the greatest divine man of them all was Moses, not only because of the miracles he performed in Egypt and during the exodus but also because of his godlike wisdom as law-giver. Even his death apparently was interpreted by some Hellenistic Jews as a kind of apotheosis.[49] Thus, the Jewish divine man shares in God's power over the cosmos; a power that, in typical Hellenistic fashion, the Jewish apologists see as giving that divine man the power to perform miracles. Such wonders are, in turn, the way a divine man can legitimate himself.[50] Miracle and divine law were thus two manifestations of the same reality for Hellenistic Judaism it would appear, and logically enough, if the law be divine, then those who interpret the law must themselves in some sense be divine men. Interpreting Jewish tradition and law, these men also shared in a power transcending the merely human[51] and could themselves thus qualify for the designation θεῖος ἀνήρ.

46. Georgi gives several examples, *Gegner,* 147, 162ff. = *Opponents,* 123–24, 133ff.

47. Cf. Georgi, *Gegner,* 148, 217–18, 261 = *Opponents,* 124, 173–74, 255–56, for examples.

48. Eleazar was the exorcisor Josephus saw in operation.

49. Suggested, along with evidence, by Georgi, *Gegner,* 159 = *Opponents,* 131.

50. Georgi, *Gegner,* 150, 154 = *Opponents,* 124, 127–28.

51. Georgi suggests this seems to have been the case with both Philo (*Gegner,* 128ff. = *Opponents,* 111ff.) and Josephus (*Gegner,* 181 = *Opponents,* 141), as well as others.

If then the category of divine man was widespread and useful in the Hellenistic world for the interpretation of such phenomena as miracles and sound advice for life, and if as a corollary the best way to identify someone to whom such powers were attributed was by the title θεῖος ἀνήρ, then the question must inevitably be raised: Did the early Christian tradition—which underlies and which has received written form in our New Testament Gospels and epistles, and which, as the language alone testifies, was intended for the Hellenistic world at large—also use the hermeneutical device of divine man in interpreting the figure of Jesus? That is, did early Christology attempt to understand and present the earthly Jesus by making use of motifs belonging to the Hellenistic concept of θεῖος ἀνήρ?[52]

Given the picture of Jesus of Nazareth as we have it in the Gospels, it should not be surprising that a number of scholars would answer that question in the affirmative. Further, given the fact that the working of miracles tended to become the chief hallmark of the divine man, it ought not to be surprising that scholars have looked to the miracle accounts of Jesus for traces of such interpretative devices.[53] And since the Gospels of Mark and John appear to place the most emphasis on Jesus' mighty acts, those are the two places where attributes of the divine man would show up most clearly if in fact that category were used as an interpretative device by the primitive church. Finally, since it is apparent that all of our Gospel writers used sources to some degree, at least in composing their narratives, the search for materials relating to the concept of divine man has increasingly turned to an attempt to recover and analyze those sources.[54]

There is as yet, however, no unanimity among New Testament scholars as to the extent to which, or even whether at all, the category of divine man played a part in the interpretation of Jesus in the early Christian traditions.[55] More light on this problem, it would appear to

52. I am drawing for this definition on Betz, "Jesus as Divine Man," 116.

53. So Betz, ibid., 117ff.; but also as early as Rose, "Herakles and the Gospels," 128.

54. For John, cf. Becker, "Wunder," esp. 141; for Mark, see Keck, "Mark"; and below, ch. 5: "Origin and Function."

55. Schweizer questions the identification on the grounds that "the figure of the wonder-worker does not emerge in written sources until the latter half of the second century, *Jesus Christus*, 127, n. 10 = *Jesus*, 127 n. 10. Howard Kee also remains unconvinced, and continues his work on understanding Mark against the background

me, could be shed if we were to gain some idea of the larger trajectory of early Christian interpretation within which the traditions contained in the canonical Gospels and epistles find their place and of which they form a part. That is to say, if we can gain some insight into the direction in which the tradition moved in the period following the production of the canonical literature, we may be able more accurately to determine the meaning and import of some directions already apparent, but in still unclear form within the traditions of the early church. Again, limitations of space prevent an exhaustive evaluation, but a review of the evidence will begin to throw some light on that larger trajectory.

III. MIRACLES OF JESUS IN THE POST-CANONICAL TRADITION

Our first step will be to survey the apocryphal gospels and acts of the second and third centuries to give some indication of the way in which some of the early fathers understood Jesus' miracles and to see how that material interprets the part of Jesus' life also dealt with in the canonical Gospels, that is, his public ministry.

There are occasions when various miracles of Jesus are recited that, as their language shows, were drawn from the canonical Gospel accounts or perhaps from tradition underlying them,[56] but in any case reflecting the form of the miracles as we already know them (*Acts Pil.* 6–8; *Ep. Apos.* 5). There are also occasions when a single miracle of Jesus, again familiar through the Gospel traditions, will be recited (sometimes in the third person; see *Clem. Hom.* 19:22 [John 9:1–34]; 2:19 [Mark 7:24–30]) through the one healed or in some other way involved.[57] In two versions of one document canonical miracles are

---

of Jewish apocalyptic writing, esp. Daniel (as indicated in his paper presented to the Gospels Seminar of the SBL in 1970, and in another paper, read in the Gospels Section of the SBL, 1971, as well as in private conversations).

56. On the existence of synoptic traditions after the Gospels were written, see Koester, *Die Synoptische Überlieferung*. We can omit the apostolic fathers from our consideration, since they contain no traditions either of Jesus or of the apostles as wonder-workers.

57. *Acts of Andrew and Matthias*; Mark 4:35–41, told by Andrew, ANF 8:519; *The Avenging of the Saviour*; Mark 5:25–34, told by the woman cured, ANF 8:474. Christ's Descent into Hell, 4:3 (XX) = *The Gospel of Nicodemus*, ch. 4 (XX); John 11:38–44, told by Hades. *Gos. Nico.* 6; John 5:2–15; Mark 10:46–52, told by recipients of healing. One who was "crooked" and a leper tell also in that same passage of being healed, but without enough detail to identify the story.

recited but with exaggerated detail, that is, how badly the corpse of Lazarus was rotted, how feeble the woman was who had the flow of blood.[58] There are also some instances where a miracle is told of Jesus that is totally different from any in the Gospels. One of them is a eucharistic miracle,[59] another deals with a stone sphinx that Jesus causes to speak and walk, and in a third Jesus appears and steers the boat in which Andrew is sailing (*Acts of Andrew and Matthias* [ANF 8:520, 519]).[60]

A more popular device for referring to Jesus' miracles is a summary of them. A number of such summaries clearly reflect the canonical tradition either in their wording or in the particular miracles to which they refer.[61] A larger number, which tend on the whole to be shorter, may reflect the canonical traditions in their language, but the wording is such that that fact is not altogether clear. That is, the summaries are so general that while some detail (e.g., healing on the Sabbath) or the general context (e.g., references to teachings found in the canonical Gospels) seems to reflect the canonical tradition, there is no certainty that the miracles being summarized must be drawn from it.[62] Sometimes the summary can be very short,[63] but normally there is reference to three or more miracles.

There is another type of summary of Jesus' miracles that seems to have as its point not so much the reminder of the kind of act of which Jesus was capable as to demonstrate that those acts were the fulfillment of Isa 35:5–6 (*Recog. Clem.* 3:60). This is quite in line with a motif of early Christian apologetic in which fulfillment of prophecy

58. The Report of Pilate the Procurator concerning our Lord Jesus Christ (one to Augustus, one to Tiberius); the material occurs at the beginning of the reports, ANF 8:460, 462.

59. Jesus produced bread and wine by striking his side; *Gos. Bart.* 2:18–19.

60. In the same document Jesus himself appeared and healed Andrew (ANF 8:524), but that is similar to the miracles reported of him in the canonical Gospels.

61. *Acts Thom.* 48; *Acts of Paul*, P. Heid., p. 79 (see *NTA*, 2:382); *Acts of the Holy Apostles Peter and Paul*, ANF 8:480; *Acts of Andrew and Matthias*, ANF 8:519; *Christ's Descent into Hell*, NTA 1:477; *The Avenging of the Saviour*, ANF 8:472.

62. *Abgar Legend* (Eusebius, *Hist. eccl.* 13:5); *Acts of Paul*, P. Heid., p. 79 (*NTA* 2:383); *Acts Pil.* 1; *Recog. Clem.* 5:10; *Clem. Hom.* 1:6 and 2:34; *Gos. Nic.* 4 (XX), ch. 10; *Acts of the Holy Apostle Thaddaeus* (ANF 8:558); Justin Martyr, *1 Apol.* 22; *Dial.* 69.

63. In Justin Martyr, *1 Apol.* 31, only healing disease and raising the dead to life are mentioned.

was used as one way of legitimating faith in Jesus. Such fulfillment was linked specifically in some cases to Isa 35:5–6,[64] but it could also be understood in a broader sense (Justin, *1 Apol.* 54; *Recog. Clem.* 1:41). Thus, fulfillment of prophecy could be used as a device to discredit the healings of Asclepius as compared with Jesus (Justin, *1 Apol.* 54; *Dial.* 69), or it could be used to demonstrate Jesus' divinity, even at a time when a direct appeal to the miraculous was no longer entirely convincing.[65]

Miracle accounts of Jesus could also be used in an allegorical or spiritualized way to indicate the present help available to those who believed in him.[66] And in one instance at least it appeared best not to be specific about the miracles at all; in true Gnostic fashion, they cannot "now" be revealed (*Acts John* 93).[67]

It would appear, therefore, that for that period of Jesus' life recorded in the canonical Gospels, that is, his public ministry, the tradition pretty well limited the development of accounts relating to this aspect of Jesus' career. While there is some attempt to set him apart from the more common magical practices of that time—for example, Jesus did his healing without drugs or herbs[68]—there seems little attempt to elaborate further his deeds in the direction of the divine man concept beyond those aspects already present in the canonical tradition. Such elaboration as there is remains limited to descriptions of those who were healed rather than to Jesus or the way he healed them.

In those areas, however, that are not covered in canonical tradition, the tendency to picture Jesus in terms more familiar to the

---

64. E.g., by Justin in *1 Apol.* 48; *Dial.* 69; Origen, *Cels.* 2:48 (I owe this reference to Lampe, "Miracles," 211). Pesch, *Jesu Ureigene Taten?*, finds traces of such a view already in Matt 11:5 (pp. 36–37) and Mark 7:37 (p. 42).

65. Arnobius and Athanasius appeal to Jesus' superior miracles as proof of his divinity (so Lampe, "Miracles," 208–9), as appears also to be the case with the *Recog. Clem.* 3:60. For Origen, the evidential value of the miracles was enhanced by the fact that they fulfilled OT prophecy (cf. Wiles, "Miracles," 222).

66. For Origen, the spiritual results of the work of the apostles represent those "greater works" of which Christ spoke (so Lampe, "Miracles," 212); *Acts Thom.* 66 interprets Jesus' miracles in terms of his present readiness to help.

67. Just prior to this, the reader is told that Jesus left no footprints when he walked.

68. *The Abgar Legend* (Eusebius, *Hist. eccl.* 1.53.5); Athanasius, *De Incarnatione*, 49 (I owe this latter reference to Lampe, "Miracles," 208).

Hellenistic world flowers. This is true in areas of Jesus' life not covered in canonical tradition, for example, the infancy gospels. Here Jesus' miracles are the equal of any the Hellenistic world knew and are notable for their lack of any genuine Christian, or even generally religious, motifs. They simply glorify the young Jesus who can and does do what is appropriate for his own convenience, physical or emotional.[69]

Such flowering of Hellenistic motifs also occurs in accounts of the activity of the various disciples following Jesus' ascension. This can be seen in the way in which these accounts are structured. The elements of the Hellenistic romance—travel, natural prodigies, miracles, erotic elements (often in a negative form like asceticism, but also in more "positive" form), separation and reunion of man and woman—are present in many of the accounts of the disciples (e.g., *Acts of Paul and Thecla*, *Acts of Thomas*). But it can also be seen in the proliferation of miracles attributed to the individual disciples. Peter cured the blind,[70] John the mortally ill (*Acts John* 23). They regularly raised the dead, sometimes murder victims (*Acts John* 51–52; *Acts Thom.* 54), often women (*Acts John* 80; *Acts Thom.* 81; the murder victim in *Acts Thom.* 54 was also a woman), and on one occasion after Peter had raised a young man from the dead, the people, we are told, "venerated him as a god" (*Acts Pet.* 28–29; Peter raised another dead man by prayer in 27). In a contest in Rome, Simon killed a boy by whispering in his ear. Peter demonstrated his superiority by restoring the boy's life (*Acts Pet.* 26; the boy's owner, Agrippa, raised him at Peter's command). Nor was Paul without the ability to raise a man from the dead (*Acts Paul* 2:11).[71]

The tendency to color such stories with elements apparently common to the Hellenistic world is further indicated when, for example, Thomas caused a demon to depart from a young woman and its exit was marked by fire and smoke (as the demon in Lucian's *Philopseudas* was described as "dark and smokey in color"; *Acts Thom.* 42–46).[72] Again, when Peter cast out a demon it knocked over a statue in its

69. Because they are more familiar than the apocryphal acts, and because they are not lengthy, I will omit any specific discussion of them here.

70. *Acts Pet.* (II, *Actus Ver.*) §§20, 21.

71. This story clearly reflects Acts 20:9ff., though it happens in Rome and the lad is Proclus, Caesar's cup-bearer.

72. Thomas cast out another demon in *Acts Thom.* 75ff., which asked to be allowed a new habitation, in the course of a long conversation with Thomas.

departure, reminding one of the story told of Apollonius of Tyana
(*Acts Pet.* 11). The wording is so similar, including the derisive attitude
of the young man possessed, that if there is no actual dependence of
one on the other, common elements of some popular story may have
been included by both authors. In Peter's case, however, the miracle is
heightened when, by means of sprinkling water and by prayer, Peter
causes the statue to repair itself (*Acts Pet.* 11).

As the example about Peter indicates, stories told of the disciples
and the apostles are not limited to stories that have parallels, however
rough, in the canonical literature. Peter, for example, caused Simon the
magician, who was flying over Rome in an exhibition of his power, to
fall and fracture his leg.[73] As further proof that his God was worthy of
faith, Peter caused a smoked fish that had been hanging in a window
to come to life, swim about, and eat the bread people threw to it (*Acts
Pet.* 12–13). John in his turn caused a shrine and temple of Artemis to
splinter and collapse, killing a priest of that cult (*Acts John* 38–42),[74]
and he was able on two occasions to empower others to raise people
from the dead (*Acts John* 24, 47; Peter did the same in *Acts Pet.* 26).

Sometimes, again in typical Hellenistic fashion, the miracles concern animals and giving them the ability to speak. Thus Peter caused
a dog to speak, who then went and summoned Simon the magician to
confront him (*Acts Pet.* 9). Thomas commanded wild asses, through
the wagon driver, to take over when the domesticated animals were
exhausted, and upon reaching his destination, Thomas had one of the
asses summon forth two women who were possessed of demons so
that they could be healed (*Acts Thom.* 68, 74).[75] There are also occasions when the accounts told of the apostles seem to be designed to
show their own personal power, as when Andrew causes seven prison
guards to die and the prison gates to open by themselves, or when
John, challenged to appear naked in a theatre and without using "that
magical name" to perform a miracle, healed a large number (*Acts Andr.
Mth.* [ANF 8:52]; *Acts John* 31–37). And in at least two instances we

---

73. In three places! *Acts Pet.* 32 (= *Martyrdom of the Holy Apostle Peter*, 3).

74. Barnabas did the same to another pagan shrine in *Acts of Barnabas* (ANF
8:495).

75. In *Acts Thom.* 78–79, the ass rebukes and then evangelizes Thomas! *The Acts
of Thomas* also contains two summaries of his miracles (20, 59), indicating his wide
renown as miracle-worker.

have what appear to be popular stories that have been included within the recital of apostolic miracles. One concerns John. In an effort to get a needed night's rest, he commanded the multitude of bugs with whom he shared his accommodation to leave the room, which they did; they dutifully remained outside the door until the next morning when John allowed them to return to the bed (*Acts John* 60–61). The other concerns Peter who prayed upon a father's request, that good might come to the latter's daughter and she promptly died. Dissatisfied with that, the father asked Peter to raise her and he did; shortly thereafter the daughter was seduced by a stranger and ran off with him. Thus, it is implied, leaving both father and daughter in a condition worse than they were in before.[76]

IV. Some Conclusions

We have now completed our rapid survey of the trajectory of development of miracle stories in the period following the writing of the canonical Gospels. We are now in a position to make some suggestions at least, or point to continuing problems, relating to the question of whether or not the early Christian tradition used the concept of divine man in interpreting Jesus. It is apparent that the apocryphal acts of the apostles have taken some strides in the direction of picturing Jesus' immediate followers in terms of popular Hellenistic imagery, including that of divine man. We have noted a number of elements above that point in that direction.

Yet it must also be noted that however florid the later accounts of apostolic activity may have been, precedents for them existed already in the canonical Book of Acts. There apostles are pictured as wonder-workers (5:12; 6:8; 14:3; 15:12); specific acts of healing are recorded (Peter in 3:6–10; 5:15–16; 9:33–35; Paul in 4:8–10; 19:11–12; 28:8–9); demons are cast out (16:16–18); dead are raised (by Peter, 9:10; by Paul, 20:7–12, an account that shares the characteristic Hellenistic ambiguity as to whether or not a real raising from death occurred); competitions of magic occur (Philip against Simon, 8:6–13); and the gospel is legitimated by miracles (Philip in 8:6–7). In many ways the apostles already function and are recognized as divine men: Peter is worshiped by Cornelius (10:25–26) and Paul and Barnabas are taken

76. *Acts of Peter*, (b), the Gardener's Daughter (*NTA* 2:278–79).

for gods (or divine men? 14:8–18). And in one section of the narrative of Paul's journey to Rome, he functions as a model divine man (with prophecies, comfort, wisdom, and miracles) both for his benefit and for the benefit of others (27:9—28:10).

The need for such accounts of the power of the followers of Jesus was in all likelihood necessitated by the religious situation in the Hellenistic world where religious competition was "won" by those who were the stronger.[77] It thus was part of the function of early Christian charismatics apparently, to perform signs and wonders to legitimate their message in the eyes of their contemporaries,[78] and the accounts of those deeds themselves became useful in such missionary competition.

Both the activity itself, to the extent that that can be recovered, and certainly the accounts of it are put within the theological framework of the power of the risen Christ to continue his work among his followers.[79] In the overwhelming majority of the accounts of the miraculous acts of the apostles contained in the apocryphal literature, the performance is preceded by prayer to Jesus, or is accomplished in his name (or both) and where that is not emphasized, the resulting faith of the onlookers in Jesus rather than in the apostles makes it apparent that such a framework is assumed. In very few cases is that framework absent, and when it is, the very secular nature of the stories indicates that in all probability they have simply been borrowed from contemporary folklore. The tendency to make the apostles into divine men is therefore carried on within the theological framework of Jesus as their Lord.

If the apostles tend increasingly to be pictured in popular Hellenistic terms as divine men, a tendency already begun in the canonical Acts, the same cannot be said of Jesus. In fact the reticence exercised with respect to the activity of the mature Jesus is quite remarkable. There appears to be no clear-cut trajectory moving in the direction of making Jesus more clearly able to compete with other Hellenistic divine men by describing him increasingly in those terms. The later

77. Georgi makes much of this point, I think convincingly; cf. as an instance, *Gegner*, 72 = *Opponents*, 53.

78. So Kertelge, *Wunder*, 28.

79. Eusebius (*Hist. eccl.* 2.3.2) refers to this point (I owe this reference to Lampe, "Miracles," 214); it was already prepared by John 14:12.

literature seems to content itself with résumés, for the most part, of the miracle activity of Jesus reported in the canonical traditions. From the accounts in the so-called infancy gospels, I think it is clearly indicated that Jesus could be transformed into such a divine man. The reticence, therefore, seems to be due less to the figure of Jesus as such than to whether or not there were firm traditions already existing about him. Whereas traditions already existing about the apostles in the canonical Acts were later embellished, traditions about Jesus that we find in our canonical Gospels tended not to be embellished. Perhaps, so one could argue, the Gospels already contained adequate evidence of Jesus as divine man, so that the need for embellishment was obviated. Yet, surely the same could be said for the apostles in the canonical Acts. But whatever the reason, the desire to portray Christian figures in divine man terms seems, in the period following the development of the canonical tradition, to have been transferred to the apostles.

When we move back to the period within which the canonical Gospels were being written we may well encounter tendencies and counter-tendencies with respect to interpreting Jesus in terms of the divine man concept. It is possible that the desire to portray Jesus as divine man had already begun to flower in the prewritten stage of the canonical traditions, or during what may well have been the stage of written sources and written fragments, between the oral tradition and the canonical Gospels. Was such a tendency so effectively countered by our canonical Gospels that the only way in which divine man conceptuality could be applied to the Christian faith thereafter was by applying it to Jesus' followers, that is, the apostles? Or on the contrary, did a tendency of seeing Jesus as divine man, already begun in the Gospel sources, carry through into our Gospels to such an extent that, since Jesus was already so clearly a divine man in the canonical Gospels, the only development possible was in terms of his apostles?

Work on these questions has been underway for some time; space precludes any summary of the individual efforts. There seems to be an emerging inclination to understand the canonical Gospels as attempts in various ways to combat the interpretation of Jesus as divine man, or to put it more carefully, to combat attempts to allow a divine man Christology to become dominant and authoritative in Christian tradition. Yet, as such work has already indicated, the problem is not susceptible of easy solution. Those who work with it find themselves increasingly confronted with the richness and variety of primitive Christian tradition, a richness and variety that appear to have characterized the life of the early Christian communities as well. Those who seek to touch such traditions must therefore realize that they are putting their fingers on evidences of pulsing life and must be prepared to reckon with all the complications by which life itself is characterized. Simple solutions to the problem of Jesus and the θεῖος ἀνήρ concept will, in all probability, be incorrect. Yet that must not serve to discourage, but to spur on, work in this area.

¶ INCREASED ATTENTION HAS BEEN DEVOTED IN RECENT YEARS TO
the problem of identifying and isolating possible pre-Johannine and
pre-Markan sources, particularly in relation to material that contains
reports of miracles.[1] In the case of Mark, doublets of such materials in
the narratives (two feedings, two miracles associated with the Sea of
Galilee, two healings using spittle, etc.), have often led to attempts to
reconstruct the parallel reports, with or without the implication that
they were the result of a twofold source underlying Mark.

Such attempts at reconstruction have characteristically assumed
that the parallelism begins with the accounts of the feedings. There
is, however, another way in which a kind of rough parallelism may be
found in the Markan narrative, namely a parallelism that begins, not
with the accounts of the feedings, but with the two accounts of miracles
associated with the sea (Mark 4:35–41 and 6:45–52).

An examination of the limits of such a Markan repetition yields
interesting results. The material in the first grouping (4:35–6:44) includes a sea-miracle, preaching, healings, and a feeding. The material
in the second cycle (6:45—8:26) includes a sea-miracle, preaching and
disputes, healings, and a feeding. There is a rough kind of parallelism
to the two cycles, but it is not exact. In the first cycle, the healings (5:1–
43) precede the account of Jesus' preaching (6:1–6), whereas in the
second block, the preaching and disputes (7:1–23) occur in the midst

---

1. For John, see Fortna, *Gospel of Signs*; for Mark, see Keck, "Mark 3:7–12," to
give but one example of each. There has, of course, been a good deal of discussion on
a point related to the material with which we are concerned, viz., the attempt to differentiate various editorial phases through which this material passed on its way to its
present shape (e.g., the whole problem of an Urmarkus). Limitations of space prevent
any consideration of that literature here.

of the healings (6:53–56; 7:24–37). The material on John the Baptist in the first cycle has no counterpart in the second, whereas the material at the end of the second grouping (8:11–21) has no counterpart in the first. And the healing at Bethsaida (8:22–26) ends the second section in a way quite unlike the ending of the first block (with a feeding, 6:34–44).

While the total material is thus somewhat dissimilar, the units that report Jesus' mighty acts are remarkably similar. In both instances, the order is: sea miracle (4:35–41; 6:45–32), three healing miracles (5:1–43; 6:53–56; 7:24–37), and feeding a multitude (6:34–44; 8:1–10). Such similar grouping of similar types of stories raises the possibility that Mark may be following a double cycle[2] of miracle stories that he found in his tradition. We shall investigate the material within which these two cycles occur (4:35—8:26), in an effort to see whether or not there are literary and linguistic indications that Mark has in fact adapted such a cycle of miracle stories to fit the purposes of his narrative.

We shall proceed in the following way. First, we shall investigate the material that does not concern itself with miracles, seeking any obvious signs of Markan editorial activity within it, to determine whether or not the author of Mark has inserted material into an order of miracle stories he found in his tradition. Our second task will be to investigate

2. Relevant terminology is worth noting. Some scholars name such a collection of miracle accounts an "aretalogy" (e.g., Koester, "One Jesus," 230–36; Robinson, "On the Gattung," 103), although some confusion can arise from the fact that this word already bears two other meanings: a celebration of the virtues and/or accomplishments of a god (his ἀρεταί; for this usage, see Grant, Hellenistic Religions, 131, 133); and a celebrative biography of some ancient worthy (for this usage, see Hadas and Smith, Heroes and Gods, passim). There is also growing investigation into the problem of the literary Gattung to which a "gospel" may belong and from which it may have been derived, seeking some light in aretalogies of the biographical variety. To use as "unloaded" a term as possible, I shall employ "cycle" to designate a general sequence of material concerning Jesus' mighty acts, and the term "miracle catena(e)" to refer to the specific pre-Markan source I am attempting to isolate. I am attempting in that way to avoid any confusion at this stage with the Gattung-question on the one hand (although my proposal, if correct, may well have implications for that problem), and with the idea that I am referring to a collection of "miracle stories" in any technical sense (e.g., as opposed, say, to "paradigms"), on the other. As I shall use it, "miracle catena" means simply a collection of stories in which the common element among them is the account of some miraculous act or event. My proposal will not, therefore, be disproved, if some of the stories in the collection do not appear to be formal "miracle stories" in the technical sense of the term.

the miracle stories themselves, to determine to what extent there has been Markan editorial adaptation of them, and whether, by stripping it away, we can come to any conclusion about the shape of the cycles in their pre-Markan form.

I. MATERIAL IN MARK 4:35—8:38
NOT DEALING WITH MIRACLES

6:1–6a, Rejection at Nazareth

It is apparent from the presence of the saying about a prophet being unacceptable in his own country in both the Coptic *Gospel of Thomas* and the Oxyrhynchus Papyrus that the saying included in this pericope was known apart from its present Markan context.[3] We may therefore be dealing with material that Mark has composed in an effort to give a framework for a saying of Jesus.[4] The fact that the saying has two parts in the non-Markan forms, whereas the first part of the saying alone is repeated in Mark 6:4, while the second part is illustrated by the disbelieving reaction of the people and the subsequent paucity of healings, may be an indication that Mark knew of both halves, but chose to cite only the first.

Further evidence of Markan editorial activity is furnished by the presence of two phrases that, in their present usage, are characteristically Markan. The one is ἤρξατο with an infinitive (in this instance διδάσκειν) in v. 2.[5] The other, καὶ ἔλεγεν αὐτοῖς, appearing in v. 4, is

---

3. P. Oxy. I, lines 31–36; *Gos. Thom.* 31.

4. So, e.g., Schulz, *Stunde*, 30–31.

5. Cf. Schweizer (*Markus*, 69 = *Mark*, 123), who calls this a "typical expression of Mark." This word, in the medial form, meaning "to begin," appears 26 times in Mark, exclusively in aorist tense, 3rd person. Of those uses, 11 appear to be integral to the narrative and serve a function within the story in which they appear. The remaining 15 appear at the beginning of pericopes, often to introduce a saying (e.g., 8:31; 10:32; 12:1) or general speaking activity by Jesus (6:34; 8:11), and often within material that for other reasons can confidently be assigned to Markan editorial activity (e.g., 1:45; 4:1; 6:55). How characteristic the aorist 3rd person form is of Mark is indicated by comparison with Luke and Matthew. Luke employs the word some 43 times, but in both active and middle forms and in a wide variety of tenses, moods, and persons; Matthew uses it only 12 times, but again with greater variety of mood and tense than Mark. Nor does either Matthew or Luke tend to reproduce the phrase when it is used in contexts that seem to be due to Markan editorial activity (cf. Mark 1:45; 4:1; 6:2; 6:55; 8:11; at 8:31, Matthew changes the infinitive), further indication that the usage

generally acknowledged to be an attachment-formula by means of which Mark introduces traditional material.[6]

The presence of these two editorial phrases may indicate that Mark found an account of Jesus' reception in his homeland and turned what may originally have been an astonishment of approval (v. 2)[7] into an account of Jesus' rejection at the hands of those closest to him, a motif present at other points in Mark's gospel as well (cf. 3:20–21, and 31–35). The presence in this pericope of two other typically Markan themes, viz., Jesus' accompaniment by his disciples (vv. 1–2a) and a kind of summary statement about Jesus' healing (v. 5b)[8] would lend weight to the conclusion that these verses (vv. 1–6a) may owe much of their present shape to Markan editorial activity.

However one may want to conceive the original of this material and the forces that gave it its present shape, there is general agreement that we are dealing with an isolated unit of material which owes its present placement to Mark, and not to the traditions existing before him.[9]

6:6b–13, The Twelve Sent Forth

Whether v. 6b serves as the end of the account of the rejection of Jesus or as the beginning of the account of the sending out of the twelve, its redactional nature is apparent; it serves simply to connect these two accounts.[10] The presence of the relatively rare expression "the twelve"

---

to which we refer is rather typically Markan.

6. So Marxsen, "Redaktionsgeschichtliche Erklärung," 262. It is rather regularly used to introduce a saying which may not follow exactly in context, but which Mark has apparently gotten from his tradition (e.g., 4:9, 11, 21, 24; 6:10; 7:9, 14, 18; 8:21; 9:1, 31). It can also be used in what are evidently editorial insertions (e.g., 4:2; 12:38); its use to introduce the second passion prediction (9:31) not only indicates that Mark is responsible for the present location, but also lends weight to the contention that ἤρξατο with an infinitive functions similarly, since the other two predictions (8:31; 10:32) are introduced with that formula. Two variations on this formula, viz., καὶ ἔλεγεν αὐτοῖς and καὶ ἔλεγεν, seem to be used by Mark in the same way.

7. So Knox, Sources, 1:47.

8. So Schweizer (Markus, 69 = Mark, 123), who nevertheless concludes that Mark did give this material its present shape.

9. A "seam" lies between 5:43 and 6:1, according to Schmidt, Rahmen, 153; cf. also Knox, Sources, 1:49; Sundwall, Zusammensetzung, 35.

10. Bultmann, Geschichte, 367 = History, 342.

(v. 7) has led to the suggestion that we have here to do with a "Twelve Source,"[11] although its existence has not been widely recognized; the phrase may also be due simply to Mark's editorial activity.[12] The characteristic Markan editorial phrases, ἤρξατο with an infinitive (v. 7) and καὶ ἔλεγεν αὐτοῖς (v. 10), are further clues to the editorial origins of this material. The pericope ends, in vv. 12–13, with precisely the kind of summary of activity that Mark himself has apparently composed, and inserted, throughout the early chapters of his gospel.[13]

The presence of καὶ ἔλεγεν αὐτοῖς, used to introduce the saying of Jesus in vv. 10–11, could argue that this pericope has, like its predecessor, been constructed around a word of Jesus that Mark found in his traditions.[14] The difficulty in the narrative, centering around the vacillating personal endings of the finite verbs (3rd person in indirect speech, vv. 8–9a; 2nd person imperative in vv. 10–11, with a transitional 2nd person in v. 9b) may well point to some kind of combination of material through editorial activity, perhaps even to the combination of two sayings of Jesus from the tradition, the one in v. 9, the other, appropriately introduced by Mark, in vv. 10–11, with the whole then summed up in vv. 12–13.

The fact that the narrative will not reach its conclusion until 6:30–32 simply reinforces the impression that the Markan editorial hand has fallen heavily on this material, to the extent that not only the order, but the material itself, owes more to his literary activity than to traditions at his disposal.

11. E.g., Knox, *Sources*, 1:21–22, who argued for this source.

12. Schweizer (*Markus*, 71 = *Mark*, 127–28), notes that mention of the "twelve" occurs mostly in redactional portions of Mark's narrative, and he points to the evanescent nature of the "twelve" in NT literature as an indication that it existed as a theological concept rather than as a historical group around Jesus, fixed in names and number. This, of course, would lend weight to the argument that this pericope owes its origin to a somewhat later stage in the tradition, perhaps the period when Mark was composing his gospel.

13. So also Schulz, "Bedeutung," 136, Such other summaries may be identified, some with more confidence than others, in 1:14–15, 32–34, 39, 45; 3:7–12, to name only those that precede 6:12–13.

14. So Schulz, *Stunde*, 30–31.

6:14–16, Herod's Opinion on Jesus

Although these verses belong in the present configuration of Mark to the story of the death of John the Baptist that follows them, we shall consider them as a separate unit. We again confront the phenomenon of a set of verses totally without necessary connection to the material preceding it.[15] While this in itself proves nothing about the degree of Markan editorial activity, it is significant to the extent that it argues against this material having existed in any kind of pre-Markan continuity. This pericope, like the material beginning in 6:1, gives no indication, either in content or form, of having been joined to what precedes it in any way prior to the writing of the gospel.

While these verses now serve as an introduction to the account of John's death, there has been some speculation that originally they may have belonged to a tradition that had different material following it.[16] Proof is lacking, however. Nor is there any measure of agreement as to the extent of Markan literary activity in these verses.

The evidence for such literary activity consists in the repetitiveness of v. 14 and vv. 15–16, with the conclusion that such literary results are to be attributed to the work of an editor expanding his tradition, in this case to make it useful as an introduction for the following story. Yet this solution is not entirely convincing. There are no typical Markan phrases indicating literary activity, such as we have observed in the preceding verses, and where such is the case, it is better not to assume Markan redaction.

If, on the other hand, we read, with the majority of the best mss, ἔλεγεν in v. 14 instead of ἔλεγον, then a better solution suggests itself, namely, that we are dealing here with a doublet from the tradition, combined by Mark.

Verse 14 and vv. 15–16 give accounts of Herod's hearing about Jesus, and indicate the conclusion he drew, but the verses differ in content. In v. 14, Herod hears in a general way about Jesus (his "name became evident"), and concludes that, to account for what he hears, in this instance apparently about Jesus' mighty acts, he must assume John has risen from the dead. In vv. 15–16, Herod hears the various

15. Schmidt, *Rahmen*, 172–73, argued that a seam is clearly visible between vv. 13 and 14; so already Weiss, *Evangelium*, 200.

16. Bultmann, *Geschichte*, 329 = *History*, 302.

opinions circulating about who Jesus is, to which Herod then adds his own view, viz., he is John redivivus. A later copyist, noting the repetition, attempted to smooth it over by including v. 14 in the series of opinions (changing ἔλεγεν to ἔλεγον), thus limiting Herod to the one expression in v. 16. The similarity between the opinions expressed in v. 15 with those expressed in 8:25 about Jesus would tend to point further to v. 15 as containing pre-Markan tradition.

6:17–29, John the Baptist's Death

It is clear that we are here dealing with material that is not drawn from what may be termed the gospel tradition proper.[17] The story is in no way tied to the career of Jesus. Whether or not it already existed in written form prior to Mark's use of it, is difficult to say.[18] The material, however, shows few if any signs of Markan editorial activity. Apparently Mark felt it suited his purpose as it stood, namely, to fill out the space between the sending forth of the twelve and their return.[19] That he may also have wanted to point to a further similarity between Jesus and John, viz., that John, too, died a violent death at the hands of his enemies (cf. also 9:12–13),[20] could account for the choice of this story to fill that interval, but it does not account for his placing it just at this point in his narrative. But that, in its way, argues for the fact that Mark is responsible for this order, since there is nothing in the mission of the twelve, and the account of John's death, to indicate any kind of pre-Markan relationship between them, either as to form or content.

Mark has apparently, then, taken two traditions dealing with Herod's opinion that Jesus is John redivivus, combined them as an introduction to the account of John's death, and inserted the whole episode between the account of the sending out of the twelve and their

17. So Knox, *Sources*, 1:50; Schweizer, *Markus*, 74 = *Mark*, 132–33; Bultmann, *Geschichte*, 328 = *History*, 301; Sundwall, *Zusammensetzung*, 37.

18. Schweizer, *Markus*, 74 = *Mark*, 132, identifies it as having come to Mark in written form; Sundwall, *Zusammensetzung*, 37, says it may have; Knox, *Sources*, 1:50, is unwilling to decide the issue either way. This last, it seems to me, is the only solution the evidence really allows.

19. So Schweizer, *Markus*, 74 = *Mark*, 132; Bultmann, *Geschichte*, 328–29 = *History*, 301–2; Knigge, "Meaning," 68, and many others.

20. Burkill, *Mysterious*, 184, gives this as the reason for Mark's inclusion of this story.

return, in order to create an interval in his narrative during which they carry out their mission.

6:30–33, *The Twelve Return*

The account of the return of the twelve, after the interlude concerning John the Baptist, contains a number of indications pointing to Markan editorial style, if not to Markan composition. Verse 30 contains the word ἀπόστολος, rare in Mark (only here and 3:14 var.), and begins with a phrase that Snoy has rather convincingly demonstrated, belongs to the Markan stock of editorial phrases, namely καὶ συνάγονται.[21] The descriptions contained in vv. 31–32—the crowds which swarm around Jesus, the motif of the sea and boats, in this instance a sea journey—as well as the phrase with which v. 31 is introduced (καὶ λέγει αὐτοῖς), point in the same direction.[22] That v. 33 is an awkward transition is recognized even by those who see in these verses some evidence of the use of sources,[23] and the resemblance between this verse and the general tenor of 6:14–56 has been pointed out by Snoy.[24] It is rather clear, then, that vv. 31–33, at least, present an attempt on the part of the author of the gospel to accomplish the change in scene from the mission of the twelve to the feeding of the 5,000. The evangelist has borrowed terminology in this passage from the account that follows (the crowds, v. 44; the verb φάγειν vv. 36, 37), creating in that way the transition.[25]

---

21. Snoy, "Redaction," 238. He points out that the verb appears in five summaries (2:2; 4:1; 5:21; 6:30; 7:1), in each instance in the introduction of pericopes where redactional activity is evident; that in each instance except 5:21 it is preceded by καὶ and begins the phrase; and that in 4:1, 6 30, and 7:1, it is in the historical present, a tense Mark seems to favor. It must be noted that these latter three instances differentiate themselves from 2:2 and 5:21, where the verb is in the aorist passive; we would also limit the redactional activity in 5:21–23 to the first verse (and some others) rather than the whole pericope.

22. Bultmann, *Geschichte*, 367 = *History*, 342, identifies vv. 31–32 as redactional.

23. E.g., Knox, *Sources*, 1:23.

24. Snoy notes ("Redaction," 240) the same use of the impersonal pl., without an indication of change in subject, along with the tendency to repeat words that had been used in an earlier verse.

25. I owe this latter observation to Snoy, "Redaction," 239. Sundwall, *Zusammensetzung*, 39, comes to the same conclusion. Schulz, *Stunde*, 30, identifies vv. 30–33 as a summary which Mark wrote.

7:1–23, *The Tradition of the Elders*

The indications of Markan editorial activity in this passage are so numerous and clear that the verses represent in almost paradigmatic form the way in which Mark has assembled his material. How little Mark is really concerned with any consistent geographic or temporal framework is indicated by the abrupt way in which the passage begins. There is no indication of its relation to the healings that immediately preceded it. The introductory formula καὶ συνάγονται is, as we have already seen, characteristic of Markan literary activity, and represents his attempt to link with his narrative the traditions that follow. Into what appears to have been an original unity in vv. 1 (2?)–8, Mark has inserted vv. 3–4, as an explanatory gloss designed to clarify for his readers the central issue of this conflict between Jesus and the Pharisees, and perhaps even to link this dispute more firmly to Isa 29:13 (LXX) by putting it in the context of general Pharisaic traditions (v. 3b).[26]

To this unit Mark has then attached a second, vv. 9–13, introducing it with his characteristic editorial phrase καὶ ἔλεγεν αὐτοῖς.[27] The repetition of point and language in vv. 8 and 9, coupled with the fact that both make their point by means of an OT quotation, are clear indications as to why Mark felt these traditions belonged together. This unit ends with v. 13a; v. 13b appears to be Mark's attempt to give a kind of generalized application of the point of this story to Pharisaic activity. The abrupt appearance of the crowd in v. 14, coupled again with the editorial phrase καὶ . . . ἔλεγεν αὐτοῖς, marks this as another seam in the material. The mention of the crowd, with no preparation for it in the narrative thus far, would argue for Mark as the author of this verse, particularly in light of his predilection for associating such crowds with Jesus in other passages which clearly are due to his literary activity.

With v. 15, a shift in point is again apparent, namely from the question of cultic purity and impurity, and the resulting contradictions between tradition and the OT, to the question of the true source of impurity as a person's inward disposition, rather than what one does or does not eat.[28] The material is not unrelated, however, and gives again

---

26. Suhl, *Funktion*, 80, argues for this point.

27. Cf. ibid., 79; Bultmann, *Geschichte*, 356 = *History*, 329; Sundwall, *Zusammensetzung*, 44, among others.

28. I follow here the argument of Sundwall, *Zusammensetzung*, 44, and tacitly

an indication of why Mark felt it appropriate to join vv. 15–19 to 1–8 and 9–35a.[29]

The core of the discussion that follows in the second half of ch. 7:1–23 appears to have its center in the point of v. 15, which may well have originally stood as an independent saying, and around which Mark then organized the remaining material. To attach this verse to a similar saying in vv. 18b–19, Mark has used the device of a private conversation between Jesus and the disciples (vv. 17–18a), a device he employs on several occasions; in this instance it allows him, by implication at least, to carry on his theme of the disciples' lack of understanding.[30] That Mark is responsible for this attachment is indicated again in v. 18a by the phrase καὶ λέγει αὐτοῖς, a variant on his usual attachment-formula,[31] and by the fact that 17–18a are expressed in typically Markan language.[32] A parallel saying to vv. 18b–19 is found in the *Gospel of Thomas* 14c, further evidence that Mark may have attached this saying to the saying found in v. 15.

The last portion to be added consists of a *Lasterkatalog*. Whether or not vv. 20 and 23 ought to be reckoned as having belonged to that tradition, or as having been added by Mark is not altogether clear. The content of v. 20, repeating as it does the point of vv. 18b–19, and of v. 23, which could be construed as an attempt to link the catalog of vices to vv. 18b–19, may argue for their Markan composition. It is likely that some attempt to complete the unity would have been made by Mark, and v. 23 may be such an attempt, although there is insufficient evidence to argue convincingly one way or the other.

---

dispute the contention of Suhl, *Funktion*, 79, that vv. 14–19 represent a pre-Markan unity.

29. E.g., Suhl, *Funktion*, 79. Marxsen, "Redaktionsgeschichtliche Erklärung," 259, has argued for a parallelism between 4:1–20 and 7:14–23, concluding that we have to do with a "form" that is more clearly preserved in 7:14ff. There is too much evidence of Markan composition within those verses to allow me to be convinced by his argument.

30. I find Carlston's argument convincing at this point, "Things that Defile," 92.

31. Suhl (*Funktion*, 79, following Marxsen) argues that καὶ λέγει αὐτοῖς comes from a pre-Markan "disciples-tradition"—to my mind unconvincingly.

32. Cf. Schweizer, "Mark's Contribution," 427, for example.

8:11–21, *Seeking a Sign, Discourse on Leaven*

This segment of Mark's gospel is made up of a series of more or less self-contained unities, held together, and concluded, by Markan editorial activity in much the same way as 7:1–23. The first such unity is comprised of vv. 11–13, which apparently circulated as an independent pericope, prior to Mark, without any indication of time or place of occurrence.[33] It may originally have been created around the saying contained in v. 12,[34] and indeed the presence of the phrase ἤρξατο (συζητεῖν), characteristically Markan, may indicate that Mark himself is responsible for this construction. But whether he framed the saying, or used a pericope that had already framed it, it is apparent that he added the concluding v. 13, in order to provide the setting for vv. 14–15, which assume Jesus and his disciples are sitting in a boat. This unity (vv. 14–15) may again have been created around an originally independent saying, contained in v. 15,[35] but lack of any characteristically Markan vocabulary in the framework of the saying would argue for Mark having found it already in his tradition in substantially its present form. To this warning of Jesus, triggered by a discussion on lack of bread, Mark has appended a second unit from his tradition dealing with the same problem, viz., vv. 16–18a.[36] The second reference to lack of bread in v. 16 seems to indicate that this was the occasion for Mark to combine these two originally independent units in this present framework.

The purpose for this combination becomes clear in vv. 19–21, which have by all appearances been composed for this situation by Mark, assuming, as they do, not only the doublet of the feeding of the multitude, but their present order (5,000 first, then 4,000) as well. As these verses make clear, the motif of the disciples' lack of understanding underlies this section, and will find its climax in the story of Peter's confession in 8:27–30. The attachment-formula καὶ ἔλεγεν αὐτοῖς in v. 21, introducing a variant on the second question in v. 17, is further indication of the Markan origin of these verses, and of a similar origin for the present configuration of these eleven verses.

---

33. Schmidt, *Rahmen*, 203.

34. Bultmann, *Geschichte*, 54 = *History*, 52.

35. Ibid., 139 = 131; Schmidt, *Rahmen*, 204.

36. Sundwall, *Zusammensetzung*, 52.

Summary on the Non-Miraculous Materials in 4:35—8:38

Of the material reviewed, only the tradition about the death of John the Baptist appears in the present narrative of Mark in substantially the shape in which it circulated in the pre-Markan tradition. It is apparent, however, that this story circulated independently of its present context in Mark and gives no indication of having been part of a series of stories that Mark has taken over and worked into his narrative. The remaining material bears indications of having been composed by Mark, or collected by him, or combined by him from diverse elements into the present configuration. To that extent, the units do not appear to belong to any pre-Markan cycles of stories in which order and content were given and whose editorial adaptation is limited to introductory or concluding remarks, or to material interpolated into their original order.

II. Miracle Stories in Mark 4–6, A First Catena

We must now investigate the material dealing with miracles in these chapters, to see whether or not the stories show the same characteristics of editorial activity we have found above, or whether they give indications of a different kind of origin and different treatment at the hand of Mark. We shall consider first the stories found in Mark 4:35—6:44.

4:35–41, *Stilling of the Storm*

There is little question that this story came to Mark from his tradition. There is some question, however, about the extent to which Mark contributed to the introduction of the story. There are evidences that v. 35 may have been provided by the evangelist in order to tie this story to the parable discourse that precedes it. The presence of καὶ λέγει αὐτοῖς, a variant of the Markan attachment-formula, would argue for this, as well as the phrase ἐν ἐκείνῃ τῇ ἡμέρᾳ, which indicates it belongs to the same day as the parable discourse. The word διέλθωμεν has been seen as the kind of word a person unfamiliar with seafaring terminology would use for a journey across the sea, although this point is not to be pressed.[37] The present shape of v. 36, with its puzzling phrase ὡς ἦν ἐν τῷ πλοίῳ, and the singular mention of "other boats" may indicate the

---

37. So Lohmeyer, *Markus*, 90.

story was originally provided with another introduction. The implied presence of Jesus in the boat already (v. 35; cf. 4:1), coupled with the apparent taking him into it in v. 35 (παραλαμβάνουσιν) also argues for a seam between vv. 35 and 36.

On the other hand, some have been impressed by the fact that the phrase "on that day," while characteristic of the editorial activity of Matthew and Luke, is not a characteristic of Mark's literary additions.[38] That v. 35 comes from the tradition is supported by the detail that reference to its having become evening (v. 35) provides motivation for Jesus' sleeping (v. 38). However, it could equally be argued that Mark felt it necessary to add mention of the evening in v. 35 precisely to account for Jesus' sleeping. In whatever way this question may be decided, it is clear from the present location of the story that Mark felt it was in some way possible to relate the stilling of the storm to 4:34, and may well have adapted the original beginning to conform to the present locus. The Markan attachment-formula with which v. 35 begins, the difficulty of "receiving" him into the boat (v. 36) when he is presumably already in it (v. 1), and the apparently unnecessary mention of the "other boats" (v. 36), which in fact reduce the danger by providing other means of help in the storm—all of these would seem to argue for this miracle having originally circulated independent of its present connection with 4:1–34.[39]

5:1–20, The Gerasene Demoniac

Whatever the origin of this story may have been, there are no clear indications of Markan editorial work in the story as we now have it. Despite the confusion as to the boat's actual landing point (Gerasa is not located on the shore of the sea, a fact that has precipitated a good deal of textual variation), it is probable that v. 1 belonged to the story as Mark received it.[40] In fact, the story is so closely linked with the preced-

38. E.g., Schmidt, *Rahmen*, 135.

39. Schweizer, *Markus*, 60 = *Mark*, 107, thinks this story circulated in connection with the parables of Jesus before 4:10a was added. The repeated presence of the Markan attachment-formula throughout 4:1–34 would argue against this.

40. So Schmidt, *Rahmen*, 140–41; Sundwall, *Zusammensetzung*, 30. For others who argue for this by implication, if not explicitly, see n. 41. This is not a unanimous opinion, however; for the idea that v. 1 is editorial, cf. Lohmeyer, *Markus*, 94; Bultmann, *Geschichte*, 224 = *History*, 210. Lack of any characteristic Markan vocabu-

ing one (sea journey to opposite shore, 4:35, 5:1; getting into [4:36] and out of the boat, 5:2) that they appear to have been linked already in the pre-Markan tradition.[41]

Nor are there any obvious points at which Markan style becomes apparent. The pleonasm of v. 4 may be due as well to the pre-written stage of transmission as to Mark's reputed fondness for this device.[42] There is a difficulty with v. 8, which is a rather clumsy insertion to justify the response of the demons in v. 7 to Jesus' presence,[43] but there is no indication that it is due to Mark's editorial activity. It may well have been there when Mark got the story, and been inserted at the stage when this story was combined with the one that preceded it. The very lack of Markan style in the story argues for Mark having gotten it in written form, and having reproduced it substantially as he received it. However one may want to explain the fact that the story ends with Jesus' command to the healed demoniac to proclaim what God had done for him, it is enough different from Mark's more usual demand for silence to argue that vv. 19–20 also belonged to the story when it came to Mark.[44] The absence of apparent Markan editorial activity would therefore tend to point in the direction of a pre-Markan source, reproduced here substantially as it lay before the evangelist.

5:21–43, Jairus' Daughter and the Woman with a Hemorrhage

We have to do here with two separate incidents that have been combined into one account. It has been suggested that the stories are re-

---

lary or phrases, plus the close connection with the preceding story, seem to me to throw the weight to the former opinion.

41. So Bultmann, *Geschichte*, 224 = *History*, 210; Sundwall, *Zusammensetzung*, 30; Schmidt, *Rahmen*, 142; Grundmann, *Markus*, 107.

42. Easton, "Primitive Tradition," 93, argued it reflected Mark's predilection for pleonasm; Lohmeyer (*Markus*, 94), on the other hand, argues that v. 4 is to be accounted for as "oral tradition set down in writing."

43. Bultmann (*Geschichte*, 224 = *History*, 210) and Schweizer (*Markus*, 63 = *Mark*, 114) simply assume it is Markan.

44. Although Mark can omit the command to silence in a healing (even in Jewish territory, cf. 5:34), and can include it in a healing in Gentile territory (cf. 7:36), this is the only time a recipient of a healing in Mark is commanded to spread the news of it. The presence of the phrase ἤρξατο κηρύσσειν, in this instance integral to the story, does not argue for Markan editorial activity. Markan editorial use of ἤρξατο with the infinitive is restricted to references to Jesus.

ported in this order simply because they happened that way. Jesus lands, disembarks, meets Jairus, accompanies him, on the way is touched by the woman, and goes on to Jairus' house, despite discouraging news from some retainers, to raise the child from death.[45]

However possible such a series of events may have been, such a solution is rendered unlikely by the fact that the two stories betray different styles of composition. Whereas the narrative material concerning Jairus' daughter uses the historical present almost exclusively and is written in short sentences with relatively few participles, the story of the woman with the hemorrhage is told in the more usual aorist and imperfect tenses, with longer sentences and a higher frequency of participial use. It is clear, therefore, that the two stories arose independently of one another, and have at some point been combined.

At what point cannot so easily be resolved. It is of course possible that Mark could have gotten them already interwoven[46] and placed them in their present spot in his narrative. But this is to raise the question of why they should have been combined in the tradition. Is there something about them that demands their early combination, since they could not circulate alone, or at least not so well? One possibility could have been the need to create a space between Jairus' request for help (v. 23) and the news that such help would no longer avail (v. 35). Yet there is no such need inherent in the story, and if the story did arise independently, it must, as stylistic considerations make clear, have been able to make its point without such a lapse of time. The journey of Jairus from his house is time enough for the child to have died,[47] and indeed, the drama is heightened if, while the father is still asking for help (v. 23), news comes that it is too late (v. 35). The present form of v. 36 (Jesus overhears the message to the father) argues for just that order, since then the one speaking in v. 35 is the father, and Jesus overhears the news that interrupts the father's pleas.[48] In its present configuration, Jesus overhears while he himself is talking to the woman, a somewhat more awkward picture necessitated by the combination of the stories. That the miracle would be enhanced by the delay in the announcement

45. See, e.g., Weiss, *Evangelium*, 195; Schmidt, *Rahmen*, 148.

46. So Grundmann, *Markus*, 113; Schmidt, *Rahmen*, 148; Bultmann, *Geschichte*, 228 = *History*, 214.

47. As Lohmeyer (*Markus*, 101) has pointed out.

48. So Sundwall, *Zusammensetzung*, 32.

of the girl's death is hard to see; a triumph over death is as miraculous whether the death be sudden or after lingering illness.

Nor is there any need for this kind of framework for the story of the woman with the flow of blood. The account is complete in itself and gains little from its present position, either in terms of necessary information or theological point, which could not be gotten were the story set in another framework. There is no compelling reason, then, why the stories had to be combined by the tradition in order for either of them to be understood or valued.

The alternative would be their combination by Mark. While such combination was not necessary for the preservation of either of the stories, such combination is surely characteristic of Mark,[49] and he may well have desired to create a space within the one narrative by the insertion of another, as he did, for example, in the narrative of the sending out and return of the twelve (6:14–29 within 6:6–13 and 6:30–33).

It is, of course, difficult to determine why Mark would combine these two stories, but an answer would be provided in part, at least, if they had already been associated in his *Vorlage*. There are enough similarities between them for the two to have been drawn together in the tradition, i.e., similarities in the *dramatis personae* (both female sufferers), the number twelve (the girl's age; the years of unabated flow of blood), as well as in vocabulary (contrast of fear and faith, vv. 33–34, 36; prominence of "daughter," vv. 23, 34; the use of cognates of "save," vv. 23, 34). If the story of the woman came first, there would also be a progression from healing a persistent illness to raising one from the dead.

There is other evidence for the suggestion that the story of Jairus' daughter followed that of the woman. The introductory v. 21 is so closely bound up with the preceding story and flows so well from it that it seems to be part of a narrative in which these stories followed one another prior to their use by Mark.[50] The one unnecessary phrase in v. 21 is καί ἦν παρὰ τήν θάλασσαν, something already known. The preceding portion of the verse flows smoothly, and emphasizes

---

49. So Schulz, *Stunde*, 29, who lists five examples, as does Burkill, *Mysterious*, 121. That this combination is due to Markan activity, cf. Lohmeyer, *Markus*, 101; Sundwall, *Zusammensetzung*, 35; Schweizer, *Markus*, 65 = *Mark*, 116.

50. Cf. Bultmann, *Geschichte*, 228–29 = *History*, 214–15; Sundwall, *Zusammensetzung*, 33.

the crowds, something necessary for understanding the story of the woman, as the repetition of their mention in v. 24 indicates. They are not necessary for the story of Jairus' daughter, although the detail of being on the seashore is helpful for that narrative (the father comes from his village to the seashore to find Jesus). We may have evidence here that v. 21ab served originally to introduce the story of the woman, and that v. 21c was included here by Mark as part of the introduction to the story of Jairus' daughter that followed.[51] This displacement then necessitated v. 24, to reintroduce the crowds necessary for the story of the woman.[52]

If v. 24 is redactional, as v. 21c may well be, there is little else that can be so identified. Verse 43a has been seen as a Markan addition, in keeping with his theory of the messianic secret.[53] Verse 43 is interesting for another reason as well, however; namely, the final injunction that the child be fed. As the Lukan revision of this material shows, Luke was aware of the awkwardness of this final statement in its Markan position. By omitting mention of the girl's walking, and putting in its place the command that she be fed, Luke makes the girl's eating to be proof of her recovery, and then concludes with the injunction to silence. In Mark, on the other hand, the command to eat does not prove that the child has recovered; her walking does that. There is therefore no reason for Mark to have added it after the injunction to silence. Apparently the story as he found it ended with that remark. But why that mention of eating at the end of the story? It points, as we shall suggest below, to the tradition that originally followed it in the Markan *Vorlage*, namely, the feeding of the multitude.

We are suggesting, then, that Mark, finding these two stories in his *Vorlage*, inserted the story of the woman, which had been the first of the two as he got them, into the story of the healing of Jairus' daughter, a stylistic act characteristic of his use of his material. He then introduced both of them with the addition of v. 21c, and smoothed the way for the story of the woman with v. 24. The two stories portray Jesus as a wondrous healer who can cure hopeless illness (v. 26) and raise the dead. They may therefore have belonged to a series of such stories

51. Lohmeyer, *Markus*, 100.
52. Meyer, "Entstehung," 40; cf. also Sundwall, *Zusammensetzung*, 32.
53. E.g., Sundwall, *Zusammensetzung*, 32; Schweizer, *Markus*, 65 = *Mark*, 116.

that began with 4:35,[54] and, like the two preceding stories, they show remarkably few evidences of redactional activity, appearing apparently in substantially the form in which Mark got them.

6:34–44, *Feeding of the 5,000*

This story of the wondrous feeding has come to Mark, in essentially the form in which he reproduces it, from his tradition. It bears none of the signs of his literary activity within the body of the narrative.

In the course of its transmission, the feeding story appears to have been accommodated to the celebration of the eucharist (the four words: taking, blessing, breaking, and giving, are similar in the miracle story and the account of the institution of the Lord's Supper, and occur in the same order in 6:41 and 14:22), although the actual form differs from the account of the last supper in Mark, and from the same kind of accommodation in the parallel story of the feeding of the 4,000 (8:6), indicating that this accommodation took place before Mark got the story.[55] Had he inserted such references, he would, presumably, have brought the phrases into closer parallel with his account of the Lord's Supper.

There is rather plainly, however, Markan editorial activity in the present introduction of the story. It is obvious from the story itself that some mention of crowds must have been associated with it, and Mark himself has here put it into such a context (6:30–33). Yet the lack of clarity in vv. 31–32, and the artificiality with which the crowds are provided in v. 33 (they anticipate in a strange way the point where Jesus and his disciples will land), indicate that this setting is due to Mark, and that therefore the original beginning of the story has been altered, if it has not disappeared altogether.[56]

The present beginning of the pericope appears to be v. 34.[57] Here again, there are indications of Markan redaction, although there is no unanimity among scholars as to its extent.[58] The presence of the

---

54. So Grundmann, *Markus*, 112; indirectly, Weiss, *Evangelium*, 180; Schweizer, *Markus*, 65 = *Mark*, 116, among others.

55. Schweizer, *Markus*, 77 = *Mark*, 138.

56. So Bultmann, *Geschichte*, 259 = *History*, 244; Sundwall, *Zusammensetzung*, 39.

57. Schmidt, *Rahmen*, 190; cf. also Knox, *Sources*, 1:23.

58. On this matter, see Schweizer, *Markus*, 79 = *Mark*, 140.

Markan formula καὶ ἤρξατο (here with διδάσκειν) indicates that Mark has here inserted a reference to Jesus' teaching activity.[59] Mark may also have been responsible for inserting the reference to sheep without a shepherd,[60] although its original presence could have motivated his insertion of the remark about Jesus' teaching activity.

There is also some indication that v. 33 has been reshaped to include mention of the deserted place. It is clear that this reference plays no part in the story itself, and in fact seems contradicted by the assumption (v. 36) that it is possible for the people to find sufficient food for themselves in the surrounding villages and fields. The question in v. 37b does not concern, as in 8:4, the impossibility of buying so much bread in that place; rather the question is how to buy it, i.e., lack of money sufficient to feed such a huge crowd. The problem is not finding food, therefore, but how the disciples could be expected to procure it. The reference to the deserted place seems to have been drawn from the account of the feeding in 8:1–10, in order to fit it into its present context of a retreat by the disciples who have finished their mission and need rest. Yet such borrowing could occur only if both traditions were known and could be drawn upon, a fact that implies rather clearly that Mark, who intended to include them both, took the reference to a deserted place from the feeding of the 4,000, and used it in the story of the feeding of the 5,000 as well. In that case, the story of the feeding of the 5,000 finds its point in the teeming multitudes who are fed by Jesus, not because they cannot find food for themselves, or because they may perish if they do not eat soon (both motifs found in 8:1–10), but apparently simply to show Jesus as one who "feeds his sheep as a shepherd," as it were.

Finally, the verb used to introduce v. 34 (ἐξελθών), without mention of the boat (cf. 5:2 and 6:54, where the verb refers to disembarking), would be more appropriate to Jesus' coming out of a house, rather than getting out of a boat. Yet that would be precisely the case, if, as we have suggested, this story is the fifth of a cycle of five that originally followed immediately upon the story of the healing of Jairus' daughter (5:43). In that case, Jesus emerges from the house, sees the crowds milling about (6:34), and feeds them, as he had commanded the little girl

---

59. Bultmann, *Geschichte*, 231 = *History*, 217.
60. Ibid.

to be fed (5:43). Mark, wanting to include more material about the preaching activity of Jesus, detached the last story (retaining the reference to feeding Jairus' daughter, which in the present context seems unmotivated), and then, when it was to be reintroduced later, created the scene of the crowds the story originally had assumed, and, under the influence of the second feeding account, added the detail of the wilderness to fit it into his scheme of how the returning disciples withdraw from the crowds surrounding Jesus (a typically Markan detail, cf. 6:33 ἀπὸ πασῶν τῶν πόλεων and 3:7b–8) in order to find needed rest.

To that extent, there is a kind of consistency of scene and narrative in the first catena of five miracle accounts, a consistency one would expect from such a collection if it were to circulate as an independent tradition. We have suggested above, however, that Mark had a second catena of miracle accounts, set in the same pattern (sea miracle, three healings, and a feeding), and we must now turn to investigate that possibility.

III. A Second Catena of Miracle Stories, Chapters 6–8

The second catena, as the first, began with a sea miracle.

6:45–52, Jesus Walks on the Sea

The presence of this narrative at this place in Mark's gospel gives rise to a number of problems with respect to Mark's sequence of events. One such problem concerns the destination of the boat in which the disciples find themselves. In v. 45, they are told by Jesus to go before him to Bethsaida, whereas in v. 53, they, now with Jesus in the boat, come to land at Gennesaret. A number of explanations have been attempted, based on the supposition that the narrative reflects accurately a historical sequence[61] (the contrary wind, v. 48, prevented the intended landing—yet the wind is stilled in v. 51; Jesus changed his mind—of which there is not one word in the narrative, etc.); yet the basic problem remains in all such explanations, namely that Jesus, who has just proved himself master of the sea, is nevertheless unable to bring the boat to its intended landing.

---

61. Snoy has a comprehensive review of the difficulties involved in accounting for this sequence on the supposition that it reflects actual events.

Another such problem is represented by the combination of εἰς τὸ πέραν and πρὸς Βηθσαϊδάν. Since εἰς τὸ πέραν in the synoptic narratives normally means a trip to the east shore from the west, and since the most recent voyage (v. 32) was also described in such terminology, a second voyage in the same direction is hardly possible.[62] There have been attempts to resolve this difficulty by dropping one or the other of those references, yet the principle of *lectio difficilior* would require both of them to remain.[63] Such difficulties in the itinerary can, of course, reflect an unconcern, even an ignorance of Palestinian geography, but that explanation hardly covers the problem contained in the sequence of vv. 45 and 53, with the mix-up of destination.

Such evidence renders it increasingly difficult to maintain that the connection of the story of the feeding of the 5,000 and the walking upon the sea antedates Mark,[64] despite the evidence of their connection in John.[65] Such incongruities would be better explained in terms of elements of geographic reference attached to independent traditions which Mark has here put together, with the resulting difficulties. However difficult it may be to reconcile vv. 45 and 53, it is easier to understand the confusion if both elements came from firm traditions in the Markan *Vorlage*, rather than one or both coming from Markan editorial activity.[66] On that basis, the conclusion suggests itself that the connection, in the present sequence, of the accounts of the feeding and the walking on the sea, is the result of Mark's activity and was not given to him in his tradition.[67] Rather, he has taken two originally independent stories and has linked them in a somewhat artificial manner.[68]

62. E.g., see Lohmeyer, *Markus*, 132, for a discussion of this problem.

63. For a review of such attempts, see Snoy, "Redaction," 210ff. His reference to the *lectio difficilior* is on 214.

64. This position is affirmed, e.g., by Lohmeyer, *Markus*, 132; Klostermann, *Markusevangelium*, 74; the stories were "presumably" joined prior to Mark.

65. Schweizer, "Mark's Contribution," 426, has recently reaffirmed this, on the basis of a common order of feeding, crossing in a boat, and seeking a sign (Mark 8:1–13; John 6:1–35). This argument depends on seeing in Mark 8:10 a parallel to the much fuller account, including a miracle, in John 6:16–21, which I regard as the basic weakness of this proposal.

66. Snoy, "Redaction," 234; cf. also Knox, *Sources*, 1:45–46.

67. See, e.g., Snoy, "Redaction," 222, 232; Sundwall, *Zusammensetzung*, 41; Best, *Temptation*, 105.

68. For a review of others who hold a similar position, cf. Snoy, "Redaction," 222ff.

That this linkage is due to Mark is further indicated by v. 52, where the astonishment of the disciples at seeing Jesus walk on the sea is explained in terms of their not having understood the meaning of the feeding (the implication being, apparently, that had they understood that, they would not have been surprised at this), a motif (disciples' lack of understanding) typical in Mark. Verse 52 thus appears to be redactional and represents Mark's attempt to link the two stories,[69] in terms, be it noted, of his own conception of the role of the disciples, rather than out of any regard for sequential or geographic accuracy.

The evidence of redactional activity in the introduction of the story of the walking on the sea (vv. 45–46)[70] is additional indication that Mark is responsible for the present sequence of these stories.

The difficulty contained in v. 45 is related to the dismissal by Jesus of the crowds. The purpose of the phrase ἕως αὐτὸς ἀπολύει τὸν ὄχλον is clearly to link v. 45 with the crowds mentioned in v. 36. It is not evident why the presence of the disciples should render Jesus' dismissal of the crowds impossible, or even difficult,[71] and the need to send the disciples away is already given in v. 46: Jesus desires to pray alone. The presence of the crowds and the need to be alone to dismiss them, puzzling in itself, is thus not necessary to explain why Jesus had become separated from the disciples (a separation necessary for the following events), and has rather plainly been added by Mark to connect this story to the incident of the feeding of the multitude. Elimination of the crowds then also clears up the problem associated with the verb ἀποταξάμενος in v. 46. In the present context, it is unclear whether the αὐτοῖς refers to the crowds or to the disciples. The verb itself would be more appropriate to leave-taking than to dismissal.[72] If the crowds of v. 45 are eliminated as redactional, then v. 46 obviously refers to the disciples, and the verb can assume its normal meaning. The elimination of the phrase concerning the crowds thus gives a clear introduction to the story: Jesus, desiring to pray alone, compels his disciples to go without him, intending to meet them again in Bethsaida. All of this reinforces

---

69. So, e.g., Snoy, "Redaction," 227; Sundwall, *Zusammensetzung*, 41; Best, *Temptation*, 105; Lohmeyer, *Markus*, 130.

70. So Sundwall, *Zusammensetzung*, 41; Snoy, "Redaction," 232; Klostermann, *Markusevangelium*, 75.

71. So Bultmann, *Geschichte*, 231 = *History*, 217.

72. See Snoy, "Redaction," 233, for a clear discussion of this point.

the suggestion that the last phrase about crowds in v. 45 is the result of Mark's attempt to link the two stories into their present sequence.

There may also be other editorial activity in the story itself. The variant of the Markan attachment-formula καὶ λέγει αὐτοῖς (v. 50) may indicate that the content of what Jesus said has been added by Mark, and the fact that Jesus intended to pass them by (v. 48) seems to indicate that the motif of rescue from the storm (v. 51) was not a part of the original story. The fact that both the words of encourage-ment (v. 50e) and the actual stilling of the wind reflect the account in 4:35–41 may be further indication that Mark has added them, having been influenced by that earlier narrative, although such a conclusion must remain tentative.

The problem of destination—Bethsaida in v. 45 and Gennesaret in v. 53—still remains, however. As we have seen, it is grotesque to assume that any author, however uninterested he may be in geographic detail, would create such a difficulty. It is equally hard to imagine that it could remain long in the tradition in such form, although that is of course possible. In a thorough and fruitful study, Snoy has suggested that v. 53 (the departure by sea, in this instance to Gennesaret) may in fact rep-resent the original conclusion to the story of the feeding of the 5,000, since the account of the feeding of the 4,000 ends in a similar way (the departure by sea, in this instance to the regions of Dalmanutha, 8:10).[73] It is, of course, quite like Mark to insert one story into another. If that is the case, it would explain how the geographical problem arose: in his desire to connect both stories to the disciples' lack of understanding (v. 52), Mark is willing to tolerate the geographical difficulties that result from that connection (i.e., the order to go to Bethsaida now precedes the arrival at Gennesaret, due to the insertion of vv. 45–51 between vv. 44 and 53), just as, in his desire to connect the two incidents, he is will-ing to tolerate the ambiguity with regard to the dismissal of disciples and crowds (vv. 45–46).

If Snoy is correct, we may understand Mark's redactional work in the following way. Two originally unrelated stories (feeding the 5,000, walking on the sea) existed in Mark's tradition (we would urge: the former ending one miracle catena, the latter beginning the other). The story of the feeding ended with Jesus and his disciples departing by

---

73. This is the thesis of Snoy, which he develops in ibid., 234ff.

sea to Gennesaret (v. 53). The story of the walking on the sea began with Jesus' dismissing his disciples (by sending them to Bethsaida) so he could be alone to pray, and it concluded with Jesus' getting into the boat with them (v. 51a). Influenced by the story of the stilling of the storm (which began the first catena), Mark added details to conform this account to it (viz., vv. 50b, 51b, although this remains an open question), and then connected it to the story of the feeding by adding the detail of dismissing the crowds (v. 45) and by tying the stories together through the motif of the disciples' inability to understand what was happening (v. 52). In this way, the two accounts were connected, indeed, as we should like to maintain, the two catenae were attached to one another.

6:54–56, Jesus Heals the Sick

There is a rather general consensus that the material contained in these verses represents a composition by the evangelist himself.[74] Although there is no command to silence as in similar summaries at 1:32–34 and 3:7–12, and despite the absence of the characteristic verb θεραπεύω (1:34; 3:10; in v. 56 the corresponding verb is σώζω), there is little reason to question that consensus.

The major problem is not the Markan origin of this material, however. Rather, the problem centers in the reason for having such a summary of healing at this point in the narrative. Both the other summaries follow a series of healing stories; in this context, the most recent healing was reported in ch. 5. Why would Mark have put a summary here? To argue that it is to create an appropriate setting for the dispute with the Pharisees that follows in ch. 7 does little to clarify the situation. Why would a general account of healing make a dispute about dietary rules any more comprehensible? Some other reason must have dictated its presence here. That Mark's use of his sources may provide the clue has been hinted at by some,[75] without their having been able to be more specific about detail. Obviously, if our thesis could aid in solving this problem, it would help to confirm what we are maintain-

---

74. E.g., Schweizer, *Markus*, 80 = *Mark*, 143; Schulz, "Bedeutung," 136; Meyer, "Entstehung," 40; Bultmann, *Geschichte*, 366 = *History*, 341, among many others.

75. E.g., Schmidt, *Rahmen*, 195; Knox, *Sources*, 1:46.

ing. To solve it, we must investigate the account of the healing of the blind man in 8:22–26.

8:22–26, *The Blind Man of Bethsaida*

The geographical datum καὶ ἔρχονται εἰς Βηθσαϊδάν (v. 22) provides the clue to the original position of this story within the pre-Markan cycle.[76] Βηθσαϊδάν is mentioned only twice in Mark, here and at 6:45. We have already noted the difficulties that attach themselves to that first reference, within the present Markan order. We have also seen the problems raised by the present locus of the summary of healing in 6:54–56. The solution to those problems, we urge, lies in the fact that the story of the healing of the blind man has been displaced from its original position in the catena, where it followed the story of the walking on the sea, and, in its place, Mark has composed and placed a generalized account of healings, since his original source also had a healing story following the sea miracle.

Such an original order would clear up several problems. The difficulty with Bethsaida as destination would be clarified, since the original order would have been: walking on the sea (the first story in the second catena), containing the notation (6:45) that they are to go πρὸς Βηθσαϊδάν, followed immediately by the story of the blind man, which begins by noting their arrival at that destination (εἰς Βηθσαϊδάν, 8:22).[77] The problem of the present locus of the summary of healings

76. Bultmann, *Geschichte*, 363 = *History*, 339, concedes that it is difficult to tell when concrete geographical data belong to the tradition and when they are redactional, using 8:22a as an example, although at other times he does assign such a detail to the editor in its present form (Bultmann, *Geschichte*, 68, 227 = *History*, 64, 213). He is followed in this by Sundwall, *Zusammensetzung*, 53; Klostermann, *Markusevangelium*, 88; Lohmeyer, *Markus*, 158–59, with the observation that there seems to be no good reason for Bethsaida to have belonged originally to the story. Schmidt (*Rahmen*, 207), on the other hand, argued for the traditional nature of 8:22a. The most important point for our argument is not the traditional nature of the present wording of καὶ ἔρχονται εἰς Βηθσαϊδάν; that phrase may be Markan. Our point is simply that the association of this healing with Bethsaida comes to Mark from his tradition, in this instance, a miracle catena.

77. Robinson ("Johannine Trajectory") has pointed to a somewhat similar phenomenon in John 2:12 and 4:46bff., regarding Capernaum. Our investigation appears to confirm his conclusion (p. 10) that "it would seem to be redactional policy, when splitting a source in order to interpolate material, that one provide an overlapping or repetitious comment," in our case, retention of the original geographical notation,

would also be clarified, since Mark may well have filled the space in his catena, space created by the removal of the story of the blind man, with similar material (i.e., healings), which in this instance he himself composed. This would also explain the omission of mention of demons and a command to silence in 6:54–56, since the story of the blind man, underlying this summary, contained neither. In the summaries in 1:32–34 and 3:7–12, on the other hand, both are included, since the stories preceding each of those summaries contained both. At this point in the second catena (after what is now 6:54–56), Mark then also inserted a section he had assembled concerning Jesus' teaching activity (7:1–23), as he had done in the first catena (6:1–33; see above, Section I). With the account of the Syrophoenician woman (7:24–31), he then resumed the order of his source.[78]

The reason for the present location of 8:22–26 is to be found in the structure of the Markan narrative. It has long been recognized that this story plays a key role in Mark's plan and fits into its present context in terms of that plan. It is preceded by a discussion (8:11–21) that, as we argued above, is largely redactional in its present configuration, the theme of which is the disciples' inability to comprehend what they have just experienced.[79] Clearly, the disciples have been blind to what has been going on about them. The story is followed immediately by Peter's confession, indicating that now, however slowly, their blind eyes are beginning to see.[80] The blind man of Bethsaida thus appears to be symbolic of the disciples[81] who, with the confession of Peter, now begin to see, if not understand entirely, the fate awaiting Jesus (cf. 8:31, and

---

Bethsaida.

78. Loisy, *Les Evangels Synoptiques*, 1:940 n. 3, suggested that originally 8:22–26 followed 6:45–52, although he did not develop it. Grundmann, *Markus*, 164, suggested that 8:22ff. originally preceded 7:31–37, since v. 37 could well refer to more than just the healing of the deaf-mute. Lohmeyer, *Markus*, 160, has also called attention to the connection between 7:24ff., 7:31ff., and 8:22ff., as miracles of the messianic time, thus adding strength to our contention that they were originally side by side in a preMarkan miracle catena.

79. So, e.g., Held, "Matthew," 207; Meye, *Jesus and the Twelve*, 70–71; Grundmann, *Markus*, 165.

80. Cf. Meye, *Jesus and the Twelve*, 70–71, 77; Grundmann, *Markus*, 208, and esp. n. 1; Schweizer, *Markus*, 88 = *Mark*, 164.

81. So, e.g., Matera, "Interpreting Mark," 130; Best, *Temptation*, 108; and indirectly, Held, "Matthew as Interpreter," 210.

the beginning of Mark's emphasis on the passion). With this story of blindness healed, the first major section of Mark's gospel appears to be concluded, and the second major section, beginning with the confession, is begun.[82]

7:24–31, *The Syrophoenician Woman*

The reference to a journey εἰς τὰ ὅρια Τύρου with which this story begins is generally recognized as redactional, its purpose being to create a Gentile framework for the stories that follow.[83] The suggestion for this region may well have come from the identification of the woman as Συροφοινίκισσα, thus suggesting to Mark that this event occurred in that region.[84] Internally, the story is more consistent if the event took place on Galilean soil; if Jesus himself is on foreign soil, then he himself is not in fact limiting the "bread" to the "children." The careful identification of the woman ('Ελληνίς, Συροφοινίκισσα) would be more appropriate if the event occurred in Galilee, than in a region where such nationality would be the rule rather than the exception.

Some have also assigned v. 27a, especially the πρῶτον, to editorial work on the part of Mark,[85] or to a still later period,[86] but the remainder of the story is rather clearly a unity. The concluding verse (31), however, is part of the geographical framework within which Mark has set his material.[87] The itinerary, as often noted, is torturous at best, and all but impossible to imagine.

What we have, then, is an account of a miracle that has been put into its present geographical framework by Mark. Yet with or without that framework, there are elements in the story that indicate it is

82. So, e.g., Luz, "Geheimnismotiv," 15; this clear intention of Mark also militates against any arrangement around the rubric "eating bread"; the "bread" in this portion of the gospel provides the opportunity for Mark to demonstrate the disciples' lack of comprehension, and is subordinated to that larger aim; cf. also Sundwall, *Zusammensetzung*, 47, on this point.

83. E.g., Lohmeyer, *Markus*, 145; Luz, "Geheimnismotiv," 21, who sees this journey as "surely intended to be programmatic," citing "only" 13:10 and 15:39.

84. So Sundwall, *Zusammensetzung*, 45, among others.

85. Cf. Schweizer, *Markus*, 85 = *Mark*, 152.

86. So Bultmann, *Geschichte*, 38 = *History*, 38; Held, "Matthew," 198.

87. E.g., Bultmann, *Geschichte*, 39, 227 = *History*, 38–39, 212–13; Luz, "Geheimnismotiv," 21; Schweizer, *Markus*, 87 = *Mark*, 154, among others.

not in its original context. The mention of the house into which Jesus withdraws, for example, is difficult to explain, because it assumes an area with which Jesus is familiar, and within which he is known. To argue that Mark supplies the house in order to provide a place where Jesus may conceal himself is to overlook 1:45b, where such a desire to remain alone is accommodated by a simple withdrawal from inhabited areas.

If, however, as we have proposed, this is the third story in a miracle catena of five stories, following the story of the blind man at Bethsaida, a better context emerges. Jesus has advised the healed man not to enter the village (8:26), which would then be the place in which the house of 7:24 is situated, with Jesus; desire for privacy due to the healing that has just occurred, a desire implied in 8:26 as well. That the area is familiar may be inferred from Jesus' command that the disciples go there to await him (6:45). Mark has displaced the story of the blind man for schematic reasons, as we saw, and inserted the dispute with the Pharisees (7:1–23), not to follow 6:54–56, a context that, as we saw, has little to recommend it, but rather to precede the story of the Syrophoenician woman, in order to illustrate the freedom that Jesus has over against Jewish legal restraints, a point at least implicitly contained in 7:25–30.[88]

Such an explanation enables us to account for the present order of Mark as one dictated by his plan for the gospel at this point: the journey to non-Jewish territory (7:24–30) to illustrate the freedom of Jesus from a narrowly legalistic Judaism (7:1–25), leading ultimately to the confession of Peter as the culmination of Jesus' activity among the people (chs. 1–8), and as the beginning of the journey to the cross (chs. 9–16). It also enables us to account for the problems inherent in the present order of stories by showing how, in their position in the original catena, they flowed more smoothly than they do in their present context, a context dictated by Mark's own conception of the career of Jesus.[89]

88. So Klostermann, *Markusevangelium*, 81; Sundwall, *Zusammensetzung*, 46, notes the difficulty of maintaining here also a connection of these stories on the basis of the rubric "eating bread," since nothing of that nature is mentioned in the following story.

89. To avoid confusion, let me assert that the unity within the catena for which I am arguing is a literary rather than historical one. That is, the order I find is an order based on literary art, not historical sequence, an order that Mark, who is operating on a different schematic projection, alters for his own purposes.

7:32–37, The Deaf-Mute

The redactional nature of the description of Jesus' journey in v. 31 makes it clear that this story was not bound to any specific locus, although the familiarity on the part of the people with Jesus, and with his healing powers, does suggest an area within which Jesus was known. It is also reasonably clear that, apart from the geographical framework, the story as we now have it is a unity, unmarked by any editorial activity, with the exception of the command to silence in v. 36.[90] The conclusion of the account in v. 37 is, on the other hand, rather generally recognized as constituting an original part of it.[91] The language appears to be drawn from an OT background,[92] and seems to be somewhat broader than one would expect as the conclusion of just one story. It has been suggested that the verse may have served as the conclusion of a series of accounts,[93] a point that would argue in favor of seeing this story itself as the final one in the triad of three miracles of healing we have suggested as belonging to this second catena. It is, further, interesting to note that the only accounts in these two catenae in which there are injunctions to silence are the story of Jairus' daughter and this account of the deaf-mute—pericopes that in both instances immediately precede the accounts of the feeding of the multitude, as we have proposed the order—and that amazement on the part of the bystanders is also limited to these two stories. Such parallel phenomena would tend to support the idea that we are dealing with parallel catenae in these miracle accounts.

Finally, if Lohmeyer is correct in arguing that this account combines the description of a conventional miracle-worker with the eschatological fulfillment of OT faith, in which divine action and thus divine reality become evident,[94] then we may have an indication that the function of these catenae was in some sense theophanic, a suggestion that will have to be pursued in more detail in a subsequent study.

---

90. So Grundmann, *Markus*, 156; Bultmann, *Geschichte*, 227 = *History*, 213; Schweizer, *Markus*, 87 = *Mark*, 154; Lohmeyer, *Markus*, 149ff.

91. So, e.g., Bultmann, *Geschichte*, 227 = *History*, 213, Lohmeyer, *Markus*, 149ff.; Schweizer, *Markus*, 87 = Mark, 154.

92. E.g., Fuller, *Interpreting*, 60–61; Evans, *Beginning*, 29.

93. So Knox, *Sources*, 1:59; Schweizer, *Markus*, 87 = *Mark*, 154; Taylor, *Mark*, 354.

94. Lohmeyer, *Markus*, 151–52.

8:1–10, Feeding of the 4,000

The account of the feeding of the 4,000 is introduced with a phrase ἐν ἐκείναις ταῖς ἡμέραις πάλιν . . .) that seems clearly to depend on the Markan context in which this is the second such account of a feeding (cf. especially the πάλιν), and for that reason is almost surely redactional.[95] Some have also suggested that vv. 9b–10 are similarly redactional, perhaps to make this story conform to the ending of the feeding of the 5,000.[96] Two points argue against this, however. First, these few words can hardly be regarded as a parallel to the much longer story of the walking on the sea, and are, in fact, a much closer parallel to 6:53, which we had reason to argue represents the original conclusion to the story of the first feeding. Secondly, there is a real problem with the destination (εἰς τὰ μέρη Δαλμανουθά), a location that, as the textual history of the verse indicates, presented problems at a very early time. The Markan summaries tend to mention either more general locations (e.g., "beside the sea," 2:13; 3:7; 4:1) or more widely-known places (e.g., Capernaum, cf. 1:21; 2:1), indicating that Dalmanutha may very well have been part of the tradition that Mark simply hands on. We should want to argue, therefore, that the form in which Mark got this story from his catena comprised 8:1b–10, thus paralleling the form of the first feeding (6:35–44, 53).

The parallelism between these two stories of feedings indicates that we are dealing with a doublet, and may even imply that they appeared in written form in the pre-Markan tradition. The fact that they appear to be variants raises the question as to why Mark would include both of them. To suggest that he included both because they circulated as a pair in the tradition[97] is a possible solution, but improved, we would urge, if they circulated as the final story, in each instance, in two catenae of miracle accounts. In this latter case, Mark would include

---

95. Bultmann, *Geschichte*, 259 = *History*, 244; Schmidt, *Rahmen*, 192, argues that the redactional addition is limited to the word πάλιν. The story would then have begun with a genitive absolute, a form with which other stories begin in the catenae we are proposing, at 5:2; 5:21; 6:35.

96. E.g., Klostermann, *Markusevangelium*, 86; Sundwall, *Zusammensetzung*, 50–52.

97. The suggestion of Sundwall, *Zusammensetzung*, 49.

both because they appeared in the two catenae he is incorporating into his narrative.[98]

IV. SUMMARY

What we have proposed is the existence of a pre-Markan cycle of miracles, circulating in the form of two catenae, identical in arrangement (sea miracle, three healing miracles, and a feeding miracle) but not in content,[99] and consisting, as far as we have been able to determine on the basis of linguistic and literary analysis, of the following verses from Mark:

Catena I	Catena II
4:35—5:43, 6:34–44, 53 (with 4:35, 5:21c, 5:43a, and 6:34bc as probably editorial, and 5:24 and 6:35b as clearly editorial)	6:45–51, 8:22–26, 7:24b–30, 32–37, 8:1–10 (with 6:45c, 50c, 51b, 7:36, and 8 is as editorial)
• Stilling of the Storm (4:35–41) • The Gerasene Demoniac (5:1–20) • The Woman with a Hemorrhage (5:25–34) • Jairus' Daughter (5:21–23, 35–43) • Feeding of the 5,000 (6:34–44, 53)	• Jesus Walks on the Sea (6:45–51) • The Blind Man of Bethsaida (8:22–26) • The Syrophoenician Woman (7:24b–30) • The Deaf-Mute (7:32–37) • Feeding of the 4,000 (8:1–10)

Mark has incorporated these two catenae into his narrative, adapting them to his own plan for his gospel, but limiting his interpolation into them to two large blocks of material (6:1–33 into the first; 7:1–23 into the second), in each instance material characterized by the teaching/disputing activity of Jesus.

98. That Mark is the first to have combined them is indicated by 8:4, where such a reaction on the part of the disciples is possible only if this account reached its present form completely independently of any awareness of the account of the feeding of the 5,000; cf. Schweizer, *Markus*, 88 = *Mark*, 156; Grundmann, *Markus*, 158. This is a further argument against Sundwall's proposal that they circulated as a doublet.

99. Edwards, "Eschatological Correlative," 14–15, indicates a similar case with the *Sätze heiligen Rechtes*, and his own "eschatological correlative" as a *Gattung*, namely that "though there is a development of a double form of the saying . . . the content of the form can and does change, while the external features of the form do not."

There remain a number of points to be considered. What, for example, is the relationship, if any, between these catenae and the "semeia source" of the fourth gospel? And what of the origin of these two catenae? What kind of *Sitz im Leben* can they have had, and what sort of function can they have performed, which caused them to be assembled? Related is the question of possible parallels to, or models for, such a catena: are they to be found in the OT? in Hellenistic Judaism? in secular Hellenistic sources?

Another group of questions centers around their pre-Markan form. Did they come to Mark in written or in oral form? Is there any discernible pattern to be found within the three healing miracles in either, or both, of the catenae?

A third group of problems centers around the use Mark made of them. If we have in fact isolated a pre-Markan tradition, the redaction-critical implications for an understanding of the Markan theology need to be explored, as do the implications of this whole matter for the synoptic problem.

Such problems, and others like them, remain to be considered. We shall undertake that task in a second study on the function of the catenae and their use by Mark.

The Origin *and* Function *of the* Pre-Markan Miracle Catenae

5

¶ IN THE LAST CHAPTER I ATTEMPTED TO INDICATE THE CONTOURS of two similar miracle catenae that Mark incorporated into his gospel narrative. In this chapter I want to pursue the broader goal of fitting the catenae into the framework of primitive Christianity. In pursuit of that goal, I will attempt to answer the kind of questions posed at the end of the last chapter, viz., what other evidence is there for the existence of these catenae and possible models guiding their formation, the origin and function (the *Sitz im Leben*) of the catenae, and the way in which Mark made use of them in the composition of his gospel.

Because necessary limitations of space have forced me to compress a good deal of material into a relatively small scope, a statement of my thesis at the outset may be appropriate: The most likely background out of which the catenae were formed is to be found in (Hellenistic-) Jewish traditions about Moses; the groups that formed the catenae drew from those traditions in ways similar to those in which Paul's opponents in Corinth drew upon them; the catenae were formed as part of a liturgy that celebrated an epiphanic Eucharist based on bread broken with the θεῖος ἀνήρ ("divine man"), Jesus, during his career and after his resurrection; and Mark sought to overcome that view of Jesus and of the Eucharist by the way in which he used the catenae in his own narrative.

NON-MARKAN EVIDENCE FOR THE CATENAE

As would be expected, the material contained in the catenae has been used in Matthew and Luke in the form into which Mark had previously cast it. One would, therefore, not expect them to have used the catenae independently of Mark. Yet the way in which Luke uses Mark 4–8 indicates that he may have been aware, if not of the catenae, at least of the fact that the outlines of the Markan repetition were identical with the materials we have assigned to the second catenae, and of Mark's use of them. Matthew, in dealing with the material in Mark 4–8, detaches the first four stories (Mark 4:35—5:43) in order to place them at other points in his narrative (Matt 8:23–34 and 9:18–26), and does not begin to follow Mark's order until the account of the rejection of Jesus in his homeland (Mark 6:1–6a; Matt 13:53–58). Luke, on the other hand, repeats the Markan order, which incorporates the first catena, without alteration, omitting only those accounts that he has used elsewhere (Mark 6:1–6, incorporated into Luke 4:16–30) or that do not accord with his purpose (emphasis on John the Baptist as forerunner of the suffering Jesus, Mark 6:17–29). All material related to the second catena he then omits completely. It would be attractive to speculate that such an exact correspondence may have been due to Luke's awareness of the existence of such catenae. But it may also be due simply to Luke's having recognized the dimensions of the Markan repetition, brought about by the latter's use of the two catenae. In the absence of further evidence, however, any solution will remain speculative.

That the author of John had at his disposal a source consisting in large measure of miracles has been rendered highly probable by recent studies.[1] There is some superficial similarity between this "semeia-source" and the pre-Markan catenae—the "first sign" in John (2:1–11) is in some sense a water-sign, and the second sign is a healing, as is the third miracle story John offers (5:1–47), which is then followed by the wondrous feeding (6:1–15)—but that is not enough evidence to link the two miracle-sources to one another in any significant way. The "semeia-source" and the pre-Markan catenae mutually reinforce the idea that such miracle-sources circulated in the period prior to the writing of the gospels, but there is nothing to link them, or indicate they owe their origin to a common source.

Christian writings post-dating the synoptic gospels do not provide significant evidence for the existence of pre-Markan catenae, since they are, for the most part, remarkably uninterested in the miraculous activity of Christ. Aside from the infancy gospels, there is little

---

1. See D. M. Smith, *Composition*; and Fortna, *Gospel of Signs,* although Fortna wants to include other narrative material in the source besides miracles.

recounting of such activity; and such as there is takes the form, for the most part, of a simple listing of healings, with an occasional specific miracle reported.[2] There is, however, one piece of evidence which may reflect an awareness of the catenae. It is found in the Christian *Sib. Or.* 6:13–15, where the order of reporting is sea miracle ("he shall walk the waves"), three reports of healings in general form (he shall deliver from sickness, raise the dead, banish pains), and miraculous feeding ("from one wallet there shall be sufficiency of bread . . .").[3] That this order is not drawn from any present order in the synoptic gospels is clear, and since in two other places in the *Oracles* the miracles of sea and feeding are reported in that order, viz., in just the opposite order in which they now stand in Mark (6:34–52 and par.), this may be a further indication that a tradition was known in which this order was followed.[4] Since that is the order in which they occurred in the catenae (with intervening healings), this may indicate that knowledge of them survived their use in Mark.

2. There is no mention of any miracle of Jesus in the Apostolic Fathers. In other early materials (excluding the "infancy gospels"), Jesus' miracles are sometimes reported in the form of summary statements which contain no clear indication that they are drawing on the canonical gospels, e.g., *Recog. Clem.* 1:41; 3:60; 5:10; *Clem. Hom.* 1:6; 2:34; Justin Martyr, *1 Apol.* 22, 31, 45, 54; *Dial.* 69; *Gos. Nic.* chs. 10 and 4 (20); *Acts Pil.* 1:6–8 (probably referred to by Justin, *1 Apol.* 48); *Acts Thadd.* (ANF 8:558); and the *Abgar Legend* (see *NTA* 1:441). As Justin (*1 Apol.* 48) indicates, such summaries may be more dependent on the idea of Christ fulfilling the prophecy of Isa 35:6 than on any specific accounts of wondrous deeds. At other times, general summaries of miracles are given which are dependent to some extent for their wording on the canonical gospels, e.g., *Ep. Apos.* 5; *Acts Thom.* 47 (see also 66); *Acts Paul* (*NTA* 2:382); *Acts of Pet. Paul* (ANF 8:480); *Acts Andr. Mth.* (ANF 8:519); *Acts Pil.* 6 (= *Gos. Nic.* 6): Christ's descent into Hell (*NTA* 1:477); and in three later sources, the *Reports of Pilate to Augustus* (ANF 8:460) and to Tiberius (ANF 8:462), and in the *Avenging of the Saviour* (ANF 8:472). In still other instances, individual miracles, drawn from the Synoptics and John, are retold, e.g., *Clem. Hom.* 19, 22 (John 9); 2, 19 (Syro-Phoenician woman); *Acts Andr. Mth.* (stilling the storm; ANF 8:519); Christ's descent into Hell (= *Gos. Nic.* 20; [Lazarus]; *NTA* 1:473); and the *Avenging of the Saviour* (woman with flow of blood; ANF 8:474). In two cases, miracles are reported that have no parallel in the canonical accounts: the *Gos. Bart.* 2, 18 (a eucharistic miracle), and the *Acts Andr. Mth.* (stone sphinx speaks and walks; ANF 8:520).

3. The text in *NTA* 2:719 reads: "He shall walk the waves, and deliver men from sickness, He shall raise up the dead, and banish many pains, and from one wallet there shall be sufficiency of bread for men."

4. *Sib. Or.* 1:356–59; 8:272–78. In these two instances, reports of healing precede the account of the sea and feeding miracles.

Pattern for the Catenae in the Hellenistic Milieu

Some light on the meaning and function of the catena would be forth-coming if its origin could be pinpointed in some specific part of the ancient world, i.e., in Hellenistic or Jewish circles. Since healings play a significant part in the catenae as Mark found them, and since Justin Martyr, for one, points to the similarity in this respect between Jesus and Asclepius,[5] the material that collected around the latter figure would be a logical place to look.

Such an investigation, however, yields little more than negative results. Pietschmann long ago observed that the reports of Asclepius' healings were designed more to encourage the reader than to report events, and have virtually nothing historical about them. He found only two exceptions to such "pious legends" among the inscriptions at Epidauros, and they were both from the Roman period.[6] Again, the mode of healing reported in the vast majority of the votive inscriptions centers on appearances of Asclepius to the suppliant in a dream;[7] the six incidents of healing reported of Asclepius before his death are clearly mythical, and occasionally etiological.[8] In no instance is there an attempt to link accounts of cures attributed to Asclepius in any kind of repeated cycle, or to form them into any kind of narrative. The accounts, in short, are quite unlike the miracle stories contained in the pre-Markan catenae. Asclepius is not present, save in dreams; there is no attempt to convey a sense of the reality of the healing through any narrative framework; and their purpose was not so much to awaken faith as to give advice on how to cure certain maladies. Indeed, Pliny reports that Hippocrates copied the inscriptions from the Asclepian temple at Cos, and after subsequently burning it down, used what he had learned in instituting his own medical practice.[9]

---

5. See Justin, 1 Apol. 22, 54; Dial. 69. The same thing is found in Acts Pil. 1; evidently this was a relatively familiar identification to early Christians, since Asclepius enjoyed a reputation as the "gentlest and most man-loving of the gods" (Aristides, Oratio 39, quoted from Edelstein and Edelstein, Asclepius, 1:410).

6. In Pietschmann, "Asklepios," 1687. He observes that "für entsprechende Beispiele aus der Zeit v. Chr. versagen die epidaurischen Steine."

7. For examples, see Edelstein and Edelstein, Asclepius, 1:439 (Ovid, Metamorphoses), and 229 (Stele I from Epidauros).

8. They are listed and described in Pietschmann, "Asklepios," 1653–54.

9. Pliny, Nat. 29.1.(2), 4 (Edelstein and Edelstein, Asclepius, 1:401–2). The

There are few other figures whose exploits could have served as pattern for the form of the catenae. Serapis performs rescues from troubled seas, allows threatened ships to land safely, and occasionally heals,[10]—acts also reported of Asclepius,[11] who in addition is reported to have raised a man from the dead[12]—but in no instance are such reports collected into the kind of order found in the catenae. There is enough difference between such accounts, and the gospel miracle stories, to give point to Kertelge's observation that the former are unlikely to have served as the model for the latter.[13] Demon-possession, for example, which plays a significant part in the gospel miracle accounts, was all but unknown in the pre-Christian Hellenistic world;[14] and the multiplication of food, while common in folklore, is characteristic of Jewish rather than Greek material in antiquity.[15] In any case, there appear to be no miracle catenae of the type Mark used circulating in Hellenistic circles that can help us in determining the kind of influences which caused them to take the form they did.

Edelsteins have followed that account with a recipe for an antidote to venomous animals, which appeared in the same temple, an indication of the purpose which such temples seem to have served.

10. For instances, see Kertelge, *Wunder*, 97 n. 353, 354; also Weinreich, *Heilungswunder*, 14.

11. See Aristides, *Oratio* 42 (Edelstein and Edelstein, *Asclepius*, 1:161); Pietschmann, "Asklepios," 1655; Weinreich, *Heilungswunder*, 14. Rescue from the sea is also used metaphorically for aid in overcoming various obstacles; cf. Aristides, *Oratio* 42 (Edelstein and Edelstein, *Asclepius*, 1:159). In this sense surely also the attribution of such power by Philo to Augustus in the former's encomium: "This is the Caesar who calmed the storms which were breaking out on every side" (I owe this reference to Kertelge, *Wunder*, 97 n. 254).

12. For raising Hippolytus, he was killed by a lightning-bolt from Jupiter, who could not tolerate such hubris; for examples of this myth, see Edelstein and Edelstein, *Asclepius*, 1:79, 80; for more general statements about his power to raise the dead, 3, 56.

13. Kertelge, *Wunder*, 41.

14. So McCasland, *Finger of God*, 68–69.

15. So Rose, "Herakles," esp. 134. The point of his article is a denial of any influence of a life, or accounts, of Hercules on the gospel narratives. For such evidence of the multiplication of food in non-Jewish sources as there is, see Eitrem, *Some Notes*, 64 n. 5.

PATTERN FOR THE CATENAE IN JEWISH TRADITIONS[16]

Any discussion of "signs and wonders" related to Jewish traditions must begin with the figure of Moses. Such activity is already emphasized in the narrative of Israel's exodus from Egypt and is then taken up and amplified in later traditions. The description of Moses in Josephus, and especially in Philo, indicates the attempt to make him appear a θεῖος ἀνήρ,[17] complete with all the virtues of such a figure, and miracle-working is then also part of the role of the expected "one like Moses."[18] In a similar vein, the deliverance of the exodus and of the messianic time is seen in typological relation,[19] with the desert wanderings on occasion serving as a prototype of the messianic time.[20]

In a development of this theme, Harald Sahlin has urged that the purpose of John's baptism was "to prepare the New Exodus of Salvation under the Messiah" (he appears quite appropriately in the desert) and that the theme of a new exodus was determinative in the thought of the primitive church. He finds such exodus typology in the Eucharist, linked to the Passover celebration, and argues that we can see, from 1 Cor 10:1–2 and Rom 6:3–4, that Christ's death and resurrection have the "same meaning for the Church as the crossing of the Red Sea has for Israel."[21] Whatever one may think of Sahlin's conclusions, it is clear, from the evidence he cites, that the Moses-saga was of great importance for the theological reflection of the primitive church.

In the light of this background, it is not surprising that a "Moses-Christology" would become a significant trend in early Christian the-

---

16. This kind of division of subject matter is made out of convenience, not out of any conviction that influences on the catenae will be either Hellenistic or Jewish, in any exclusive sense. Kertelge is surely correct when he observes that it is antecedently probable that the primitive Christian miracle tradition had been influenced by both traditions by the time it reached Mark (*Wunder*, 209 n. 36).

17. Concerning Josephus, see Meeks, *Prophet-King*, 138–42; concerning Philo, see 102–6. Georgi (*Gegner*, 148 = *Opponents*, 124) describes Moses as "der θεῖος ἀνήρ schlechthin" ["the θεῖος ἀνήρ par excellence"] for Jewish tradition. For a similar judgment, see Meeks, *Prophet-King*, 176.

18. Meeks, *Prophet-King*, 163–64; Hahn, *Hoheitstitel*, 388–89.

19. Sahlin, "New Exodus," 82–83.

20. Linton, "Demand," esp. 122.

21. Sahlin, "The New Exodus," 91.

ology,[22] related, because of "signs and wonders," to the earthly career of Jesus.[23]

The elements of such a christology in Matthew need not be rehearsed. That such a christology was also evident in John and Luke is likewise hardly to be disputed.[24] In that light, the absence of such a Moses christology in Mark is all the more interesting, and leads one to raise the question, at least, whether such an omission may not have been intentional on Mark's part, perhaps due to some apologetic interest. Light will be shed on this problem as our discussion progresses.[25]

A prime example of the influence of the Moses tradition is to be seen in the account of the wondrous feeding, with which the catenae conclude. The manna miracle held great interest for Hellenistic Judaism,[26] so it is not surprising that reflections of the Moses tradition are to be seen especially in the account of the feeding of the 5,000.[27]

Mark 6:34a may be a reference to Num 27:16–18, with its leaderless masses;[28] the "green grass" of v. 39 may be an eschatological blooming of the desert as the "one like Moses" repeats the manna miracle;[29] the division into 100's and 50's in v. 40 may reflect the ordering of Israel in Exod 18:13–27.[30] Persuasive arguments can also be marshaled in favor of the thesis that John's account of this event has been deliberately shaped in the light of Moses and the wilderness tradition.[31]

The event with which the catenae end seems thus to have been shaped against the background of a Moses tradition. In view of the order of events that constitute the catenae, it is of further interest to

22. So Georgi (*Gegner*, 216–18 = *Opponents*, 172–74) in a largely positive discussion of Hahn; for a summary of the latter's position, see *Hoheitstitel*, 404.

23. Ibid., 396.

24. For Luke, see Hahn, *Hoheitstitel*, 382ff; for John, see Meeks, *Prophet-King*, passim.

25. I owe this judgment to Hahn, *Hoheitstitel*, 400.

26. See Kertelge, *Wunder*, 134, n. 545.

27. Hahn, *Hoheitstitel*, 391.

28. So Montefiore, "Revolt," esp. 136; and Friedrich, "Die beiden Erzählungen," esp. 19. However, van Iersel ("Die wunderbare Speisung") argues against such an association (esp. 188).

29. So Friedrich ("Die beiden Erzählungen," 18ff.), again disputed by van Iersel ("Die wunderbare Speisung," 188).

30. G. Friedrich, "Die beiden Erzählungen, 17–18; see also Kertelge, *Wunder*, 133.

31. Cf. Meeks, *Prophet-King*, 98; Stauffer, "Antike Jesustradition," esp. 29.

note that the two major miracles associated with the exodus—passing through the sea and the wondrous feeding in the desert—comprise the kind of miracle with which the catenae begin and end, viz., a sea-miracle and a feeding-miracle.[32]

The figures of Elijah and Elisha also suggest themselves to any consideration of miracle traditions in the OT.[33] The story of the Syro-Phoenician woman (Mark 7:24–30) and the raising of Jairus' daughter (5:35–43) have frequently been cited as showing an influence from the Elijah cycle,[34] but less widely recognized is the fact that, in later Jewish tradition, Elisha, because of his "double portion of the spirit" (2 Kgs 2:9), was regarded as a greater worker of wonders than Elijah.[35]

The rough parallelism between the accounts of Elisha's wonders, and the material contained in Mark 4–8 has on occasion suggested to some scholars that such parallelism is more than accidental.[36] Since such a parallelism requires considerable re-interpretation of the obvious point either of the Elisha or the Jesus tradition, along with some re-arranging, it has not found widespread acceptance. It is interesting to note, however, that Hartmann's reflections have led him to posit a double miracle tradition in Mark that coincides almost exactly with the outline of the catenae I have proposed, although he attributes the original order to Peter's preaching which underlies the gospel.

It is again interesting to note, in this connection, that the first miracle reported of Elisha is a water-miracle (2 Kgs 2:12–14). While this act reflects more immediately a similar act by Elijah (2 Kgs 2:8–10), it was almost surely also influenced by the story of Moses and the exodus through the sea. Thus, it too would tend to reinforce the idea that the catenae are influenced, at least in their opening story, by an

32. Five miracles are reported from Egypt to Sinai in Exodus 13–17, but they are of somewhat different content than those in the catenae—there are no healings in the Exodus account—so that the sheer fact of five miracles in the wilderness account and in the catenae does not indicate any clear relationship.

33. These anecdotes, probably originally circulating apart from any collection, seem also to betray a certain "Moses motif," more pronounced perhaps in the case of Elijah; cf. Heising, "Exegese," esp. 86–87 for a brief discussion and further literature.

34. E.g., Flammer, "Syrophoenizerin," esp. 470–71; Kertelge, *Wunder*, 116–17, 152.

35. A glance at the index of Ginzberg, *Legends*, will confirm this.

36. Cf. Hartmann, *Aufbau*, 144–51; Heising, "Exegese," 93; Flammer, "Syrophoenizerin," 469–72. For a discussion and evaluation of this idea, see Brown, "Jesus and Elisha."

OT account that had begun to assume importance for collections of miracle stories long before the Jesus tradition began to coalesce.

Later Jewish tradition records wondrous deeds of a number of rabbis, but with very few exceptions, the kinds of stories reported are of little value for our discussion.

Many of the miracles have to do with rain, and the effect of prayers to God for it to start or cease.[37] Perhaps the most famous of these is Ḥoni the Circle-Maker, of whom it is also reported that he slept for a period of 70 years.[38] The rabbi about whom the most miracles are reported is Ḥanina ben Dosa, about whom a large variety of miraculous acts are reported. Most important for our purposes is a cycle of five miracle stories that have been assembled around him.[39] The content of the miracles is entirely different from those of the catenae, however, and the only relationship would consist in the number five, a slim reed upon which to support any conclusions.

Both later Jewish traditions, and the catenae, probably share a common influence from the OT, rather than in any way exerting influence upon one another, so far as I have been able to determine.

In summary, it would appear that OT accounts of wondrous acts, particularly those reported of Moses, but including those attributed to Elijah and Elisha, are closer in kind to the individual miracles contained in the catenae, their order in it, and the origin of a cycle of miracles as such, than the sort of miracle stories reported of those wonder-workers of the Hellenistic period who, from a chronological point of view, could have had some influence on the gospel traditions. The sea-miracle and the wondrous feeding, which enclose the catenae, are also reported of Moses, and an influence from that direction seems more likely than from Hellenistic stories of rescue at sea, since no act of providing food is associated with such a sea-miracle in any non-Jewish narrative.

37. See Ḥoni, *b. Ta'an.* 19a, 23a; R. Ḥiyya b. Luliani, *b. Ta'an.* 25a; R. Jonah and Ḥanan ha-Nehba, *b. Ta'an.* 23b; Ḥanina b. Dosa, *b. Ta'an.* 24b (to name but a few).

38. *b. Ta'an.* 19a, 23a.

39. The cycle of five stories: *b. Ta'an.* 24b–25a; the story of Ḥanina's goats bringing home bears on their horns, found as the fourth in the cycle, is also referred to in *B. Meṣ'ia* 106a; other miracles, not included in the cycle, are told of him in *b. Ber.* 33a, 34b; *b. Pesaḥ* 112b–113a; *b. Yebam.* 121b; *b. B. Qam.* 50a.

The Function of the Catenae

In the absence of compelling evidence pointing to a model for the pre-Markan catenae from which we might deduce its function, we shall have to determine the function from the material within the catenae themselves. The nature of that material, viz., miracles, provides the decisive clue, since the function of miracles in the Hellenistic world was rather clearly epiphanic,[40] and that function has also been taken over into the gospel miracles, and more particularly, those in Mark.[41]

More interesting, from our standpoint, is the fact that, given the generally epiphanic character of the Markan miracle accounts, some of them have been singled out in the course of scholarly investigation as being more clearly epiphanic in nature than others. The stories contained in Mark 4:35—5:43 have been seen as differing in style and motif from the preceding miracle accounts, and have been identified as epiphanic.[42] The stilling of the storm (4:35–41) clearly belongs to this type of story, as the reaction of the disciples makes clear (v. 41).[43] Interestingly, the first story of the Johannine semeia-source is also clearly epiphanic (explicitly so in 2:11a), suggesting a possible similarity in function if not in ancestry.

The story of the Gerasene demoniac is also clearly epiphanic, with its contest of strength between divine and demonic powers.[44] Jesus' walking on the sea (6:45–52) belongs quite obviously to this type of story as well,[45] as does the account of healing the deaf-mute (7:32–37). In fact, v. 37 appears to be a kind of epiphanic conclusion to more than one story,[46] and may well have served to conclude and sum up the

40. Kertelge, *Wunder,* 167. "Epiphany" in this connection points to the visibility of divinity or divine power in some person or act.

41. So Schulz, *Stunde,* 68, 82; Betz, "Jesus," passim; Kertelge, *Wunder,* 167, among others. That the Markan miracles betray the christological interests of the primitive community is not to be denied, but neither does that fact alone rob them of their epiphanic character.

42. E.g., Kertelge, *Wunder,* 90; W. Grundmann, *Markus,* 102.

43. So Kertelge, *Wunder,* 93, 96, 167; that such stories about rescue at sea form a virtual topos for the θεῖος ἀνήρ traditions, and that such men also arouse reactions of fear and amazement, will become important for this study later on. On these points, see Betz, "Jesus," 116, 172.

44. So Kertelge, *Wunder,* 106, cf. also 107–9; Schulz, *Stunde,* 70.

45. E.g., Kertelge, *Wunder,* 147–48; the comments on Mark 4:35ff. also apply here.

46. Dibelius, *From Tradition,* 76; Lohmeyer, *Markus,* 152; Kertelge (*Wunder,* 160)

three healings of the second catena (8:22–26; 7:24b–30, 32–36). The two feedings (6:34–44, 8:1–10) have also been singled out as belonging to this category, especially in light of their likely relationship to the OT miracle of the manna, one account of which (Exod 16:1–21) contains an explicit reference to an epiphany of Yahweh (vv. 9–10).[47]

Given, then, the epiphanic character of the stories contained in the catenae, it is clear that one of the functions of those catenae would have been to point unmistakably to Jesus as a kind of *deus praesens,* as one in whom divine power is at work.[48] In the first catena, he shows himself Lord over demons (5:1–20), sickness (5:25–34), and death (5:21–23, 35–43); in the second as one who, in his healing presence, does "all things well" (7:37, as the conclusion to the three preceding healings). In both catenae, he is Lord of creation, as shown in his mastery of the sea,[49] and the wondrous provider of food.

The fact that both catenae end with an account of feeding multitudes will also not have been accidental in relation to their function. The similarity between the two Markan accounts of the wondrous provision of food and the material in the NT referring to the primitive celebration of the Eucharist has often been noted:[50] the similarity in language between Mark 6:41 and 14:22, a similarity mirrored in 8:6 as well; the parallelism between 1 Cor 11:24 and Mark 8:6 (particularly in the use of the verb εὐχαρισεῖν ("to give thanks"), absent from Mark 14:22); the changes that Matthew and Luke undertake, especially with respect to Mark 6:35 and 41, seemingly motivated by the attempt to emphasize the parallelism between the feeding and the Eucharist;[51] the Johannine order, in which a lengthy discussion of the meaning and validity of the Eucharist is attached to the feeding of the multitude. The regular elements associated with the Eucharist in the primitive

---

calls attention to the similarity between v. 37 and Gen 1:31.

47. I owe this reference to Heising, "Exegese," 82.

48. Cf. Schulz, *Stunde,* 70; Keck, ("Introduction," esp. 368) also recognized the fact that apart from the Markan framework, a collection of miracles would have this character.

49. See ch. 1: "Jesus and the Storm-Tossed Sea."

50. E.g., Sundwall, *Zusammensetzung,* 50; Lohmeyer, "Abendmahl," esp. 252; "Die urchristlichen Abendmahl," 9:282; Clavier, "La multiplication," 451; Jenkins, "Markan Doublet," esp. 107; Flammer, "Die Syrophoenizerin," 477; Kertelge, *Wunder,* 135, 140.

51. See especially the detailed discussion by van Iersel, "Die wunderbare Speisung," 171ff.

church (a regular meal, an eschatological celebration, provision for the poor and the hungry) are also found, at least implicitly, in the Markan accounts of the feeding;[52] catacomb art represents the Eucharist exclusively in the form of a wondrous feeding.[53] All of these elements bear witness to the connection between these meal accounts and the Eucharist.

Boobyer has attempted to deny such similarity, on the basis of the occurrence of similar words in other accounts of meals in the NT which are in no cleat way associated with any eucharistic celebration, and on the basis of the similarity between Jesus' procedure at the feedings, and that of any pious head of a Jewish household presiding over the daily common meal.[54] Van Iersel, in a careful examination of Boobyer's arguments, concluded that the language of the Markan feeding accounts is in fact closer to the Eucharist than Boobyer or his examples would allow.[55] Lohmeyer had already pointed out that the miraculous provision of food for the multitudes reduces, if not eliminates, any serious comparison between Jesus' action and that of the pious Jewish housefather.[56] That Mark did not pattern his narration of the feedings after his account of the Eucharist is clear enough, but the many eucharistic overtones in the feeding narratives, coupled with the apparent eucharistic interpretation of them by the authors of Matthew and Luke, as well as others in the primitive church, make a flat denial of eucharistic references difficult to maintain.

On the other hand, the dissimilarity in actual wording between Mark 6:41 and 8:6, and 14:22, indicate that Mark is probably not responsible for the eucharistic overtones of the two feeding accounts. Had he been particularly interested in that similarity, he would in all likelihood have conformed the former verses more closely to 14:22 than is now the case. There is thus good reason to believe that the eucharistic reflections in the feedings are pre-Markan, and that the tradition Mark is employing saw those two accounts as related in some way

---

52. So Lohmeyer, "Abendmahl," 233–34.

53. Lohmeyer, "Die urchristlichen Abendmahl," 9:310 (among other places).

54. Boobyer, "Eucharistic Interpretation," esp. 162–63, 168–69.

55. Van Iersel, "Die wunderbare Speisung," 168–69.

56. "Abendmahl," 224; cf. also Ziener, "Brotwunder," esp. 285.

to the eucharistic celebration.[57] But how are those reflections to be accounted for? The most likely explanation lies in the suggestion that, at some point prior to Mark, the stories of the feeding had their locus in a liturgy accompanying a eucharistic celebration, either as an auxiliary to it, or as part of the catechism accompanying it, the point of which was to clarify the meaning and import of that celebration.[58]

Such a conclusion throws considerable light on the use and function of the two pre-Markan catenae. They apparently served as part of the interpretive liturgy accompanying a eucharistic meal.[59] But more, the epiphanic nature of the miracles attached to the account of the feeding would indicate that the liturgy was intended to call the participant's attention to the presence of Christ himself at the meal. As he was revealed in his mighty acts as a *deus praesens*, so he is revealed in the meal as present among the participants. This would have the further implication that for the participants the eschatological age had already begun, that the Christ whose reality was seen in the miracles was now at hand in the celebration of the Eucharist.

The miracles that precede the accounts of the feedings would again confirm this. Lohmeyer called attention to the fact that the healings that we have assigned to the second catena are miracles of the messianic time, an insight strengthened by the apparent relationship between the conclusion of the miracles in Mark 7:37 and Isa 35:5-6a.[60] The epiphanic emphasis of the miracles in the first catena is indicated by the repeated presence of cognates of φόβος ("fear/awe"; Mark 4:41; 5:15, 33, 36), regularly associated in the NT with epiphanic manifestations.

Such an understanding of the Eucharist has left its traces in other parts of the writings of the primitive church. Luke 24:13-35 points not only to the presence of the risen Jesus at common meals of the

57. So van Iersel, "Die wunderbare Speisung," 179; Kertelge, *Wunder*, 183.

58. Cf. van Iersel, "Die wunderbare Speisung," 179-81, 194; Heising, "Exegese," 90; Kertelge, *Wunder*, 136; Dibelius, *From Tradition*, 95; Jenkins ("Markan Doublet," 110) who uses the term "auxiliary." Van Iersel ("Die wunderbare Speisung," 183) suggests that the stories of the feedings failed to achieve greater rounding-off as miracles because such development came to a halt when the stories were placed in the service of a eucharistic liturgy.

59. Flammer ("Syrophoenizerin," 476-78) calls attention to the appropriateness of including Mark 7:24-30 in a eucharistic anamnesis.

60. Lohmeyer, *Markus*, 160.

Christians,[61] but specifies that his presence is in fact recognized in the very eucharistic act itself (v. 35),[62] thus making that celebration epiphanic in nature. Acts 10:40–41 links the manifestation of the risen Lord to eating and drinking with him. John 21:1–14 is a further account of Jesus revealing, himself at a meal, and the story is specifically identified by the writer himself (v. 1) as having that purpose. Revelation 3:20 may also reflect such an understanding, and 1 Cor 11:26 seems to have been formulated in direct opposition to a view of the Eucharist that laid a too-exclusive emphasis on the epiphanic element in the celebration.[63] A similar view of the function of early Christian common meals is implied in the longer ending of Mark (16:14a), and a fragment from the *Gospel of the Hebrews* pictures the risen Jesus revealing himself to his brother James by providing for him a meal with decided eucharistic overtones.[64]

It would appear, therefore, that the pre-Markan miracle catenae have their *Sitz im Leben* in the eucharistic liturgy celebrated by some group or groups within the primitive church, a liturgy that used epiphanic events in the life of Jesus to give substance to its epiphanic interpretation of the eucharistic meal. Such a conclusion, however, in its turn raises two further questions, to which we must give detailed consideration: What sort of community would have developed such an understanding of the Eucharist? What sort of Eucharist did they celebrate, if the Last Supper did not play the decisive role in their interpretation of it?

WHAT SORT OF COMMUNITY WOULD HAVE
INTERPRETED THE EUCHARIST IN AN EPIPHANIC WAY?

The exclusive concentration upon the miracles of Jesus in the catenae, along with the epiphanic nature that characterizes them, point to a theological view that was current in the Hellenistic world and that was

---

61. Betz, "Ursprung," esp. 16.

62. So Hahn, *Hoheitstitel*, 387.

63. So Reicke, *Diakonie*, 265.

64. *NTA* 1:165; Stauffer ("apokalyptischen Festmahl," esp. 265) finds a similarity between the epiphanic feedings, and the epiphany of Israel's messiah at a festal meal in 1QSa 2, 12, 14, 20. Both Schmidt ("Ahendmahl," 1, 12) and Lietzmann ("Abendmahl," 1, 31) called attention to the epiphanic function of the Eucharist in the earliest liturgies of the church.

used to designate men who had similarly marvelous powers, viz., the concept of the θεῖος ἀνήρ. Since the idea of epiphany will be basic to any christology that sees in Jesus a θεῖος ἀνήρ,[65] it would seem highly probable that such a christology characterized the belief of those Christian groups within which the catenae were formed.

The characteristics of the θεῖος ἀνήρ can be summarized briefly: a wondrous birth, a career marked by the gift of overpoweringly persuasive speech, the ability to perform miracles, including healing and foreseeing the future, and a death marked in some way as extraordinary.[66] In these categories, every philosopher or exorcist was a candidate, and as a result the whole concept could become the object of ridicule. But whether designated "hero" or θεῖος ἀνήρ, this cluster of concepts did represent a way of understanding extraordinary men in terms of their relationship to divinity, and on that basis, it can be a useful tool in research into NT development.

The presence of material in Mark bearing the stamp of θεῖος ἀνήρ characteristics has been widely noted, but more importantly for our problem it has been widely seen to have come into the Markan tradition at a time prior to the writing of the gospel.[67] In several other instances, it is manifest in precisely those miracles that belong to the pre-Markan catenae.[68] There is reason to believe, then, that the communities from which the catenae came saw in Jesus a kind of θεῖος ἀνήρ, sharing the power of God, which he made visible in his acts, and perhaps serving as a kind of "model" for the activity of those who followed him and, in some measure, shared in the epiphany that characterized him.[69]

---

65. Betz, "Jesus," 120.

66. In addition to Bieler, ΘΕΙΟΣ ΑΝΗΡ, see further Betz, *Lukian*; Eitrem, "Heros"; Hadas and Smith, *Heroes and Gods*; M. Smith, "Prolegomena"; and Meeks, *Prophet-King*.

67. On this point, see Keck, "Mark 3:7–12," esp. 350; Schulz, *Stunde*, 67–69; Kertelge, *Wunder*, 89; Weeden, "Heresy." Weeden's argument would be more persuasive, had he found evidence that Mark's opponents had called upon the disciples in support of their position, rather than validating it by an appeal to the Holy Spirit (154). To risk discrediting the entire apostolic tradition simply to characterize his theological opposition seems an unlikely device for Mark to have used.

68. E.g., Robinson, "Kerygma," 133; Keck, "Mark 3:7–12," 358.

69. So Koester, "One Jesus," esp. 232; Schulz, *Stunde*, 77; Kertelge, *Wunder*, 28; the activities reported of Peter, Philip, and Paul in Acts confirm this point as well.

A question immediately rises: Is the existence of such a community likely? Is there any evidence that such a view could be held within the contours of the primitive church? An affirmative answer to such questions is made possible by the work of Prof. Dieter Georgi of Harvard University; a résumé of the portions of his work relevant to our discussion must be undertaken.[70]

In attempting to discern the contours of the opposition facing Paul as he wrote the material contained in 2 Corinthians, Georgi, following hints in 2 Cor 3:7–18 and 11:22, examines the nature of Jewish apologetic tradition in the Hellenistic world. In that apologetic, Moses emerges as the greatest religious hero of the Jews, and therefore as the greatest of the Jewish θεῖοι ἄνδρες.[71] He is the one who gave the Law, which displays his intimate relationship to the cosmic order, and thus to God.[72] He is also the one who entered, and won, a contest of miraculous power with the Pharaoh, again proving his share in the divine power over the cosmos.[73]

When Moses displays this divine reality, however, he also shows it to be a human possibility. In that way, Moses makes evident the exalted possibilities open to any one who attaches himself to Moses and his tradition.[74]

The focal point and goal of all Jewish propaganda was the service of the synagogue, and the Scriptural interpretation of the diaspora synagogue is reflected in the Hellenistic-Jewish apologetic.[75] Following practices common to that time, traveling Jewish missionaries made their living from propaganda activity, as well as from begging, and found shelter when necessary within the synagogue itself.[76] As Moses' career shows the nature of his power to understand God's will, so the extraordinary nature of the message of the traveling missionaries was

---

70. Georgi, *Gegner* = *Opponents*. This will of necessity be a very brief summary of the conclusions relevant to this particular problem and will not be able to give any indication of the wealth of detailed evidence and careful research which characterize the volume as a whole.

71. *Gegner*, 149, 152 = *Opponents* 124, 126; cf. also Meeks, *Prophet-King*, 104, 138.

72. Georgi, *Gegner*, 152 = *Opponents*, 126.

73. Ibid., 151 = 125 ; cf. also 154, 160 = 127–28, 134.

74. Ibid., 262, 264 (cf. also 181) = 256, 258 (cf. also 147–48).

75. Ibid., 87–88, 96, 98–108, 130–37 = 84–85, 89–90, 90–98, 112–17.

76. Ibid., 110–12 = 99–100.

shown by extraordinary demonstrations of power, a practice common among Hellenistic missionaries for other cults.[77] Thus the person and ability of the missionary played a key role in his success, and superiority was often shown by competition among the missionaries, the one displaying the most impressive charismatic acts proving the superiority of the power in which he participated.[78]

Against such a background, the nature of the opposition Paul faced in Corinth begins to emerge. Drawing upon the Jewish apologetic just outlined, these Christians saw in the earthly Jesus a θεῖος ἀνήρ comparable to Moses.[79] But as Moses had represented in his divine power a possibility open to other men, so apparently did Jesus for the group in Corinth[80] On that basis, they may well have arrogated to themselves divine qualities, understanding the nature of their apostolate in terms of their understanding of the θεῖος ἀνήρ christology.[81] Confronting Paul, they seem to have felt that the inevitable competition of apostles had shown them to be the superior group.[82]

The christological corollary of such a position is the blurring of the distinction between the historical Jesus and the exalted Lord. Paul's opponents drew no sharp line between the earthly and the glorious Jesus with the result that the career of the earthly Jesus underwent a glorification that all but denied the decisive significance of the cross upon which Paul laid so much emphasis.[83]

The manner in which Georgi outlines the contours of the group Paul opposed in Corinth presents an understanding of Jesus showing a marked similarity to the kind of understanding to which the catenae also point. The Moses christology of the Corinthian opponents[84] seems

---

77. Ibid., 114, 191 = 101, 154–55.

78. Ibid., 72, 134, 192–200 = 53, 115, 155–59.

79. Ibid., 259, 282–84, 286 = 254–55, 271–72, 273–74.

80. Ibid., 261 = 255–56.

81. Ibid., 224–25, 254 = 232–33, 251–52.

82. Ibid., 229–34 = 236–38.

83. Ibid., 285–87, 290–92 = 273–75, 276–77; see also Reicke (*Diakonie*, 278–82) for a similar judgment on the position of Paul's opponents, although he identifies them as docetic-gnostic Jews (282) and assumes they were the same group Paul combats in 1 Corinthians, views that Georgi does not share.

84. Paul also seems to reflect such a christology when he compares the bread and the cup to the manna and the water in the wilderness, 1 Cor 10:3–4.

to be reflected in the miracles that begin and close the cycle (water and desert feeding), suggesting that the christology informing the catenae may also have seen in Jesus an epiphanic figure along the lines of Moses, the θεῖος ἀνήρ.[85]

Such a christology would also explain how a collection of miracles could be used in a eucharistic liturgy. Seeing the power and divinity in the earthly career of Jesus, the θεῖος ἀνήρ, such communities could celebrate his glorious presence at their communal meals without the need to interpose an account of the inauguration of those meals specifically anchored in Jesus' death and subsequent glorification. The feeding of the multitudes in a miraculous way would recall the θεῖος ἀνήρ, Moses in the wilderness, and furnish the way to interpret the θεῖος ἀνήρ, Jesus providing food for his followers. The communal meal would thus become epiphanic of this glorious Jesus, whose glory was already visible during his career as θεῖος ἀνήρ. A celebration centering on the glorious Jesus, risen from the dead, could thus quite appropriately be anchored in an event of Jesus' earthly life, rather than in his death; and this appears to be what the catenae do.[86]

We are not arguing, of course, that the catenae formed part of the eucharistic liturgy of Paul's opponents in Corinth. We are simply pointing to those opponents as evidence that the kind of community that one could have expected to develop the catenae did in fact exist within the primitive church, and may well have represented a more widespread movement than would at first appear to be the case. The kind of θεῖος ἀνήρ christology that the catenae presuppose and display may, at one point, have been popular among the many that characterized primitive Christianity.

A further question is implied in all this and must now be discussed in more detail. The catenae appear to have been related in some

85. Georgi has called attention to the similarity between the christology of Paul's opponents and that of "einer bestimmten Schicht der synoptischen Tradition" ["brings to mind the christology of certain layers of the Synoptic tradition"] (*Gegner*, 289 = *Opponents*, 276).

86. This is not to affirm that those who held such a view knew nothing of Jesus' passion, simply that they did not invest it with the theological importance which Paul, and, as we shall see, Mark did. Emphasis on the θεῖος ἀνήρ Jesus, now the glorified Lord, would draw attention away from his ignoble death; but it is hard to conceive of a Jesus tradition that would have been altogether ignorant of his death; see the article by R. E. Brown, "Jesus and Elisha."

way to a eucharistic celebration, tied to a θεῖος ἀνήρ christology. What sort of Eucharist would it have been, and what evidence is there that such a Eucharist may in fact have been celebrated?

WHAT SORT OF EUCHARIST IS PRESUMED BY THE CATENAE?

The evidence contained in the writings of the primitive church concerning the form and meaning of the Eucharist is notoriously ambiguous. It is clear from 1 Corinthians 11 that Paul understood the meal differently than current practices there interpreted it, and his extended recitation of tradition may point to his introduction of a new emphasis.[87] Mark has traditions that both presume the Passover setting (14:12–16) and that do not (14:22–25), and the latter passage may contain a polemic against a Eucharist in which the cup played an insignificant part (14:23).[88] Luke–Acts may give evidence of three eucharistic traditions: the primitive meals in Acts, the D account in Luke, and the full text.[89]

Several attempts have been made to account for this state of the evidence. Hans Lietzmann sought to trace back two types of eucharistic celebration to the very beginning, one based on a continuation with the risen Lord of the common meals shared with him before his death, the other remembering Jesus' last meal and subsequent crucifixion.[90] E. Lohmeyer developed this thesis by linking the first type to a Galilean origin, the second to Jerusalem,[91] a thesis somewhat modified by Marxsen, who sees a Palestinian type celebrating table fellowship with Jesus, and a Hellenistic type based on the sacramental importance of the elements themselves.[92] Opposition to such a dual origin of the Eucharist has also been expressed. B. Reicke thinks the evidence simply shows two different ways of referring to the Eucharist, due to the desire to emphasize different points, but he maintains that from the

---

87. See Lohmeyer, "Abendmahl," 217; Lietzmann, *Mass,* 332; Heitmüller, "Abendmahl," 24.

88. Lohmeyer, "Abendmahl," 9, 186; Heitmüller, "Abendmahl," 31.

89. For a summary of such evidence, see Lietzmann, *Mass,* 331–32.

90. Lietzmann's views are summarized ibid., 204–5. Cullmann modified this view, finding one form of the Eucharist based on a meal-fellowship with the risen Lord, the other on the Last Supper of Jesus with his disciples ("Meaning").

91. Lohmeyer, "Abendmahl," 239, 242; idem, "Die urchristlichen Abendmahl," 93–94.

92. Marxsen, *Lord's Supper,* 26–27.

beginning there has been one unified Eucharist.[93] Schweizer has made a similar point concerning the impossibility of demonstrating the existence of two fully different kinds of Eucharist.[94] There is as yet no consensus on this matter, other than that the evidence is complex.

Corresponding to the variety of evidence concerning the Eucharist, moreover, is the plethora of evidence in the gospels pointing to the importance of meals, both actual and illustrative, in the mission of Jesus. Meals with Pharisees and sinners, ordinary and extraordinary provisions of bread, meals as a central element or an illustration of reward in parables and sayings—all point to the central role played by meals in the gospel traditions.[95] This tradition of meals, particularly of common, non-extraordinary meals, is also reflected in the accounts of the Eucharist. Mark 14:22–24 reflects the picture of the Jewish "housefather" presiding at the common evening meal,[96] a practice also reflected in the account of the meal shared with the risen. Jesus in Luke 24:30.[97] Such reflections of common meal practices would seem to suggest that the eucharistic origins are in some way related to them.[98] Indeed, the repetition of eucharistic meals would, as Lohmeyer argued, appear more likely if they were related to repeated common meals, rather than to a unique final meal.[99]

There is, further, certain evidence to link the idea of the presence of the risen Lord to the eucharistic celebrations. In addition to the account of the disciples on the Emmaus road, Luke 24:36–43 recounts a meal of the eleven and some others with the risen Lord. In Acts 10:41 Peter recalls meals that he and others had with the risen Jesus, and a

93. Reicke, *Diakonie*, 291, 397.

94. Schweizer, "Das Abendmahl eine Vergegenwärtigung," esp. 94–95, 99; idem, "Abendmahl," 16.

95. Cf. Lohmeyer, "Die urchristlichen Abendmahl," 9:202–3; 10:92–93; idem, "Abendmahl," 218–23; Perrin, *Rediscovering*, 102–8. Lohmeyer ("Die urchristlichen Abendmahl," 9:209), following Albert Schweitzer, also argued that underlying all of these meals is the tradition of the messianic meal.

96. Cf. Heitmüller, "Abendmahl," 27; Lohmeyer, "Abendmahl," 226.

97. So Betz, "Ursprung," 16.

98. Ibid.; see also Perrin, *Rediscovering*, 104, 107; Cullmann, "Meaning," 10; Lohmeyer, "Die urchristlichen Abendmahl," 9, 303; Lietzmann, "Abendmahl," 31; Heitmüller, "Abendmahl," 37–38.

99. "Die Urchristlichen Abendmahl," 9:281.

general reference may be contained in Acts 1:4 to such events.[100] The joy that is described in connection with the common meals in Acts 2:46 is also best accounted for in relation to Jesus' resurrection rather than to his death, although of course the latter need in no way be excluded here. Paul's argument with the Corinthians against their customs in celebrating the Eucharist, especially the emphasis on Jesus' death in 1 Cor 11:26, seems to indicate an emphasis in Corinth on the resurrection, apparently to the point of ignoring the death; such ignoring seems to be what Paul is trying to overcome.[101] John 21:13 preserves the memory of a meal with the risen Jesus, and Rev 3:20 may also reflect an awareness of that meaning of early common meals.[102] Schmidt has suggested that the eucharistic material in *Didache* 9–10 is closely related to Acts 2:46, since a special meaning of Jesus' death is absent in the *Didache*,[103] and surely the thanksgiving (10) would most easily be understood against the background of the joy at Jesus' resurrection. Even the later Acts of Thaddeus preserve the tradition that the Twelve "ate and drank with him after his resurrection for many days."[104] The serious questions that can and have been raised about the synoptic dating of the Eucharist as a kind of "Christian passover meal," also call into question the necessity of linking the Eucharist to the death of Jesus, and, to that extent, give evidence to the possibility at least of a celebration tied not to Jesus' death, but to his resurrection.[105]

Coupled with the exclusive reference to the presence of the risen Lord and the joy that characterized the common meals of the early Christians is the absence of any mention of wine at those meals. There is other evidence that bread was the main element shared in such common, eucharistic meals: *Acts Pet.* 2, 5; *Clem. Hom.* 14:1, 4; *Acts John* 85, 109, 110; *Acts Thom.* 27, 29, 133 (49 and 120–21 are also sometimes so regarded; on 49, see below; 120–21 seems to contain a reference

---

100. So Cullmann, "Meaning," 8, 11–12.

101. See Reicke, *Diakonie*, 279; he sees a connection between the joyous meals of Acts 2:46 and the eucharistic celebration in Corinth (289–90).

102. On this latter point, see Cullmann, "Meaning," 7.

103. Col. 12; cf. also Wiegand, "Abendmahl," 15.

104. This citation is found in ANF 8:559.

105. See the discussions of this point by Lohmeyer, "Die urchristlichen Abendmahl," 9:204, 305; Marxsen, *Lord's Supper*, 18; Schmidt, "Abendmahl," 10; Heitmüller, "Abendmahl," 30, 38; Cullmann, "Meaning," 12–13, 16.

to wine, although it is ambiguous); *Gospel of the Hebrews*, fragment 7 (*NTA*, 2:165; in some collections it appears as fragment 8).[106] In addition, it is clear in *Didache* 9 that greater emphasis was laid on the bread, as 9:4 indicates, in the Eucharist celebrated by the group that shared that tradition.[107] Schweizer has argued that while bread may be emphasized, the exclusion of wine cannot be deduced from that. That bread may be used as *pars pro toto* for both elements is shown in the *Acts Thom.* 49, where the "bread of blessing" is immediately identified as the "Eucharist of thy holy body and blood."[108] Yet the emphasis on bread is often accompanied by a reference to a second element, i.e., water, which seems to exclude wine as beverage. If bread were used as *pars pro toto* for bread and wine, why then the mention of water? Clearly, this evidence cannot be quite so easily dismissed.

It must also be observed that in no instance of a "bread Eucharist," is there a reference to the death of Jesus as in any way providing the basis or point of origin for this celebration. If there is a point of origin, other than the common meals shared with Jesus prior to his death, it would seem to be located in the accounts of the wondrous feedings.

Lohmeyer argued regularly for this connection. The feedings provided a better basis than the Passover celebration for the three points that characterized primitive meals: a normal meal to satisfy hunger, an eschatological celebration, and a care for the poor and hungry.[109] This would also explain why Acts always characterizes these meals as the breaking of bread, since that was the main element in them. The Johannine account of the feeding confirms this, followed as it is by John's "eucharistic" discourse. Further, the repetition in the eucharistic material in the *Didache* 9:3–4 of the word κλάσμα for bread, a word found in the gospels only in the feeding of the multitudes, shows a link

106. Cf. Schmidt, "Abendmahl," 11; Lietzmann, "Abendmahl," 31; Lohmeyer, "Die urchristlichen Abendmahl," 9:277, 310; Cullmann, "Meaning," 10; Kretschmer, "Abendmahl," 40.

107. Richardson (in Lietzmann, *Mass*, 299) argues that the Eucharist known to the Fourth Gospel was also such a bread Eucharist, and that the liturgy in *Didache* 9 has its origin in a rite where the distribution of bread was the focal point, along with recitation of the Lord's prayer (405–6). On the absence of wine, see also Lohmeyer, "Die urchristlichen Abendmahl," 9:193; Heitmüller, "Abendmahl," 30.

108. Schweizer, "Das Abendmahl eine Vergegenwärtigung," 88–89.

109. Lohmeyer, "Abendmahl," 233–34.

between the Eucharist and the feedings in the *Didache*.[110] One may not want to find such arguments as proof for Lohmeyer's Galilean tradition, but such evidence, coupled with the catacomb art that regularly portrays the Eucharist with the figure of the feeding of the multitude, does indicate some connection at least in the earliest traditions, between the Eucharist and wondrous feeding.

Seen against the background of that kind of eucharistic celebration, a celebration that, as we know, could engender the kind of excessive behavior that Paul combats in Corinth, the rather one-sided emphasis of the eucharistic accounts in the canonical writings on the death, rather than on the death and resurrection of Jesus, becomes clearer.

It is surprising, on the face of it, that the extent to which the accounts of the "institution" of the Eucharist in the synoptic gospels and Paul avoid all mention of Jesus' resurrection. This is all the more surprising because the whole gospel tradition has been shaped in the light of that event, and as documents of the Christian faith they owe their origin precisely to it. It is not self-evident therefore, that the accounts of the Eucharist, as we have them in their explicit form in Paul and the Synoptics, should so resolutely omit any mention of the risen Lord in connection with that celebration, particularly in the light of the explicitly eschatological element attached to those words (e.g., Mark 14:25), and in view of the many other references that connect eucharistic joy to joy at the knowledge of Christ's resurrection.[111] Literature dealing with the origins of the Eucharist has been strangely silent on this anomaly.

There are, furthermore, indications that the canonical accounts of the Last Supper contain polemical elements that emphasize the connection of that meal to Jesus' death. First Corinthians 11:26 is such an instance. It is rather clearly a Pauline additum, attached to the parallel words about the bread and the cup shared in memory of Jesus.[112] In this instance, we can clearly see the danger that Paul is attempting

110. Lohmeyer, "Die urchristlichen Abendmahl," 10:91.

111. Such an omission cannot be accounted for by citing unwillingness on the part of tradition to have Jesus predict his resurrection, since he does just that in the predictions of the passion (Mark 8:31; 9:31; 10:34; and par.).

112. Cf. Reicke, *Diakonie,* 257; Lietzmann ("Abendmahl," 33) argued that this connection is what Paul had received from the Lord.

to combat with such emphasis. That same emphasis is present in the Synoptics, with their location of the Eucharist in the repetition of the last meal before Jesus' death, and its exclusive reference to that impending event, although the view being combated is not so clear as in Paul. We would argue, however, that the same problem has called forth the same solution. Paul's separation of meal and sacramental elements in 11:34 also opens the way for greater emphasis on the two elements as representing Jesus' body and blood, and thus his death.[113] This is carried out in the Markan account, where the meal-context has disappeared from the words about the elements, although it is still present in the introduction (14:22).

A further indication of the attempt to link the Eucharist to the death of Jesus may be found in the attempt to place its origin on the "night of the betrayal." It is clear from John and the *Didache* that such an interpretation was not universally accepted even during and after the period within which the canonical gospels were being written. On that basis, the Pauline mention of the night of the betrayal (1 Cor 11:23) might possibly also be seen as a theological interpretation of the Eucharist. Further, if as seems likely, the Johannine dating of the last meal of Jesus with his disciples on the night prior to the Passover is correct, the Markan dating of the Eucharist as coinciding with the meal should similarly be seen as a theological interpretation, an interpretation that Matthew then followed.[114] This view receives further substantiation if, as some have suggested, Mark 14:22–25 has been inserted into a narrative that originally did not contain mention of the eucharistic institution as a part of the passion story.[115]

We have now seen evidence pointing to a kind of eucharistic celebration different from the one represented in Paul and the synoptic gospels. It is a meal remembering with joy the risen Lord whose presence is celebrated each time the meal is shared. It is patterned upon and recalls the meal-fellowship with Jesus enjoyed by his disciples prior to his death and which was re-established after his resurrection when he again ate with them. It seems to have found its center in the breaking and eating of bread as the chief element in the meal, rather than in the

113. So Lohmeyer, "Abendmahl," 246; Reicke, *Diakonie*, 255.

114. So also Richardson (in Lietzmann, *Mass*, 296); Marxsen, *Lord's Supper*, 17–18.

115. Marxsen, ibid., 18–19.

regular use of bread and wine. And it may have found the instituting event in the account of the wondrous feedings rather than in Jesus' last Passover meal with his disciples.

Such a Eucharist has some points that would allow it to lend itself to observance by the kind of community that we posited earlier, which saw in Jesus a θεῖος ἀνήρ whose glorious earthly life was remembered and whose presence as the risen Lord was revealed and celebrated at a common meal. The fact that precisely the Corinthian community, which seemed to have such a christology, also appears to have observed that sort of Eucharist lends weight to the suggestion that such a view of Jesus and such a Eucharist went together. The conclusion of the catenae with the account of the feeding would also link it with a Eucharist that saw its warrant in the activity of the earthly Jesus, and specifically in his meal-fellowship with those who followed him. The possibility that the catenae may have formed part of a eucharistic liturgy is thus enhanced to the extent that eucharistic practices existed for which such a collection of events would be meaningful.

If that is the case, we must next ask about the way in which Mark used the catenae and about his motive for using them the way he did. Much of this has already been implied in the arguments up to this point, and this final section may then also serve as a summation.

THE MARKAN USE OF THE CATENAE

If, as we have been urging, Mark included in chs. 4–8 of his gospel material, which originally had been collected and arranged for inclusion in liturgies accompanying celebrations of the Eucharist, it is obvious from the use that Mark has made of them that he does not share the understanding of the Eucharist originally embodied in such material. The catenae gave expression to a theology that saw in Jesus a glorious θεῖος ἀνήρ who manifested himself as such by his deeds during his earthly life, and who is present in his wondrous power at the eucharistic celebration. Mark obviously does not share that theology, and he has countered it by the way he has used the catenae in his own narrative.

In the first place, he has relocated the material within the context of Jesus' earthly life and effectively separated it from any context in which it could continue to throw light on eucharistic understanding and practice. In doing that, he has also separated out any hint that Jesus as θεῖος ἀνήρ is the one present at the Eucharist. Mark has located the mighty deeds of Jesus within the context of the earthly activity of Jesus, a context he himself largely limits to the first eight chapters, and has attached the Eucharist to another kind of event in Jesus' life, viz., his suffering and death.

This would mean, of course, that while Mark does include material that in its original intention presented Jesus as θεῖος ἀνήρ he has used it in a way which de-emphasizes that aspect of its theology. That is, its importance for Mark seems limited to Jesus' earthly career and does not inform his idea of the continuing presence of the risen Jesus with his people. That presence is to be characterized, as Mark sees it, more by humility and suffering than by wonder-working and glory, as the sections on discipleship, especially those following each of the three predictions of the passion, make clear. Could this also account for his unwillingness to include appearances of the risen Jesus at the conclusion of his account? Be that as it may, Mark's intention to combat a θεῖος ἀνήρ christology may also contribute to the formulation of those passages normally seen under the rubric "messianic secret." An investigation of that point would lead us beyond the bounds of this article, however, and so cannot here be pursued.

A second, and related way, in which Mark has transformed the intention of the material contained in the catenae is to be seen in his insertion into the catenae of two blocks of material that present Jesus in his role of teacher-proclaimer, material that Mark himself has assembled apparently for this purpose (6:1–33; 7:1–23). In this way Mark is correcting what he apparently felt was a one-sided emphasis on Jesus as the wonder-worker, by showing that Jesus engaged in proclamation as well as in acts of power.

Since teaching was also a part of the characteristic activity of the θεῖος ἀνήρ, it could be argued that Mark has not abandoned, but simply broadened, the θεῖος ἀνήρ typology to include this other activity as well. Since, however, the Jewish world that Jesus inhabited knew of leaders whose primary function was teaching (i.e., rabbis and scribes), recent studies in Markan christology have, I think rightly, found the chief evidence for a θεῖος ἀνήρ christology in the mighty deeds of Jesus. The extent to which that category plays a part in Mark's presentation of Jesus as proclaimer-teacher could perhaps be gathered from a careful analysis of the way in which Mark presents Jesus as teacher, particularly in the material he has assembled in 6:1–33 and 7:1–23. Such an analysis would again take us beyond the bounds of this present investigation.

A third way in which Mark has countered the theology implied in the catenae is more directly related to its eucharistic function, particularly as that function is related to the story of the wondrous feeding, with which the catena-form ended. A careful analysis of those pericopes will prove instructive.

A comparison of the form in which the feedings occur in the synoptic gospels reveals that the motif of the fish is reduced in both Matthew and Luke, and that corresponding with that there is in Luke and Matthew an increased emphasis on eucharistic motifs. That is to say, Matthew and Luke have interpreted the feedings in Mark in a eucharistic way.[116]

Matthew omits any mention of fish after 14:19a (thus omitting Mark 6:41c and 43b) in the account of the 5,000. In the account of the 4,000, Matthew has taken the reference to fish from Mark 8:7, as the different word for fish ἰχθύδια shows, but he has patterned the mention of fish after his first narrative (cf. 14:17 with 15:34; and 14:19 with 15:36, where the word for fish reverts to ἰχθύς); and he has omitted Mark 8:7, where the fish receive a special blessing and an independent distribution. It is clear from this that Matthew intends both narratives to make the same point over against Mark: less emphasis on fish and a correspondingly greater emphasis on the Eucharist.

Luke 9:12–17 also omits Mark 6:41c and 43b, thus focusing exclusively after 9:16a on the bread, one of the elements in the Eucharist. Van Iersel has called attention to the change that both Matthew and Luke make in Mark's introduction to his first account (6:35): καὶ ἤδη ὥρας πολλῆς γενομένης ("And when it grew late"). Matthew changes it to ὀψίας δὲ γενομένης ("When it was evening"), thus making it specifically an evening meal, introduced with the same formula as the Last Supper (Matt 26:20). Luke changes it to ἡ δὲ ἡμέρα ἤρξατο κλίνειν

---

116. I am drawing, in the following discussion, on the careful research embodied in van Iersel ("Die wunderbare Speisung"), although, as will become apparent, I shall want to differ from the conclusions that he draws from that research. On the eucharistic emphasis in Matthew and Luke in the feeding accounts, see his discussion on 170ff.

("Now the day began to wear away," 9:12), a formulation closely re-
sembling Luke 24:29 (the Emmaus story), which has clear eucharistic
overtones. These are the only two places in Luke where this formulation occurs, and this change also points to Luke's desire to interpret
the feeding in a eucharistic way.[117] The second account of the feeding
(Mark 8:1–9) is omitted by Luke.

Such treatment of the fish-motif in Mark immediately raises the
question about the place played by the fish in the two accounts that
Mark has preserved. The account in Mark 8 restricts the fish to one
sentence (v. 7), and in such a way that the sentence itself seems intrusive. In addition, the mention of fish is framed in parallelism to the
phrase about the bread (v. 6b) in such a way that the reason for such a
parallelism has not been clearly apparent.[118] If one were intent on adding the mention of fish to a story told about bread alone, that would be
one way to do it.

The account in Mark 6 also gives indications of peculiarity in the
way the fish-motif appears. Of the three times fish are mentioned (6:38,
41, 43), the latter two have been noted as also somewhat intrusive, perhaps explained by the fact that they have been added later to an earlier
form of the account.[119] The inclusion of fish in Mark 6:38 is somewhat
peculiar in that Jesus' question asks only about bread (38a), whereas
the answer includes bread and fish. That may indicate an editorial addition at this point as well, although the linguistic structure of the verse
may not compel one to that conclusion.

The question that now arises is this: how is the intrusive nature
of the mention of fish in the two feeding accounts in Mark to be explained? Van Iersel, noting that Matthew and Luke emphasize the eucharistic connotations in their accounts of the feedings, concludes that
this tendency must already have been at work in the Markan redaction. Therefore, he suggests that the words ἀναβλέψας εἰς τὸν οὐρανὸν
. . . , ἵνα παρατιθῶσιν αὐτοῖς ("and he looked up toward heaven . . .
in order to set before them") in Mark 6:41 have been added in order
to emphasize the importance of the bread, and hence to link the story

117. Van Iersel, "Die wunderbare Speisung," 170

118. As van Iersel himself admits, "Die wunderbare Speisung," 176. Kertelge clearly
sees the same problem (*Wunder*, 140), as does Jenkins ("Markan Doublet," 98).

119. Cf. Kertelge, *Wunder*, 136, 131; van Iersel, "Die wunderbare Speisung,"
174–75.

to the Eucharist. Mark thus began the tendency that is then carried further in Matthew and Luke.[120] The difficulty with such a conclusion, however, as van Iersel himself notes, lies in the fact that in v. 43, the mention of fish (which he himself admits to be "nachgetragen") points in just the opposite direction, viz., away from an emphasis on the eucharistic bread.[121] Furthermore, the assumption of eucharistic emphasis in the Markan redaction suffers from additional embarrassment in the account of the feeding of the 4,000, where Mark 8:7, more patently an addition than anything in the account in Mark 6, works precisely counter to the proposed tendency. Here again, attention is called to the fish, and to that extent distracts from the bread.[122]

The difficulty clearly lies in the assumption of Markan eucharistic emphasis. What the evidence clearly points to is just the opposite. Mark is not trying to call attention to the Eucharist; rather, his redactional activity, in each case calling attention to the fish, is rather clearly intended to *de-emphasize* the eucharistic reflections in the two feeding accounts.[123] Once that point becomes clear, the difficulties that van Iersel finds with 6:43 and 8:7 disappear, and the Markan intention emerges clearly: in each instance, he has sought to obscure heavy emphasis on bread alone.

Given that insight, it becomes apparent that the two catenae that Mark had before him, each ending in an account of a feeding, emphasized not only the eucharistic connotations in those reports, but a very particular Eucharist, viz., a bread Eucharist, with all its associations of an origin its the earthly life of Jesus, who for the catenae was already the glorious θεῖος ἀνήρ. Mark, on the other hand, sought to call attention to the importance of Jesus' death prior to his glorious state, and one of the ways he does that is to cast the Eucharist in a different framework than the catenae, viz., in the framework of Jesus' last meal

120. van Iersel, "Die wunderbare Speisung," 175; cf. also Kertelge, *Wunder*, 135.

121. Van Iersel writes: "Dazu soll jedoch bemerkt werden, dass diese Hinzufügung nicht der Tendenz entspricht, die Fische in den Hintergrund zu drängen" (ibid., 175).

122. With regard to the Markan addition of 8:7, van Iersel is forced to admit: "Aus welchem Grund dies geschah, ist nicht ganz klar" (ibid., 176).

123. That two different words for fish occur in the two accounts in Mark (ἰχθύς in ch. 6, ἰχθύδιον in ch. 8) cannot be used to argue against the Markan origin of both insertions. That such a difference could be tolerated, both by tradition and by Mark, is indicated in 1:12–13, where two different words for "desert" occur, virtually side by side.

with his followers prior to his death. He accomplished that by inserting into an earlier passion story an independent account of the institution of that meal (14:22–25), thus grounding the Eucharist in that event in Jesus' career. He then took the catenae, which originally had functioned within a eucharistic liturgy, de-emphasized their eucharistic overtones by calling attention to the presence of fish in that meal as well, and placed them within the eucharistically benign framework of the earthly career of Jesus. To emphasize this new locus for the events contained within the catenae, he inserted material drawn from the other characteristic activity of Jesus, viz., his proclamation-teaching. In that way, Mark was able to preserve the valuable material contained in the catenae about Jesus' career, while at the same time subordinating them to his own understanding of Jesus and of the Eucharist.[124]

The question whether or not the pre-Markan form of the feeding accounts contained eucharistic emphasis must therefore be answered in the affirmative. This eucharistic emphasis was toned down by Mark, but once the inclusion of the catenae within a framework unrelated to the origin of the Eucharist had been accomplished, later authors were free to revive the eucharistic connotations still latent in those stories. That of course is precisely what Matthew and Luke, each in his own way, have done, as van Iersel has shown.

Mark's theological program, the resources he had with which to work and the problems he felt himself called upon to resolve, thus begin to emerge from our consideration of the kind of catenae he incorporated into his gospel and of the use he made of them. It is from the careful sifting of such evidence that the redaction history, and thus the theology, of Mark can eventually be discovered.

124. There are obvious christological implications in this discussion, and their direction should, at least by implication, be clear. Lack of space prevents further development at this point.

Miracles *and the* Historical Jesus: A Study *of* Mark 9:14–29

6

❡ TWO ASSUMPTIONS ARE OPERATIVE IN THE FOLLOWING DISCUSSION to the extent that they determine the methodology to be employed and the outline to be followed. For the sake of clarity, they will be set out as the introduction to this article.

INTRODUCTION

The first assumption concerns the nature of the synoptic gospels. It is assumed that three levels can be distinguished with regard to the materials contained within them. The first level to be distinguished is that of the finished gospel, i.e., the redactional level. The material on this level is the material as it now lies before us, having been given its final form by the evangelist-redactor, and betraying the theological interests that motivated him in constructing the gospel as he did.[1] Results achieved by working on this level will have the highest degree of probability, since we can have the work of the authors before us, and, in one case, one of the sources used (Mark). The second level to be distinguished is that of the traditions employed by the evangelists in the composition of their gospels. The material on this level must be disentangled from the interpretative overlay imposed on it by the gospel author, both through his redactional work, and by his ordering of those traditions. Results achieved by working on this level will have some degree of probability, to the extent that the theological interests and redactional style of the various evangelists can he isolated and then separated from the traditional material. At present, the results of form- or tradition-critical

1. Without prejudice to the question of whether or not the synoptic gospels are the product of one author, or of a "school," and without prejudice to the question of the identity of the authors, they will be referred to simply as "Matthew," "Mark," and "Luke."

work do not appear to have achieved the level of probability of work done on the redactional level. The third level to be distinguished is that of the historic events that gave rise to the traditions. The material on this level must be disentangled from the shaping it received in the process of traditioning, a shaping that made that material useful in the primitive church. The results achieved on this level have the lowest degree of probability, partly because of the nature of the material, which resists being reduced to "bare" (i.e., non-interpreted) history, partly because there is as yet no unanimity about how the material is to be approached. While there is some agreement that the criteria of "dissimilarity" may yield results characterized by some degree of historical probability, certain defects inherent in that approach indicate that the results achieved by its application will contain certain distortions.[2]

Such a characterization of the gospel materials has as its corollary a methodological assumption, namely, that no historically probable conclusions can be reached until the material has been traced back through its redactional and traditional levels. Before that process has been completed, the question of historicity cannot legitimately be raised. Much of the confusion inherent in the search for historically reliable material about Jesus of Nazareth in the synoptic gospels is the result of asking historical questions of the material on level two (traditional) or level one (redactional).

The second assumption concerns the form of the miracle story in the gospels. The formal structure of the miracle story, as isolated by form-critical studies—the problem stated, the solution given, the proof indicated, each element capable of expansion in detail[3]—will be assumed as the minimal pattern necessary to tell such a story. More

2. Historical probability demands that material of Jewish cast attributed to Jesus be suspect, since Jesus so offended those who practiced Judaism that they conspired in his death, and that material of Christian cast be suspect, since the early church may have read its own ideology back into Jesus' career. Yet the result, a non-Jewish Jesus unrelated to the theological reflections of his followers, is strangely unhistorical. A more sophisticated approach, yet to be developed, is necessary for work on this level.

3. Because of its apparently accidental quality, the "acclamation" that may or may not be found at the conclusion of a miracle story is here regarded as part of the "proof." It is a public manifestation that the miracle has taken place, which may or may not be included in the narrative. To regard it in that way appears to me more in conformity with the evidence, than to assume it is an integral part of the miracle-story form, and then assume its deletion when it is not present. Its inclusion appears to be optional; cf. Tagawa, *Miracles et Évangile*, 93 n. 4.

specific discussion of this methodological assumption and its application will be included in the following discussion.

On the basis of the first assumption (the gospels contain material at three levels), the paper will be divided into three major sections, corresponding to the redactional level, the traditional level, and the historical level. The paper will attempt to indicate some of the evidence, and some of the steps, through which one must work, if methodologically reliable results concerning the historical Jesus are to be achieved.

THE REDACTIONAL LEVEL

Unlike some of the other miracle stories in the canonical gospels,[4] Jesus' healing the possessed boy is not mentioned or developed in later Christian literature. There is a story in the apocryphal *Acts of Thomas* (§§ 75–81) that has a similar chain of events (after Thomas casts the demons out of two women, they become "like dead people," and are raised by Thomas, after prayer), but there is no indication that the story is in any way dependent on the account of the possessed boy.[5]

There is thus no indication that later interest in the story would have caused modifications in the story in the gospels, to make that story conform to later interests.[6] We can, with some confidence, assume that the stories as now presented in the three synoptic gospels represent substantially the form given them by the respective evangelists.

Which of the synoptic accounts reflects the earliest form of the story? Here we face ambiguous evidence. On the one hand, form critics have assumed that greater detail indicates a later stage in the tradition. On that basis, Mark, with more detail, would represent a later stage of the tradition than Matthew and/or Luke, who have less-detailed versions. Is there any evidence that Matthew and/or Luke had access to an

---

4. The stories of the woman with the flow of blood (later names "Veronica" or "Berenice"), and of Lazarus fascinated later tradition (e.g., the various Reports of Pilate), and other miracles of Jesus are identified, even described in later Christian writings (e.g., *Ep. Apos.* 5). References to Jesus' miracles are surprisingly rare in later Christian literature (see ch. 3: "Gospel Miracle Tradition and the Divine Man"), and the account of the boy possessed is, to my knowledge, mentioned only in the synoptic gospels.

5. Philostratus tells of a young man from whom Apollonius cast out a demon, but the similarity with the story in Mark 9 ends there (*Life* 4.20).

6. The variant readings in Mark 9:29 will be discussed below.

earlier form of the tradition than the form found in Mark (from "Q"? from a special source?)?

Matthew has a shorter version of the story, but that is characteristic of his style. He regularly shortens Markan miracle stories, reducing their detail in order to make a theological point.[7] Matthew has also rearranged some of the material in order to reduce the confusion of the Markan story (cf. Matt 17:15b, derived from Mark 9:22a and placed earlier in Matthew's form of the story), and has omitted material, apparently for the same reason (e.g., Mark 9:14–16, 20–21, 22b–24). Matthew has thus produced a story whose major emphasis is the disciples' failure.[8] The father's doubts no longer figure in the narrative; from the beginning he is a believer.[9] Thus, the disciples remain as the central figures. The question is: can they heal?[10] The point of the story in Matthew appears to be instruction to the disciples that faith can do all things, their failure being due to their little faith.[11] The story in Matthew is thus a unity in all its details, and the ending that, as we shall see, is a Markan appendage (9:28–29), is here integrated with the story, and serves as its climax.[12] The Matthean form of the story therefore seems to owe more to theological reflection than to dependence on an (earlier) independent source.

Matthew's version could thus be dismissed as a typically Matthean modification of a Markan miracle story, were it not for the fact that Luke, contrary to his normal tendency,[13] also presents a shorter version of the story, omitting many of the details also omitted in Matthew. One can hardly argue, in the light of Luke's omitting a detailed description of the disease (Mark 9:21b–22a), that the slight addition in Luke 9:39c

7. For a good discussion, see Held, "Matthew," passim.

8. So e.g., Fuller, *Interpreting*, 81; Held, 188. I have made no attempt to be exhaustive in citing secondary literature, either supportive or otherwise. Such citations as are given are meant, unless otherwise noted, to be representative.

9. Cf. Held, "Matthew," 191.

10. Ibid., 191, 271.

11. Cf. ibid., 292–93.

12. So ibid., 189. Matthew's identification of the boy's problem as σεληνιάζεται is reflected in the language of Lucian, *Philops.* 16 (καταπιπτόντας πρός τὴν σελήνην). While this could reflect later language on Matthew's part, it is hardly sufficient to allow any conclusions to be drawn.

13. So ibid.

represents an enrichment of detail.[14] Further, the notation that it was an only son (Luke 9:38) may be more typically Lukan (cf. 7:12; 8:42) than due to traditional accretion. Does this omission of common detail by Matthew and Luke then argue for their knowledge of an earlier form of the story, perhaps from "Q"? Two observations argue against such a conclusion. First, the point of Matthew's story is simply omitted by Luke. The point in Luke is not the disciples' faith, as in Matthew, but simply the miracle as such, and the conclusion that this act of Jesus points beyond him to God is a typically Lukan motif for a miracle story (5:25–26; 7:16; 13:13; 17:15; 18; 18:43). Absence of a conclusion to the story common to both Matthew and Luke thus argues against accounting for their shorter versions as due to dependence on a common, non-Markan source. Thus, although both Matthew and Luke have shorter versions of the story, each has created his shorter version to express motifs typical of his own theological understanding. Each story, therefore, though it makes a different point and comes to a different conclusion, is a literary unity, indicating each owes its present shape more to editorial activity than to dependence on a common source.

The second observation arguing against a common source for Matthew and Luke is this. The Markan story is confused in its details, and invites the very omissions Matthew and Luke have made. While Luke does not normally shorten Mark's miracles, he does commonly omit doublets (cf. Mark 5:1–20 with Luke 8:26–39). The present shape of Mark's story would account for the omissions of detail, and recourse to a common source to explain Matthew and Luke seems unnecessary.

If, then, Mark is the source of the narratives in Matthew and Luke, it is also clear that Mark himself has adapted a still earlier source in order to fit it into this point in his narrative. There are a number of indications that such adaptation has taken place.

First, details in the story do not fit the geographic context in which it now stands. The last geographic notice placed Jesus and his disciples in "the villages of Caesarea Philippi" (8:27), and they are not reported as returning to Galilee until after this exorcism had taken place (9:30). In its present context, therefore, the event occurs in the region of Caesarea Philippi, not in Galilee. Yet the details of the opening of the story—the

14. Contra ibid., 192.

crowds familiar with Jesus (v. 15); the knowledge of Jesus and/or his followers as exorcists (v. 17; cf. 3:15; 6:7, 13); the presence of disputatious scribes (v. 14)—point more naturally to the area in which Jesus had to that point been most active, i.e., Galilee. Either, therefore, Mark has added such details to a story originally told of Caesarea Philippi (to what purpose?), or more likely, Mark is responsible for putting a story originally cast in Galilean terms into its present context.[15]

Further indication that Mark is responsible for placing the story here, following the transfiguration, is to be found in the textual variants for ἐλθόντες and εἶδον in v. 14. The singular forms, with good textual attestation, indicate the story at one time told of Jesus' return to his disciples. Later copyists completed the adaptation of the story to the present return of Jesus with Peter, James and John (9:2, 9–12), by changing the singular to plural. Such an explanation seems more likely than the assumption that an original plural was changed at some point to the singular (why?).

Mark may be responsible for further redactional work in the introduction of the story. Verse 15 bears indications of Markan style (καί εὐθὺς, the astonishment of the crowd), and its inclusion disturbs the flow of the narrative. Without it Jesus asks the cause of the dispute (v. 16) that he has come upon (v. 14). On the other hand, no obvious purpose is served by the addition of v. 15 to the story; it provides no essential clue to the point Mark wants to make. Thus, no definite decision can be made about its origin.

The case seems clearer with vv. 28–29. Here the signs of Markan style—Jesus alone in a house with his disciples, who ask for and receive an explanation of what has just happened (Mark 4:10–12; 7:17–23; 10:10–11)—are evident. The purpose of this addition is also clear: in this way, Mark has adapted the story to fit into this section (8:27—10:45) whose theme is the instruction of the disciples.[16] That this is Markan adaptation is further indicated by the fact that while the point

15. Mark appears to have done a similar thing with the story of the Syrophoenician woman (7:25–30) by taking a story originally located in Galilee (thus the interest in her as Syrophoenician—why would that be noteworthy in Syrophoenicia?) and putting it in a non-Galilean framework (7:24, 31).

16. This point, rather than Jesus' impending suffering, seems to be the organizing theme for this section. The nature of the material indicates that it was probably intended as instruction for the church.

of vv. 28–29 is the power of prayer, the point of the story is the power of faith (vv. 19, 23–24; so also Matthew understood it). Had Mark wanted to continue that emphasis, he knew the tradition by means of which to do it (cf. 11:22–23; it is the one Matthew later chose). In that light, Mark's choice of prayer as the final emphasis seems deliberate. The best explanation appears to be that such an emphasis met a particular need in the community for which Mark was writing.[17] Later tradition added the phrase: "and fasting" (καὶ νηστεία).[18]

The problems of this pericope are not exhausted with considerations of its introduction and conclusion. There is evidence within the story itself that is difficult to account for. There are (1) two descriptions of the lad's sickness (vv. 17–18; 22a); (2) the crowd is present (14) but later assembles (v. 25); (3) the disciples play a key role in vv. 14–19, but are ignored in vv. 20–27; (4) the dumb spirit (v. 17) is later described as deaf and dumb (v. 25); (5) one motive for the healing is provided in v. 24 (help for the father's unbelief), another in v. 25 (the assembling crowd); (6) the symptoms of the illness (vv. 18a, 20b, 22a) have nothing to do with dumbness (vv. 17b, 25) or deafness (v. 25); (7) v. 18 uses a vocabulary (ῥήγνυμι, τρίζειν, ξηραίνειν) different from that used in 20, 26 (κυλίειν, [συν] σπαράσσειν).

Such evidence leads to the suspicion that this story as it now exists is a composite, probably of two earlier miracle stories.[19] The contrasting elements can be distributed in such a way that two stories would emerge, the one encompassing roughly vv. 14–20, the other vv. 21–27.[20]

17. There is also a difficulty with this conclusion, however. The need to pray in order to do miracles is surely not characteristic of Mark. It would also be easier to understand why Mark put an exorcism in a section on instruction if the exorcism already had been so adapted. The indications of Markan style tend to outweigh such difficulties, however.

18. A similar addition was made to 1 Cor 7:5. Fasting later becomes an important feature for the Christian miracle-worker: Paul prays and fasts for Thecla's miraculous deliverance (*Acts Paul* §23); Peter fasts before his contest of miracles with Simon (*Actus Ver.* §22); Irenaeus reports that dead have been raised when an entire church engaged in fasting and prayer (*Haer.* 2.2).

19. So, e.g., Bultmann, *Geschichte,* 226 = *History,* 211; Held, "Matthew," 187; Fuller, *Interpreting,* 34; so also in the commentaries on Mark by Schweizer, Taylor, and Nineham, ad loc. Others have argued for an original story which has been expanded; e.g., G. Schille, *Wundertradition,* 30 n. 83; Kertelge, *Die Wunder Jesu,* 175–76; Schenk, "Tradition und Redaktion."

20. The items numbered 5 and 6 in the list above are not thus accounted for; we

The point of the former would be the contrast of apprentices with the wonder-worker; the point of the latter the paradox of unbelieving faith.[21] The presence in Mark's gospel of other miracles, combined either in such a way as to make it clear a combination has occurred (5:21–43), or, in a way similar to our pericope, in such a way that the two stories are more or less carefully interwoven (5:1–20; 6:45–52), lends further weight to this hypothesis. The tendency to combine miracle stories continued beyond Mark (cf. Matt 14:22–33).

If there is some consensus that two stories have been combined, there is less consensus concerning the point at which they were combined, i.e., by Mark, or at some time prior to his having received the tradition.[22] While there is no conclusive evidence either way, there is some indication that they were combined before Mark received them.

Let us take as our model a passage generally acknowledged to be an instance where Mark has combined two stories: 11:12–25. In this instance, both stories clearly retain their original integrity as units from the tradition. All elements of the miracle story are present (vv. 11–14, 20–21), and the story of the temple cleansing is complete (vv. 15–19). This is also true of other instances where Mark has apparently combined traditions (e.g., 3:20–35; 6:7–32): the two traditions tend to retain their own identity. The same phenomenon is apparent in an instance where Matthew has combined two stories (Matt 14:22–33). I would add Mark 5:21–43 as another instance where Mark has combined two traditions,[23] although not all scholars would agree Mark is responsible for their combination.

On the other hand, when two stories are interwoven, as they are in our pericope (e.g., Mark 5:1–20; 6:45–52), the signs of Markan editorial work tend to be confined to the introduction and conclusion of the combined traditions (5:1–2a, 20; 6:45a, 52). This would indicate that Mark received the traditions already combined, and confined his editorial work to framing them in such a way as to fit them into his narrative. In a similar way, the signs of Markan editorial work in our pericope are largely confined to the introduction (vv. 14–15, or parts

---

will return to them at a later point in our discussion.

21. So, e.g., Bultmann, *Geschichte*, 226 = *History*, 211; Fuller, *Interpreting*, 34.

22. Combined before Mark: Bultmann, *Geschichte*, 225 = *History*, 211; Nineham, *Mark*, ad loc.; by Mark: Schweizer, *Markus* = *Mark*, ad loc.

23. I have outlined my reasons for that conclusion above in ch. 4: "Isolation."

of them) and the conclusion (vv. 28–29). Such evidence again tends to indicate that the traditions were combined before they got to Mark, and that Mark has adapted the combined traditions to fit his narrative framework and purpose.

We would conclude, then, that the point of this pericope as it now stands in its Markan context centers not on the miracle as such, but on the disciples as miracle-workers, and their failure, with the resulting instruction to them. This point, already implicit in the story, has been made explicit by vv. 28–29, added very likely by Mark, who has then included this story in his section on Instruction to the Disciples (8:27—10:45).[24]

PRE-MARKAN TRADITION

Our next step is to inquire about the modifications that this story underwent in the course of its transmission prior to its incorporation into Mark. We have argued that the form in which Mark obtained it is basically its present form, without vv. 28–29, and with a modified introduction in vv. 14–15, although it is difficult to say with any certainty how that introduction was originally shaped. If the Markan language (καὶ εὐθύς, ἐκθαμβήθησαν) gives us a clue about v. 15, then the story will have begun with Jesus approaching his surrounded disciples, and, perceiving a dispute, asking the reason for it. In that form, the thrust of the story will have been the contrast between the disciples and Jesus as miracle-workers (vv. 18b–19, 25–27), and a subordinate contrast between unfaith and faith (vv. 19, 23–24), with the point being the greatness of Jesus as wonder-worker, contrasted to his powerless disciples[25] and the faith/unfaith of the father.

Our previous analysis has also made clear, however, that the story in that form betrays indications of an original combination of two stories, and we must now attempt if possible to retrace the process of that combination.

---

24. Cf. Held, "Matthew," 74; Bauernfeind, *Worte*, 74 n. 1. As already indicated, this theme is more appropriate for the material than the narrower designation, Instruction about Jesus' Suffering.

25. Klostermann, *Markusevangelium*, 101, identifies stories with similar points in 2 Kgs 4:31–37 (Gehazi and Elisha) and Lucian of Samosata, *Philops.* 36 (the sorcerer's apprentice).

If the story as Mark got it was in fact an earlier combination of two miracle stories, the attempt to disentangle those two accounts would be a logical place to begin. As a number of scholars have noted, v. 20 begins an account which gives the appearance of a more or less coherent miracle story. The problem is apparent in v. 20, and is amplified in vv. 21–22. The solution is given in some detail in v. 25, and the proof that the spirit does in fact leave is furnished in vv. 26–27.[26] The remaining material in the pericope does not furnish so complete a story. The problem is clearly outlined in vv. 17–18 in a setting quite different from its outline in vv. 20–22 (in v. 17 a crowd is present, in v. 25 it is clear that Jesus and the father have been alone; the self-destructive urge of the demon in v. 22 is absent in v. 18; the dumb demon in v. 17 becomes deaf and dumb in v. 25; different vocabulary is used in describing the problem in vv. 18 and 20), but the solution and proof are not readily distinguishable. This would not be surprising if two stories were combined, since the similarities that would motivate the original combination would lead to the elimination, in the combination, of similar elements. We could guess, therefore, that the solution and proof were similar to vv. 25–27, i.e., a successful exorcism.

There is, however, some evidence that makes it possible to do more than guess at the remaining form of the second miracle story. Verses 26b–27 bring more than is necessary for the first story. As it now stands, there is a two-fold solution (the demon is exorcised; Jesus takes the boy's hand to raise him) and a two-fold proof (the demon exits; the boy arises). There is the additional problem of what seems in the story to be a second miracle: the boy who was "as dead" (problem) is seized by the hand (solution) and arises (proof). Such a doubling of elements is quite unusual in a miracle story, and some of those elements may have been retained from the second story when it was combined with the first. If that is the case, the second miracle would consist as follows: description of the problem (vv. 17–18) and the result of a seizure (v.

<hr/>

26. This evidence led Kertelge, *Die Wunder Jesu*, 175–76, to see the original form of the pericope in vv. 20–27, comparing v. 20, καὶ ἤνεγκαν αὐτὸν πρὸς αὐτὸν with Mark 2:3; 7:32; and 8:22 as the beginning of a healing and then attributing to Mark the addition of vv. 14–19 as well as 28–29. Interestingly, φέρειν in those examples is used only in the present tense. As indicated, I prefer the explanation that two stories were combined.

26b); the solution, v. 27a (Jesus takes hold of the lad's hand to raise him) and the proof, v. 27b (the boy arises).

Included in the first story would be the contrast between the disciples' inability to heal, and Jesus' power to do it (v. 18b); included in the second the contrast between Jesus' confidence and the father's wavering faith (vv. 23–24).

In these two stories are contained elements that betray theological reflection on the miracle story itself. Thus, v. 19 sees in the disciples' failure their lack of faith, a point not inherent in the miracle story itself; their failure is simply reported (v. 18). Verses 23–24 amplify the father's request for help (v. 22b), a normal element in the miracle story as it appears in the gospels and elsewhere,[27] into comments on the nature of the father's faith. But whereas the dialogue in vv. 23–24 proceeds clearly within the story, v. 19 is unclear as to its referent: who is unfaithful? the crowds? the disciples? the father himself? all together? It appears that v. 19 is not so clearly integrated into the story as vv. 23–24. We will return to this point later.

If, then, as seems likely, vv. 23–24 are an insertion into an earlier miracle story,[28] we have, with its removal, a recognizable account of an exorcism. The problem is clearly indicated (v. 20), and its difficulty is heightened by the information that the child has been so afflicted since childhood (v. 21b), and that the spirit is lethal (v. 22a). Jesus, not wishing to perform the healing with a crowd present (cf. Mark 7:33; 8:23), then pronounces an epipompe[29] with the regular apotropaic formula that the demon is not to enter again the person from whom it is being driven out.[30] The success of the expulsion is indicated by the act of the demon leaving,[31] in this case, convulsing the boy one final time.

27. That such a request for help can exist independently of such theological reflection is indicated in Mark 1:40. The only difference is that there the doubt concerns Jesus' willingness to help, not his ability to do so.

28. So, e.g., Fuller, *Interpreting,* 61–62; Schille, *Wundertradition,* 32.

29. For a discussion of the place of various forms of dismissal (ἐπιπόμπη, ἀποπόμπη, ἀπολῦσις), cf. Wünsch, "Geisterbannung," 16–23.

30. This phrase is included because that is part of the exorcistic formula, not because of the episodic nature of the possession (contra Branscomb, *Mark,* ad loc.). For examples of this formula, cf. Josephus, *Ant.* 8.2.5; Philostratus, *Life* 4.20; on this particular verse, see Bauernfeind, *Worte,* 39.

31. That demons give such indication of their departure, cf. Mark 5:13; Josephus, *Ant.* 8.2.5; Philostratus, *Life* 4.20; *Actus Ver.* §11.

Into this account, the discussion about faith has been inserted (vv. 23–24). The point of this insert, however, is unique in gospel literature, in that the clear implication of v. 23 is that Jesus can do this act because he has the requisite faith![32] The response of the father—that his faith is insufficient—is never corrected. Nowhere is there any indication that the father's faith ultimately rose above its ambiguity. In their present form, vv. 23–24 present the contrast between the powerful wonder worker and the impotent seeker. Jesus is powerful because of his faith, as v. 23 clearly implies, and the faith of the father, far from ultimately proving sufficient (a point nowhere made in the narrative), is a clear counter-point to the effective faith of Jesus that alone, through the expulsion, is proved sufficient.[33] The story, with its insertion, thus clearly belongs to a level of theological reflection other than, and, as our analysis has shown, quite likely prior to, that of the synoptic authors.

This implication about the source of Jesus' power (his faith) found little support in the continuing theological and Christological reflections of the primitive church, as its absence in other gospel traditions clearly shows. Such a Christology therefore needed correcting, and it is precisely such correction that occurred when this miracle story was combined with another, similar story which did not share the objectionable Christology. Further correction was provided to the combined stories by the addition of v. 19. Here the question of faith and unfaith is linked to a broader spectrum, and to a spectrum more congenial to the maturing theological reflections of the community. The sovereign picture of Jesus, implied in vv. 23–24, is continued in v. 19, but not attributed to his faith.[34]

At some point in the traditioning of this material, therefore, two miracle stories about the healing of a demon-possessed boy[35] were

32. So Lohmeyer, *Markus*, 190.

33. The more acceptable form of this theologoumenon is found in Mark 10:27. Matthew and Luke, unwilling to reproduce 9:23, do use 10:27, indicating the latter's more acceptable form for later theological sensitivities. Remnants of this understanding of Jesus' own faith are found in Heb 12:1–3, esp. v. 2; cf. also 4:15; 5:7–9. The speculations of some scholars that Jesus, in requiring of his hearers a decision of faith, must himself have earlier made a similar decision, have no evidential value for this problem.

34. The OT echoes of v. 19 show that Jesus is here being linked more closely with God himself; cf. Deut 32:20; Num 14:27; Isa 65:2. So also Lohmeyer, *Markus*, 187.

35. I have refrained from calling the problem "epilepsy," an identification I find

combined, and the implication of vv. 23–24, that it was Jesus' faith that gave him the power to perform miracles, was "corrected" by the general statement about the faithlessness of the present, corrupt generation (a common NT description; e.g., Mark 8:38; Matt 12:39; Acts 2:40; Phil 2:15). In that way, the sovereignty of Jesus was preserved,[36] but the attention was shifted away from the (believing) Jesus to the unbelieving father, and the reason for the disciples' impotence now also becomes, by implication, their lack of faith (v. 19).

To summarize: a story that originally recited an exorcism of Jesus was interpreted by the addition of material that explained Jesus' power to do exorcisms (his faith), but explained it in a way that was, in the developing and maturing tradition, unsatisfactory. The story was then re-interpreted through the device of combining it with another, similar story, which at that point apparently bore no theologically interpretative elements. To this combination, and probably at the same time it was made, a statement about faithlessness was added (v. 19), which was intended to point the new story in a more acceptable direction. In that way, a miracle story previously uninterpreted (vv. 17–18, 20?, 26b–27), and a miracle story (vv. 20–22, 25–26a) previously unacceptably interpreted (vv. 23–24) were given a new interpretation by their combination, and by the addition of a new statement about faith (v. 19) that turned the point from Jesus' faith to the lack of faith of the

---

questionable at best, despite its long tradition. Mark's account of the symptoms is hardly clinical: his descriptions of the seizures do not match (vv. 18, 20), and the causative demon (deaf, v. 17b; dumb and deaf, v. 25) is unrelated to either set of symptoms. In ancient descriptions of epilepsy, e.g., that of Hippocrates, most of Mark's symptoms are listed, but so are many others Mark omitted (e.g., choking, twisting hands, rolling eyes, discharging excrement; Hippocrates, περὶ ἱερῆς νούσου, X). While Hippocrates concedes the disease can be fatal to children, it is not because they may fall into fire or water, but because their veins are too small to allow the dangerous phlegm to pass through, thus fatally chilling and congealing their blood (XI). While children may fall anywhere with their first seizures, they soon learn when a seizure is coming, and can then protect themselves (XV). While Hippocrates combats the idea that the disease is of divine origin, the popular diagnosis, he never hints people thought it was due to a malevolent demon, as Mark clearly does (vv. 22, 25; Hippocrates said it was hereditary, V). It was clearly not Mark's intention to "diagnose" the lad's disease as epilepsy, and such modern diagnostic attempts in my opinion help little if at all in understanding this story.

36. So, e.g., Bultmann, *Geschichte,* 169: "in diesem Wort (spricht) der epiphane Gott" = *History,* 157: "it is a God of an epiphany who is speaking."

disciples, thus also throwing new emphasis on the ambiguous faith of the father.

With such an analysis, we have recovered the earliest identifiable form of the traditions contained in Mark 9:14–29, i.e., two miracle stories, one more easily recoverable than the other, which, in their original form, it would appear, circulated without specific theological interpretation.[37]

THE HISTORICAL LEVEL

We are now at a point where we can ask a question on the historical level, i.e., can we determine to what extent the earliest recoverable form of the tradition reflects an actual historical occurrence? In order to insure that we do not reach conclusions based on a misreading of the kind of situation within which these miracle stories about Jesus circulated, it will be helpful to consider a sampling of non-NT miracle

37. While it is entirely possible that some of the miracle stories told of Jesus may have included explicit elements of theological interpretation from the beginning, in addition to the implicit Christological impact of a story about one whose acts manifested such power, the existence of miracle stories in Mark that apparently came to him with no explicit theological interpretation at all, and that he reproduces with no theologically interpretative introductory or concluding comments (1:29–31; 8:22–26), shows that stories could circulate in that form, and be used even as late as Mark. The overwhelming majority of miracle stories in the gospels do contain explicit theologically interpretative elements, either in the framework into which they have been put (e.g., Mark 1:21–28), or by the inclusion within the story of such theologically explicit material (e.g., Mark 2:1–12), indicating that very early in the traditioning process, miracle stories as such were found to be less useful than miracle stories whose theological interpretation was included within the story itself. The growth of other elements of the tradition (e.g., the parables) indicates that part of the traditioning process included theological interpretation becoming part of the materials themselves. For that reason, it seems more likely that the miracles with such interpretative elements included within them represent a later stage of the tradition than stories that do not have them. That miracle stories could exist without explicit theological interpretation is demonstrated not only by the Markan narratives cited, but also by the examples in secular literature of such stories. Inherently it would also seem more likely that miracle stories with no theological interpretation would acquire it, than that stories that began with such interpretation would be stripped of it. The continuing process of theological interpretation of the miracles continues as Matthew and Luke retell the miracle stories they get from Mark. I did not come upon the work of Petzke and Schille, until after I had formulated such conclusions, but I gladly acknowledge their work which confirms such reasoning (e.g., G. Petzke, "Historizität," 367–85; Schille, *Wundertradition*, 19 n. 33 et passim). For an opposite view of the development of these traditions, see Roloff, *Kerygma*, 146–47.

stories that also existed in the Hellenistic world. Such a consideration will also keep us from finding historical elements in NT traditions by means of judgments we would be unwilling to make on similar, non-NT traditions.[38]

We shall limit ourselves to two examples. One of them is simply a collection of miracle stories, without any narrative framework, which nevertheless has undergone a process of traditioning, viz., the stories from stele "A" of the Temple of Asclepius at Epidauros.[39] The other is a narrative that includes within itself miracle stories that have undergone a process of traditioning, viz., Philostratus' *Life of Apollonius of Tyana*.[40] In each case, we will ask about the kind of process of traditioning that has taken place, and what that then allows us to say about the final form of the tradition, and the kind of historical judgments they make possible.

The stories of the healings by Asclepius were inscribed on a series of stone steles, of which six still remained when Pausanias visited the temple site in AD 165. Of these, three and parts of a fourth have been recovered. The steles were of approximately the same size, and the form of the letters, as well as language and content, indicate that the material engraved on the steles is the end-product of a unified redaction.[41] As the first story on stele "A" indicates, some of these stories at least were taken from votive plaques that bore witness to the healing attributed to the agency of Asclepius. The diverse nature of the information in the various stories, however, indicates that not all of them were derived from such sources.[42]

The point of the stories is clearly to show the power of the god Asclepius. The story normally tells of the person's coming to the sanctuary, entering the temple for the rite of incubation, during which frequently a dream foretells the healing, or even the process by which the healing takes place, and then paying the votive offering. This last

38. Again, although these reflections were undertaken independently of the work of Petzke, I gladly acknowledge their confirmation in his writing.

39. On the possibility that similar collections of miracles of Jesus may have been incorporated into the gospel of Mark, see above, ch. 4: "Isolation" and ch. 5: "Origin and Function."

40. For a thorough analysis of this material, see Petzke, *Traditionen*.

41. So Herzog, "Wunderheilungen," 2.

42. Idem, 56–57.

item, although sometimes specified (e.g., stories W 3, 4, 7 in Herzog's cataloging) is not always mentioned in the accounts of the miracles. Although most of the stories concern healings, other miracles are reported, e.g., a broken drinking cup was restored by Asclepius, and then presented to the temple as a votive offering (W 10).

Not all the stories mention the incubation period (e.g., W 8, where a dumb lad suddenly answers a request addressed to the father for a pledge to pay a votive offering; W 16 where a lame man, robbed, runs after the thief), indicating that anything happening in the temple area was regarded as due to the power of Asclepius.

The way the stories are told also indicates that they were intended to encourage those who were ill that they could be healed, and that skepticism was out of place (e.g., W 2, 3). Nothing was beyond help to those who "believed" (e.g., W 9 tells of a man with empty eye sockets who, though ridiculed for his belief that he would see again, was nevertheless healed). The importance of this theme is indicated by the fact that the third and fourth stories on stele "A" make the same point, viz., that skepticism is out of place.

The purpose of the stories is thus not simply to awaken amazement at what had been done through Asclepius, but to give advice to those seeking similar help: they should believe, should do what the god advised, and should pay the proper votive offering (W 7 recited the punishment of one who withheld such an offering).

A formal analysis of the miracle accounts shows that what we have termed "intrusive" theological elements with respect to gospel miracle stories are also present in many of the stories found at Epidauros. In W 3, the discussion of unbelief and ridicule, and the god's changing the suppliant's name to Apistos, are unnecessary for the story, and indicate an adaptation of the form of the miracle story. There are accounts that bear the unadapted form of the miracle story (e.g., W 6, the removal of a mole from a suppliant's face; W 15, the cure of a cripple who then carried a large stone), but they appear in the minority. There is of course no sure way of tracing such adapted stories to an unadapted original form, but again, the presence of unadapted stories may point to an earlier stage of transmission. The difficulty in this instance consists in the fact that, if Herzog is correct in his analysis of language and inscription style, these stories have been given their form and order by a religious propagandist of Asclepius from sources (i.e., the plaques) that did not undergo a period of oral transmission. Perhaps the first story, told to indicate the source of the other stories, and thus presumably drawn from the plaque itself by showing the unadapted form of the miracle story, gives evidence that the plaques themselves were normally unadapted.

In any case, what we have at Epidauros is a collection of miracle stories told of a god, told in a form similar to those of the gospels, and betraying a process of theological adaptation. They thus provide the same springboard for historical judgment, formally, as the stories told in the gospels.

With our second example, the miracles of Apollonius of Tyana, we face a slightly different situation. These miracle stories have been included in an account that contains stories of Apollonius' travels, his wisdom, his activities, and his trial before the emperor on charges of magic. All of this Philostratus, at the behest of the empress Julia, attempted to present in a more elegant form than had theretofore been accomplished (I, 3), with the expressed purpose of showing that Apollonius was not a "magos," but had achieved what he did by reason of his wisdom (I, 2). Philostratus informs us that he used a number of written sources (those of Damis, of Maximus, and the will of Apollonius), and warns against the books of Moerangenes, which he says, were composed in ignorance of the true circumstances of Apollonius' life (I, 3). Earlier (I, 2) he had also mentioned that he had gathered information from cities and temples with which Apollonius had been associated, thus perhaps implying oral sources. Yet when he specifies his sources, he mentions only written materials, so too much weight cannot be put on those earlier statements. Thus, the materials Philostratus used and edited had already been previously edited, and he stands separated by some two hundred years from the subject about which he writes.

In our analysis, we will restrict ourselves to a consideration of miraculous deeds, and will ignore instances in which Apollonius demonstrates foreknowledge (e.g., IV, 6, 24; V, 13, 18; VI, 32), or in which he is wondrously transported from one location to another (e.g., IV, 10; VIII, 10). Some of those miracles were accomplished by persons other than Apollonius, e.g., the Indian sages Apollonius visited (III 38–39).

Some of the stories are formally incomplete, i.e., one of the formal elements is missing in the present narrative. For example, in the story of a boy possessed by a demon, no proof is cited that the letter given his mother by an Indian sage in fact effected the exorcism (III, 38). The solution is omitted in two stories, one of a man restored to sight whose eyes had been put out, the other a man whose paralyzed hand was cured (III, 39). Since these stories are told in somewhat summary fashion about Apollonius' stay in India, their incomplete form may well be due to Philostratus' literary activity. Another story in the same series has a dislocated proof, i.e., we hear first that the woman was cured, and only then the problem and its solution (III, 39).

Other stories, however, are formally complete miracle stories. Apollonius delivers himself and his companions from a "vampire spirit" (φάσμα ἔμπουσα; II, 4); he forestalls a plague in Ephesus by having the plague demon in the form of an old beggar stoned (IV, 10); he exorcises a demon-possessed boy (IV, 20); he reveals for what she is and rebukes a vampire with whom one of his students was in love (IV, 25); and he delivers a village from a satyr that had plagued its women for ten months (VI, 27). Although details are often expanded (the problem: IV, 20, 25; the solution: VI, 27; the proof: IV, 10), and although Philostratus can reveal the purpose for his telling a particular story (to give further evidence of the existence of satyrs: VI, 27; to correct information about a famous act of Apollonius: IV, 25), the stories remain "unadapted" in the sense we have been using that word, i.e., they do not contain elements unnecessary for the miracle story that allow it to make another point than the recitation of a miracle.

The two remaining stories are of more interest to the concerns of this paper. They are: the raising of the young bride-to-be (IV, 45) and the cure of a boy and the mad dog that bit him (VII, 43). In the first story, the normal form of the miracle story is easily discerned. The problem is the death of a young girl of consular family at the hour of her marriage, a death that has plunged the whole of Rome into mourning. The solution consists of Apollonius, who has met the procession, telling the pallbearers to put down the bier, and after asking her name, touching her, and whispering something secretly (τί αφανῶς) over her. The proof tells of the girl awakening, speaking and returning to her father's house. The reaction in this instance consists in the father giving Apollonius a monetary reward.

Into this story two insertions have been made. The one compares the girl's return to her father's house to the similar act of Alcestis when she was brought back to life by Hercules. In that way Apollonius, indirectly at least, is compared to that god. The other tells that Apollonius gave the reward he had received to the girl for her dowry. In that way Apollonius' generosity is emphasized, and he is shown indirectly to be unlike magicians who had the reputation of requiring large sums for their services. Philostratus added a rationalizing conclusion questioning whether the girl was really dead, or had a spark of life undetected by all but Apollonius.

We have, then, in this story phenomena similar to those we detected in Mark 9:14–29, i.e., the adaptation of a formal miracle story to serve another purpose than simply to recite an event.[43]

The second story is a combination of two stories centering around a lad and the mad dog that bit him. Again, both stories display the formal characteristics of the miracle story, although in the combination, the problem of the second story—that the dog was mad—is assumed to carry over from the first. The problem is a boy who has acted like a dog for thirty days after having been bitten by an unknown mad dog. Apollonius describes the dog to Damis, who fetches it. After taming the dog, Apollonius caused it to lick the wound where it bit the boy, thus providing the solution. The proof takes the form of the boy returning to his father, recognizing his mother, saluting his comrades and drinking water. In the second story the mad dog (problem) is sent across the river by Apollonius (since, we are informed, a drink of water will cure a mad dog), and that solution receives its proof when the dog, now on the other side, barks (a thing we are told mad dogs rarely do), lays back its ears, and wags its tail.

Into the first story there is inserted Apollonius' statement that the soul of Telephus of Mysia has been transferred into the boy, and that thus the Fates have imposed on the boy what they had imposed on Telephus. Since the problem is adequately explained by the bite of the mad dog, and since the soul of Telephus is ignored in the solution, this insertion is either to prove the transmigration of souls, or to demonstrate Apollonius' superior wisdom. It plays no part in the miracle story, and oddly enough is inserted into the account of the solution rather than the problem. Once again, it would appear, we have

43. Petzke has pointed to this story as one of the clearest examples of Philostratus' reworking of an older tradition (*Traditionen,* 129–30). He has also compared this story with Luke 7:11–17 in "Historizität.

the adaptation of a miracle story through the inclusion of an interpretative element unnecessary to the story itself. We also have what
appears to be a rationalizing statement of Philostratus concerning the
reason why Apollonius had the dog swim the river, i.e., drinking water,
something presumably the swimming dog could not avoid, cures mad-
ness in dogs.[44]

In addition to the interpretative inclusion, we have here a combination of two miracle stories, with the consequent omission of one
of the formal elements (in this instance, the problem) in one of the
stories.

Here again we have observed traditional and literary phenomena
similar enough to the material in the gospels to demand that the judgment applied to one instance of this material be applied to all.[45] We
must turn now, after this brief survey, to our major problem: what can
we say on the historical level about Jesus as miracle-worker.

The Historical Jesus

Any attempt to come to historical conclusions about Jesus of Nazareth
on the basis of the traditions contained in the gospels is fraught with
difficulties, as is well known. Yet those difficulties are compounded
in our case, because of the content of the tradition, viz., a miracle.
However reliable the process may be judged to be, by means of which
we reached our conclusions about the original form of the traditions
contained in Mark 9:14–29, any attempt to move from those conclusions to conclusions about their historical reliability will be suspect
because of their content.

It is possible, and scholars have done it, to deny the reality of that
content on a priori grounds. That is, miracles are impossible, and therefore any stories about miracle-workers are also historically unreliable,

44. So also Petzke, *Traditionen*, 133–34.

45. While there are many reports of miracles and miracle-working rabbis in the
Jewish literature of this period, the formal characteristics of those stories are in some
important respects different from those of the non-Jewish Hellenistic world, and for
that reason they have not been taken into account in this paper. For a good survey
of the Jewish materials, see Blau, *Zauberwesen*. On the formal differences between
the stories of rabbinic miracle-workers, and those found in non-Jewish Hellenistic
literature, see above, ch. 3: "Gospel Miracle Tradition." This is a problem-area that has
been badly neglected, and needs further careful investigation.

and are the product of fantasy, or over-zealous propaganda. The current state of the natural sciences, it is often argued, makes acceptance of such events impossible.

Yet such judgments can no longer be held with the assurance they once were. It has now become evident, through the discipline of the sociology of knowledge, and the studies in the influence of habit and language on the perception of reality, that "reality" as it is conceived and perceived can and will differ in different circumstances, and different historical periods. The question is not "what is reality" in the abstract, but "what functions as reality" in a concrete historical period.[46] Studies in the intentionality of perception have shown the extent to which functioning reality is influenced by internal (subjective) expectations about external (objective) stimuli.[47] Simply stated, human beings react to reality as they perceive and understand it. Hence, a type of event, entirely "unreal" by one set of criteria, could have decisive influence on an entire historical era, if that type of event were perceived as real, i.e., if it "functioned as reality."[48] One ought therefore to abandon the intellectually imperializing attitude of standing in judgment over another age's perception of reality. There is no objective (i.e., trans-historical) guarantee that we are any closer to perceiving "true reality" (basically a meaningless abstraction) than they.[49] The question, therefore, of the "reality" of Jesus' miracles cannot be solved on the basis of an a priori denial based on criteria of a twentieth-century construct of reality that is itself based on the perceptions of reality that the natural sciences anticipate and credit as "real."

Aside from such a priori considerations, however, there is another problem that intrudes itself into the discussion of whether miracles be-

46. For a good discussion of this point, cf. Petzke, "Historizität," 368–69, 378–80.

47. For a more detailed discussion of the point, cf. ch. 5: "Language, Perception and Reality" of my *Introduction to the New Hermeneutic*.

48. This seems in fact to have been the case with the Hellenistic world, where even decisions of state were influenced by various divinations and auguries. This particular view has sedimented itself into our word "inaugurate," which means to consult the omens as the first step in some activity.

49. Schille points out that "historical probability" is a useless critical criterion in the investigation of the miracle tradition, since it automatically excludes any unusual historic act or event (*Wundertradition*, 11–12 n. 8). As a criterion, it is totally unsuited to cope with any "reality" which differs from a given twentieth-century construct of that "reality."

longed to the activities of the historical Jesus, namely, the similarity of the accounts of miracles told of him, and those told of others. We illustrated this point in our discussion of the transmission and adaptation of the stories from Epidauros, and those about Apollonius of Tyana.[50] That means simply that whatever historical judgments we make about this kind of story in the gospels we will also have to make about this kind of story wherever it occurs.[51] That means in its turn, among other things, given the way in which we have seen miracle stories develop, i.e., with explicit theological interpretation added at a later stage in the tradition, that doctrinal conclusions cannot be used as a criterion of the validity of such a report. Doctrinal material is designed to interpret the story, and cannot therefore be used as a criterion in judging historical events. Thus, the fact that a miracle may point to Jesus as the one in whom forgiveness may be had (Mark 2:1–12), or as one in whose teaching the power of God is at work (Mark 1:21–28), or as an indication of the final salvific act of God for man,[52] may not be used to argue for the uniqueness of the miracle as such, with the ensuing judgment that that kind of qualitative difference allows us to say Jesus' miracles happened, while those reported of others did not, or were mere appearances. The miracles of Jesus, in short, may not be affirmed or denied on the basis of the Christian interpretation that has been given to these stories, as though that interpretation allowed one to make a different historical judgment on the miracles of Jesus than, say, the miracles of Apollonius of Tyana. It is therefore, I would argue, historically impermissible to try to judge the reality of Jesus' miracles on the basis of the doctrines that the tradition has used those stories to support. The theological truth of those doctrines may not become a support for the historical truth of the miracle.

One must therefore either judge all reports of such miracles from the Hellenistic age as false, including those reported in the gospels, or one must allow for the reality for more Hellenistic miracles than simply those reported of Jesus. Yet that appears to be precisely the attitude of

50. For further discussion and examples on this point, cf. above, ch. 3: "Gospel Miracle Tradition," 38–40.

51. Prof. Petzke has been at some pains to make this point both in his book on Apollonius of Tyana (e.g., *Traditionen*, 180–81, 384, et passim) and in "Historizität" (e.g., 368, 382–83, et passim). The point must be taken seriously.

52. So, e.g., Delling, "Das Verständnis," 271.

the gospel tradition. There is evidence that the primitive church was quite aware that others beside Jesus performed that kind of deed (e.g., Mark 9:38–39, par. Luke 9:49–50; Matt 12:27, par. Luke 11:19). It is also clear from the gospel traditions that the miracles had little if any probative value with respect to Jesus. Those who observed such deeds could come to the conclusion that Jesus was in league with Satan (Mark 3:22 and par.) as easily as they could conclude that such deeds showed his relationship to God (e.g., Luke 5:8–9). Indeed, Matthew has, I think deliberately, cast the issue of ambiguity over his collection of miracle stories in chapters 8–9 by ending the collection precisely with such a reference to their lack of specific probative value (Matt 9:32–34).[53] To try, therefore, to find exclusive validity in mighty acts reported of Jesus, or to assign them high probative value, not only goes counter to the historical evidence from the Hellenistic world, but against certain synoptic traditions as well. It is apparent that conclusions about Jesus' significance were drawn from evidence other than the historical reality of his mighty acts.[54]

The most likely conclusion, then, given the total perception of reality operative in the Hellenistic world, with all that that implies about the perceptions and expectations of that reality, would be that the historical Jesus did in fact perform deeds such as the exorcism reported of him in the early traditions underlying Mark 9:14–29, which were accepted as reality by his contemporaries, and thus functioned as such. To that extent, this passage from Mark has historic foundation in Jesus' career.[55] Whether or not the traditions that combined to form Mark

53. I base my conclusion that Matthew has done this deliberately on the fact that this is the only miracle story he has chosen to give twice (see 12:22–24), and on the fact that it is the final story in a carefully constructed sequence of a teaching session and then a healing session, which have programmatic value in Matthew's understanding of Jesus (cf. 4:23). Matthew makes clear his organizing principle by the inclusio formed by 4:23 and 9:35, containing a teaching (chaps. 5–7) and a healing (chaps. 8–9) unit. To conclude so carefully constructed a sequence with a story whose point is precisely the ambiguity of the mighty acts of Jesus is, I assume, deliberate.

54. It would be as short-sighted to be alarmed at the fact that Jesus was not the only wandering preacher in the Hellenistic world as it would be to be alarmed that he was not the only one about whom mighty acts were reliably reported. It is not the act of teaching, but its content in relation to his person that makes him significant as a teacher. The same is true of his mighty acts and, for that matter, of his death on a cross.

55. I suspect that one of Mark's tasks was to rehabilitate the picture of Jesus by

9:14–29 reliably reflect the specific historic act of healing a young lad is a more difficult question to answer, but in the absence of compelling reasons to reject it, I find no cause to do so.

Judgment on the amount of reliable detail in the earliest form of the stories we have recovered is difficult to reach. As I indicated earlier, similarity between the symptoms here reported, and those of epilepsy, cannot be used to validate the details, since the details themselves are confused.[56] Certainly the present form of Mark 9:14–29 will not provide us any clue as to the reliability of that detail.[57] There is a long history to those details and that report, as I have sought to indicate, and historical knowledge is recoverable only at the end of such an analysis as we have undertaken, not at its beginning. But the conclusion of such an analysis of Mark 9:14–29 can be positive: Jesus did heal a young lad in a way identified in his world as casting out a demon, and any historical picture of Jesus that does not include his activity as exorcist will be a distortion.

---

re-emphasizing his activity as teacher in a time when he was known, in some circles at least, primarily as one who performed mighty acts, but argumentation of this point leads beyond the bounds of the current study.

56. Cf. n. 35, above.

57. This position is still occasionally espoused; e.g., Cranfield, "St. Mark 9:14–29," 57 n. 1; Wilkinson, "The Case of the Epileptic Boy," 40.

Miracles *and* Discipleship
in Mark 10:46–52

7

¶ THE STORY OF THE RESTORATION OF SIGHT TO A BLIND BEGGAR named Bartimaeus occurs at a point in Mark where Jesus is about to begin his activities in Jerusalem. It would be important to examine this account for no other reason than that. In addition to its locus, however, the story presents other problems which give it promise for the critical investigator: the appearance of the (for Mark) enigmatic title "son of David," and the difficulty in identifying the formal structure of the story, to name but two. Our investigation will proceed in the following way: after seeking to determine how much of the story came to Mark as tradition, and how much that tradition may have developed in the course of its transmission, we shall ask about its formal characteristics as a "miracle story." We shall then ask about the significance of its present placement in Mark's gospel, which will also involve an inquiry into the importance for Mark of the title "son of David." Finally, in an effort to gain perspective on the force of the Markan narrative in which this story is placed, we shall compare it very briefly with some material from the gospel of Luke, after which we may be in a position to draw some tentative conclusions on the nature and meaning of this pericope.

STAGES OF TRANSMISSION

Our first step, then, is to attempt to trace the various stages through which our story has moved. As is often the case, Matthew and Luke, by their treatment of Mark, indicate where they found difficulties with the prose of that gospel.[1] Since such narrative difficulties often betray

---

1. Although some scholars question that Mark was the first Gospel to be written, and was a source for Matthew and Luke, I will assume the broader consensus of schol-

seams in editorial adaptation, or anomalies created by the combination of traditions, they are worthy of careful investigation.

The first such problem concerns the double notation of locus, Jericho. Cast in a form frequent in Mark,[2] the first indication (καὶ ἔρχονται εἰς ’Ιεριχώ, "and they come to Jericho") is commonly held to be due to Mark's editorial activity.[3] Both Matthew and Luke noted the awkward situation thus created, and solved it in different ways, Matthew by noting that the event occurred after the group left Jericho (20:29), Luke saying it occurred prior to entry (18:35). As they now stand, these notations on location enable Mark to continue his narrative of Jesus on the way to Jerusalem.

A second problem is the over-loaded genitive absolute, by which the disciples are included in the narrative. This too touches on a theme Mark has been pursuing, namely the trip of Jesus with his disciples to Jerusalem.[4] Again, Matthew and Luke corrected the difficulty, Matthew by making the genitive absolute plural (in Mark, the participle is singular: ἐκπορευομένου, "he was leaving") to include the disciples, and then giving a separate notice about the crowd (20:29), while Luke omitted reference to both groups of people.

A third difficulty centers in the name of the blind beggar, Bartimaeus. This is the only story in which the recipient of a miraculous healing is named in Mark, and with one exception (Jairus, 5:22, although D omits the name there), the only miraculous healing where anyone save Jesus is named. The interpretation of the perhaps Aramaic "Bartimaeus"[5] with the Greek phrase ὁ υἱὸς Τιμαίου ("the son of Timaeus") could be understood as Mark's interpretative addition,

arship that Mark was in fact a source for the other two Synoptics.

2. Mark uses the present tense of ἔρχεσθαι ("come") to introduce a location in 3:20; 6:1; 8:22; 10:1; 11:15, 27; 14:32.

3. So Burger, *Jesus als Davidssohn*, 62; Koch, *Bedeutung*, 130; Räisänen, *Messiasgeheimnis*, 151; Robbins, "Healing," 228; Schweizer, *Markus*, 127 = *Mark*, 224, to mention but a few. I make no claim to completeness in these references; I merely want to indicate characteristic views.

4. See Koch, *Bedeutung*, 130. The fact that the disciples play no further role in the story strengthens the suggestion that Mark added them because of the theme he was pursuing in this part of his gospel; cf. also Burger, *Jesus als Davidssohn*, 60; Schweizer, *Markus*, 127 = *Mark*, 224.

5. Although a Greek name, Βαρτιμαῖος could be an Aramaic shortened form of the name Τιμόθεος, i.e., טמאי; so Klostermann, *Markusevangelium*, 123.

were it not for the fact that in all other such instances, Mark gives the Aramaic word first, and then the interpretation.[6] Furthermore, as the story now stands, the Greek reader will not identify the two names, and will probably assume the blind beggar, whose father was Timaeus, bore the name Bartimaeus.[7] Matthew and Luke, perhaps aware of these problems, omit any reference to the beggar's name.

It would seem probable, therefore, that Mark, in fitting this story into his narrative, provided the first mention of the location in order to get Jesus to the place near which the story occurred, and added the reference to the disciples, and perhaps to the crowd,[8] who accompanied Jesus. The story itself will have included reference to the fact that as Jesus was leaving Jericho, he passed a blind beggar who was named Bartimaeus, and who was sitting by the roadside.[9]

Within the story itself, some scholars have found evidences of Markan composition, although there is less unity there than there was concerning the opening verse. The use of ἤρξατο with an infinitive, normally a Markan construction (both Matthew and Luke modify it here), has been thought by some to betray Markan editorial work.[10] The difficulty is that if this phrase does introduce a Markan insertion, it represents Markan use of a title, son of David, which is, to say the least, not a normal title for Jesus in this gospel.[11] A second place where some have thought to see Mark's hand is in the crowd's rebuke to the blind man. Such scholars see here the typical Markan enjoinder to silence to anyone who utters the true mystery of Jesus, i.e., the "messianic se-

6. Cf. 3:17; 5:41; 7:11, 34; 12:42; 14:36; 15:16, 22, 34, 42; see also Lohmeyer, *Markus*, 224; Roloff, *Kerygma*, 122.

7. That the name was derived from Aramaic סמיא, meaning "blind," is probably a later allegorization; see Klostermann, *Markusevangelium*, 123; Roloff, *Kerygma*, 122 n. 50.

8. Mention of the crowd may be due to Mark, but the crowd does figure in the story itself, and the use of the word ἱκανός ("great") in the sense of πολύς ("many") is unique to this verse in Mark; it may therefore belong to the pre-Markan tradition.

9. Again, the word προσαίτης ("beggar") is unique to this verse in Mark, and in the NT is found only otherwise in John 9:8. It probably also came to Mark with the story.

10. E.g., Robbins, "Healing," 231, 235; cf. also Kelber, *Kingdom*, 95; Burger, *Jesus als Davidssohn*, 62–63. It is more common for Mark to employ one, rather than two, infinitives after ἤρξατο, although two are found in three other places in Mark: 14:19, 33 and 71. It is also used by other authors, e.g., Luke 3:8.

11. See Räisänen, *Messiasgeheimnis*, 148–49; Kertelge, *Wunder*, 180–81.

cret."[12] If these are Markan insertions, then most of vv. 47–48 will have been due to Mark, and we can find, or should be able to, valuable clues to Mark's christology.[13]

Two points, however, would argue against these verses representing Markan insertions. First, as we shall see, the title "son of David" is not significant for Mark's understanding of Jesus. It is difficult to understand why Mark would want to insert a title that bears no meaning for him. On the other hand, he may have placed the story here just because the title was already present in it, in an attempt to say something about its relevance to Jesus, and particularly to Jesus' fate in Jerusalem. We shall have to return to that problem. Second, the attempts of the crowd to silence Bartimaeus have little in common with other instances of the "messianic secret."[14] It is rather bizarre to have a crowd desire to preserve a secret (from whom?), and in fact, this element in the story is probably intended more to demonstrate the persistence of Bartimaeus in the face of opposition, than to silence his confession of Jesus as son of David. Such persistence is the point of at least two other miracle stories in Mark (5:25–34; 7:25–30), one of which (5:25–34) also has in common the saying of Jesus: "Your faith has saved you." It seems likely therefore, that the substance, if not the form, of these verses was also to be found in the story as Mark got it from the tradition.[15]

Finally, there is general agreement that the final words of the pericope, ἐν τῇ ὁδῷ ("on the way"), have been added by Mark to call

12. E.g., Burger, *Jesus als Davidssohn*, 60–62; cf. Räisänen, *Messiasgeheimnis*, 149 n. 25, for other references.

13. Robbins has attempted to do just that in "Healing."

14. Cf. Räisänen, *Messiasgeheimnis*, 150–51; Burkill, "Strain," 33; Lohmeyer, *Markus*, 224; Robbins argues that the rebuke points not to the motif of secrecy, but to "depict those around Jesus as acting without understanding" ("Healing," 235). In the other instances he cites, however, it is disciples, not crowds, that show this tendency (8:32; 10:13), and though the disciples are present in Mark's story (cf. v. 36) they are *not* mentioned here.

15. So Kertelge, *Wunder*, 180; Roloff, *Kerygma*, 124; Theissen, *Wundergeschichten*, 146. Other tensions have been found in the story, e.g., the changed attitude of the crowd (threatening in v. 48; comforting in v. 49), the two titles Bartimaeus uses for Jesus (son of David, vv. 47–48; *rabbouni*, v. 51), the absence of any reaction from the crowd, despite their importance for the story (vv. 46–49), but none of these are sufficient to demand that a redactor have created them; for a good discussion on this point, cf. Theissen, 146.

attention once more to the way Jesus is now going, namely, to the passion.[16] Hence, it would appear that aside from the introduction and conclusion, Mark has reproduced the story pretty much as he received it, including the title, "son of David."[17] Had it been one of Mark's major redactional intentions to introduce that title by means of this story, one must wonder why he did not also make that title explicit in the following story, the entry into Jerusalem. The parallel account of that entry in Matthew (esp. 21:9) shows how easily redactional change could introduce the title. That Mark did not employ that simple device probably means that he, unlike Matthew, had no interest in the title, was not working with it himself, and hence we may conclude, its presence in our story means it was already contained in a story that Mark employed at this place for other reasons.

Where the story may have originated is difficult to determine, as is, on literary grounds, any development it may have undergone prior to its inclusion in Mark.[18] The presence of Aramaic words—ῥαββουνί ("rabbouni"), Βαρτιμαῖος ("Bartimaeus")—may point to a Palestinian origin for the story,[19] although the word used to describe Bartimaeus' act with his cloak (casting off rather than putting on) is clearer with regard to Greek than Palestinian custom.[20] The original purpose of the

---

16. So Kertelge, *Wunder*, 180; Koch, *Bedeutung*, 131; Roloff, *Kerygma*, 126; Luz, "Geheimnismotiv," 24–25, to mention a sampling. Some have argued that the whole of v. 52 is Markan (e.g., Robbins, "Healing," 227–28), but I would agree with Koch that the phrase καὶ ἠκολούθει αὐτῷ ("and followed him") belonged to the story as Mark found it, and helped influence Mark to put it here, although for reasons that differ from Koch's analysis (*Bedeutung*, 129).

17. Cf. Burger, *Jesus als Davidssohn*, 59.

18. Roloff is able to detect two stages of pre-Markan tradition—to the earliest story (vv. 46b, 47, 51–52) there were later added vv. 48–49—although the reasons are not entirely convincing (*Kerygma*, 122–23).

19. Schweizer, *Markus*, 128 = *Mark*, 224, argues that the presence of both "Bartimaeus" and "the son of Timaeus" may show the story originated in Palestine, with the translation of the name added when the story passed into the Greek tradition.

20. Ἀποβάλλειν in the sense of casting off a garment is frequently mentioned in Greek literature, in the sense of lightening a load and making quicker movement possible (Lohmeyer, *Markus*, 226). While the idea is present in Mark 13:16, this use of ἀποβάλλειν is not found in the Bible. The biblical idea of girding for labor (e.g., Jer 1:17; Acts 12:8) uses the word ἐπιβάλλειν, a reading with some textual evidence. Grundmann (*Markus* 221) observes that if the tradition were originally Palestinian, ἐπιβάλλειν would be the original. The meager textual evidence argues for an original ἀποβάλλειν although of course this could also be due to adaptation to a Greek en-

story is also difficult to determine on literary grounds, since it contains both a miracle and words normally associated with discipleship.[21] All of this indicates that a further step is necessary if we are to understand the original provenance and intention of this story, and it is to that form-critical analysis that we must now turn.

NARRATIVE FORM

As I have tried to show elsewhere,[22] one can usefully describe the elements necessary to narrate a miracle story as the *problem* that is to be resolved, the *solution* that in fact resolves it, and some kind of *proof* or demonstration that the problem has in fact yielded to the solution. Although few stories in Mark contain only those elements (one such is found in 1:30–31), those elements are regularly present in NT miracle accounts, as they are also in nonbiblical stories of that kind in the Hellenistic world. The elements are regularly expanded by a request for help, added detail about any of the three elements, and a public acclamation of the wondrous deed, although such expansions are not necessary to the structure of telling a miracle.

Even allowing for such expansion of detail, however, the story of blind Bartimaeus in Mark is a problem. The miracle itself is attached almost as an afterthought to Bartimaeus' stubborn refusal to be intimidated by the crowd, and the solution is virtually no solution at all. It is simply a dismissal after a comment by Jesus identifying that stubbornness as faith. The proof is limited to three words (καί εὐθὺς ἀνέβλεψεν, "and immediately he received his sight"), although perhaps Bartimaeus' ability to follow Jesus is to be taken as an indication that he can now make his own way, and need not be confined, as he formerly was, to sitting beside the road along which other people moved.

---

vironment. Both Matthew and Luke omit the phrase ἀποβαλὼν τὸ ἱμάτιον ("cast off the cloak").

21. Despite Klostermann's assertion (*Markusevangelium,* 124) that both σώζειν ("save") and ἀκολουθεῖν ("follow") are without religious significance in this context, both do belong to the language of discipleship (for σώζειν, see Mark 8:35; for ἀκολουθεῖν, 1:18; 8:34b), and may indicate the pre-Markan intention of the story.

22. See ch. 6: "Miracles and the Historical Jesus" in which I apply this form of analysis to miracles reported in Philostratus, *Life of Apollonius,* and to some accounts found on the steles at Epidauros, the temple of Asclepius. I also used it to analyze some miracles in Mark in "Jesus as Miracle Worker," ch. 8 in *Mark.*

Matthew and Luke have both taken steps to conform this story more clearly to the miracle paradigm. Luke eliminates part of the dialogue between the blind man and the crowd, puts an empowering word as solution before Jesus' statement about faith, and adds to the proof (as he frequently does) an acclamation, in this case both by the blind man and the crowd. Matthew similarly has Jesus, not the crowd, summon the blind men (Matthew has two), and adds the detail of a healing gesture to the solution: Jesus touches the eyes of the blind men. When both Matthew and Luke omit the name of the one healed, they conform to the normal practice that the only person named in a miracle account is Jesus.

All of this means that the attempt to locate a "pure miracle story" at the basis of this account, to which details were then added, is difficult in the extreme. Some scholars have tried to reconstruct such an underlying miracle story,[23] but that entails not only the omission of parts of the story as it now appears in Mark (e.g., the dialogue between Bartimaeus and the crowd, vv. 47–48), but also the reassignment to Jesus of words now credited to others (e.g., v. 49),[24] and even the reintroduction of elements now absent in Mark's account (e.g., a healing gesture by Jesus).[25] We can leave aside for the moment the fact that all such constructions presume as an earlier form of Mark's story a story now very similar to the ones in Luke and Matthew, which on other grounds seem dependent on the Markan narrative. What emerges from such an analysis is the clear indication that the story of blind Bartimaeus as it now stands in Mark had as its intention something other than the narration of a wondrous healing by Jesus. A healing is present in the story, but in such abbreviated form that it appears to have been subordinated to some other intention.

That fact emerges even more clearly if we compare Mark 10:46–52 with the one other story of the healing of a blind man in Mark, which is found in 8:22–26. This latter account is a parade example of a miracle

23. E.g., Robbins, "Healing," 232; Burger, *Jesus als Davidssohn,* 45–46; Roloff simply identifies this story as "eine reine Wundergeschichte" (a pure miracle story) and lets it go at that (*Kerygma,* 121). Koch (*Bedeutung,* 128), on the other hand, feels, as did Bultmann (*Geschichte* 228 = *History,* 213), that such reconstruction is all but impossible.

24. Robbins, "Healing," 232; Burger, *Jesus als Davidssohn,* 45.

25. So Robbins, "Healing," 233.

story. *Problem* (v. 22, along with the request for help), *solution* (vv. 23–25a) and *proof* (25b–26)[26] emerge and can be disengaged with clarity and precision. The blind man remains anonymous, and passive, and Jesus is clearly the center of attention as he overcomes this particularly difficult case of blindness (cf. vv. 24–25a). Such a comparison makes all the more evident the unique elements in the story of Bartimaeus: he is named, he is the center of the story, and he emerges as a follower of Jesus. It is his persistence, not that of Jesus (cf. 8:23–25a), which ultimately allows the healing to occur.

It is precisely this diminution of the elements of a miracle story in favor of elements of a "biographical-legendary"[27] nature that may give a clue to the kind of story with which we here have to do. If we may characterize as "legend" those stories in which someone other than Jesus is named, and hence have interest focused on them, and in which the actions of that person will teach the reader what to emulate or avoid,[28] then this story of Bartimaeus, whose persistent faith, even to the point of following Jesus, is eminently worthy of emulation—this story would be much more nearly characterized as "legend" than "miracle story."

If that comparison of Mark 10:46–52 with 8:22–26 showed the structural differences between the former account and a regular miracle story, a comparison with Luke 5:1–11 may clarify the way in which a miracle can function within a "legend." It is clear in Luke 5 that although a miracle is included, it is not the main point of the narrative.[29] Nevertheless, as Luke tells the story, one gets the impression

26. Although 8:26 has been understood in the sense of a command to silence, it is worth noting that such a command does not appear. It is merely inferred from the command not to re-enter the village. On the other hand, the man's ability to return home in a way different from that by which he came to his present location (via the village, v. 23) would be proof that he could now see, and hence could obey that command. So simple an order, difficult in the extreme for one blind but no problem for a sighted person, may thus be intended as proof that the cure was in fact effective, rather than as an indirect command to silence.

27. Koch, *Bedeutung*, 218.

28. On such a definition, the story of Zacchaeus (Luke 19:1–10) would be a legend with positive point (the reaction to Jesus, v. 8), while the story of Peter's attempt to walk on the water (Matt 14:28–31) would present a lack of faith to be avoided; cf. further Koch, *Bedeutung*, 129 n. 16. Although I differ from Koch on a number of points, his work triggered the reflections contained in this paper.

29. How little the miracle is the actual point of the story can be seen in the fact that

that the concluding positive response of Peter is related to the miracle
he experiences. One could analyze the elements in Luke 5:1–11 in the
following way: after an editorial introduction (1) in v. 1, the scene is set
(2) in vv. 2–3. A dialogue ensues in which the central character, Peter,
is engaged in a kind of verbal conflict with Jesus (3) in vv. 4–5a, which
is then resolved (4) in v. 5b. The chief character, Peter, acts (5) in v. 6a
and then the miracle is described (6) in vv. 6b–7. A second dialogue
between Peter and Jesus occurs (7) in vv. 8–10a, followed by a word of
comfort (8) in v. 8b, and the story concludes with the reaction of the
central character, Peter, to these events (9) in v. 11. If we analyze the
story of Bartimaeus, we will find that all of these nine elements are
present, that in all but two instances they occur in the same order, and
that all the material in the story of Bartimaeus can thus be accounted
for. After the editorial introduction (1) in v. 46a, the scene is set (2) in
v. 46b. A dialogue ensues in which the central character, Bartimaeus,
is engaged in a kind of conflict (3) in vv. 47–48, although in this case it
is a dialogue between the crowd and Bartimaeus, rather than between
Bartimaeus and Jesus. The conflict is resolved (4) in v. 19 and a word
of comfort is spoken (8), although again it is spoken not by Jesus, but
by the crowd. The chief character, Bartimaeus, acts (5) in v. 50, and
there follows a dialogue between Bartimaeus and Jesus (7) in v. 51. The
miracle is then reported (6) in v. 52a; and the story concludes with the
reaction of the central character, Bartimaeus, to these events (9) in v.
52b.

    Several items are worth noting here. In Luke, both dialogues occur
between Jesus and Peter; in Mark, the first is between the crowd and
Bartimaeus. In Luke, the word of comfort is spoken by Jesus, in Mark
by the crowd. If someone in the course of the tradition, for whatever
reason, substituted the crowd for Jesus in the Markan account, the two
stories would be very similar. Just that substitution has been repeatedly suggested by scholars who have examined this pericope.[30] Again,

---

the *solution* (v. 4) is given before the *problem* (v. 5a) is mentioned, a clear indication
that the miraculous act is being told in the service of some other idea, in this case, the
call of Peter.

30. If both of these elements were reported of Jesus, he would be open to the
charge of callousness toward the beggar (v. 48) and of inconstancy (v. 49) for having
changed his mind so quickly. The tradition does in fact seem to protect Jesus from
such difficulties as it is handed on, as a comparison of the Synoptics will show.

two elements have been put in another place in the Markan account: the word of comfort and the report of the miracle, displacements that have the effect of separating the comfort from the mighty act, hence de-emphasizing the miracle. In the Markan account, the miracle is less prominent than in the story in Luke. The important point here, however, is this: those elements that distort the story in Mark as far as the normal miracle story is concerned are precisely the elements that cause it to resemble most closely the story in Luke, and the story in Luke is the story of the call of a disciple.[31] Is it possible that the healing of blind Bartimaeus may also have functioned originally as the account of how he became a disciple of Jesus? Several indications point in that direction.

Chief among them, of course, is the general configuration of the story that we have just discussed: it is shaped to point more to Bartimaeus' persistent faith than to the restoration of his sight,[32] and the general form is similar to a story in Luke that is an account of how Peter became a disciple. If this had originally been a story of that kind, it would explain why the blind beggar has a name, and why interest focuses so intently upon him. That a person could thus become a disciple of Jesus, and not be included in a list of the twelve is clear from the account of the call of Levi (Mark 2:13–14). Obviously the tradition knew of more disciples, and the origin of their call, than were included in lists of the twelve.[33] Again, such an assumption about the original nature of the story of blind Bartimaeus would explain why, singularly in Mark, the recipient of a miracle followed Jesus, why his faith is so much the issue, and why the miracle assumes secondary importance. It may also explain the presence of the enigmatic title "son of David," showing the readiness of Bartimaeus to acknowledge in Jesus one

31. Luke does include others in his final observation that "they followed him," but the call itself is concerned solely with Peter (cf. v. 10b, where both verbs are in the singular), as he has been the central figure in the story.

32. So also Hahn, *Hoheitstitel*, 262 n. 1; Koch, *Bedeutung*, 130–31; Burkill, "Strain," 34 n. 9. In this same vein, it is interesting to note that in the story of the Canaanite woman where persistence is also the issue, Matthew has inserted the title "son of David": perhaps it indicates that Matthew recognized a connection between the title "son of David" and faith as persistence. See also Kingsbury, "Son of David," 599.

33. Matthew of course eliminated the problem at least in part by changing "Levi" to "Matthew" (9:9) so he would appear in the list of twelve (Matt 10:2–4; cf. Mark 3:14–19).

worthy of following. It could also explain the presence of the second title, ῥαββουνί, whose only other use in the NT (John 20:16) clearly denotes master-disciple relationship, and which, in its more common form, ῥαββί ("rabbi"), appears as address in the synoptic tradition exclusively between Jesus and his followers.[34] In addition to all this, if, for some reason, Mark were reluctant to present discipleship in the light cast upon it by the story of Bartimaeus, we could account for certain anomalies in the story concerning the crowd, viz. their active role, but above all, the fact that they, not Jesus, summon Bartimaeus to Jesus. As we noted above, were Jesus substituted for the crowd, he would function in Mark 10:46–52 almost precisely as he does in Luke 5:1–11, the story of the call of Peter.

If this story was originally meant to tell of the way one Bartimaeus came to be a follower of Jesus, i.e., a form of "call story," the question that immediately arises concerns its placement in Mark: why was it placed so late in the narrative, so long after the stories of the way other disciples came to follow Jesus (viz. 1:16–20; 2:13–14; cf. 3:14–19)? Was it because he wished to use this story to bring into his narrative the title "son of David" as in some way appropriate to Jesus' entry into Jerusalem? Or was it his view of the nature of discipleship and/or miracle that caused him to put it where he did? We must turn to an investigation of those questions. We begin with the title "son of David."

Son of David

Scholars have suggested two interpretations of the title "son of David" in the NT that are based on traditions found in the OT and developed in the Hellenistic period. The first of those traditions sees in the title "son of David" primarily the designation of a politico-nationalistic figure. The expectation that Israel's glorious future was tied to a descendant of David is based in 2 Sam 7:12–16, and what may be the clearest expression of the form that expectation took for the Judaism of the NT period can be found in the *Psalms of Solomon*, particularly 17:4, 21–32. Here the "son of David" is ruler and king, who will wreak vengeance on Israel's enemies and re-establish the hegemony of Jerusalem.[35]

---

34. See Roloff, *Kerygma*, 122.

35. In no case does it appear that this "son of David" was to be anything other than a human ruler; he was, despite references to David's descendant as God's son in

It is in light of such a background that some scholars have understood the title "son of David" in the NT to be largely a political designation, referring to the nationalistic hopes of a conquered Israel.[36] As an example, Burger points to Luke's omission of the title in his account of Jesus' entry into Jerusalem as motivated by a desire to avoid just such political overtones.[37]

A second possibility of understanding "son of David" draws on Solomon's growing reputation in the Hellenistic world, among Jews and gentiles alike, as a practitioner of the magical arts. Solomon's reputation was based on 1 Kgs 5:9–14 (Eng. 4:29–34), which was increasingly interpreted as magical knowledge (e.g., Wis 7:15–22) in the Hellenistic period (e.g., Josephus, *Ant.* 8.2.5) and beyond.[38] Since in the NT those who address Jesus with this title are primarily those in need of exorcism or healing,[39] and since the messianic King in Judaism was never identified as a wonder-worker, some scholars have suggested that the title "son of David" in the synoptic gospels reflects rather the traditions about Solomon, the healer and exorcist *par excellence*, than the political traditions of David's descendant.[40]

The absence of Jewish expectations that the messianic king would work miracles has led some scholars to suggest that the use of the title "son of David" in the NT owes more to post-Easter Christian reflections on Jesus than to any clear OT or Jewish traditions.[41] Only against

---

Ps 2:7 or 2 Sam 7:14, never understood in Judaism as a divine figure. For an excellent discussion of this problem, see "Der jüdische Hintergrund" in Burger, *Jesus als Davidssohn*, 16–24.

36. So, e.g., Cullmann, *Christology*, 133. For a contrary view, see Hahn, *Hoheitstitel*, 261; both scholars refer to Mark 12:35–37, a passage to which we must return below.

37. Burger, *Jesus als Davidssohn*, 127; the passage in question is Luke 19:28–48.

38. This development is admirably traced in Duling, "Solomon," who includes in addition to the passages mentioned the *Testament of Solomon*, and some Aramaic incantation bowls. On the bowls, see also Gordon, *Adventures*, 170–71; Fisher, "Son of David."

39. So Duling, "Solomon," 235.

40. Fisher has argued most strongly for this, primarily on the basis of the Aramaic incantation bowls. Their late date—ca. 600 AD—makes them of questionable value in this regard, however, despite the tenacity of magical traditions through the ages. On the view that the messianic King was not identified in Judaism with miracles, cf. Hahn, *Hoheitstitel*, 262.

41. So Hahn, *Hoheitstitel*, 263; Burger (*Jesus als Davidssohn*, 45–46) accepts this suggestion and develops it.

a Christian background can we understand the combination of the traditions of Jesus as miracle-worker, and as descendant of David. In that light, Räisänen argues that it was for christological reasons that Mark placed the story of Bartimaeus where he did. Because both Mark and his readers would have understood the title as messianic,[42] its placement here would help Mark develop Jesus' christological significance. Matthew shows that the title did have some resources for a christological portrayal of Jesus, but was that also true for Mark? Was it in fact for its positive christological significance that Mark chose to place its first use in his gospel at this place? To answer that question, we must look at the use of the title "son of David" in Mark.

That Mark understood Jesus as son of David always has as its counter-pole the saying of Jesus in 12:35–37, where the simplest interpretation remains: the Christ (for Mark clearly Jesus) is not the son of David the scribes await.[43] In order to set that apparent meaning aside, one must turn to 10:46–52, and argue either that the title was added by Mark, hence assuring its positive significance,[44] or that Mark valued it because of some other clue in the story (the supposed secret in v. 48, or the faith in v. 52 which is supposedly expressed in Bartimaeus' identification of Jesus as son of David). The next occurrence, Mark 11:9–10), is then understood in the light of the Matthean changes, one of which is to include the title itself (Matt 21:9), and one is then ready to find in 12:35–37 the opposite of its most obvious meaning, namely that it supports the idea of messiah as son of David.

If we begin the investigation, however, not with the ambiguous statements about Jesus as son of David (in 10:46–52 the title is abandoned in v. 51; in 11:1–10 it does not appear), but with the passage that most unambiguously speaks of Jesus as son of David, namely 12:35–37, and work from the clearer to the unclear passages, the results will be quite different. The point then appears to be the growing denial of Jesus as son of David, rather than a growing affirmation of that fact. Let us pursue such an investigation, to see what light it sheds on Mark's understanding of the title "son of David."

---

42. Räisänen, *Messiasgeheimnis*, 149.

43. So already Wrede, "Jesus als Davidssohn," 168.

44. This is the position argued for by Robbins, "Healing."

It is generally acknowledged that 12:35–37 came to Mark from his traditions.[45] It is also generally acknowledged that the intention of the passage is to say that the scribes are wrong when they say that the Christ is the son of David, although most scholars quickly qualify such an acknowledgment.[46] Yet there are other passages in Mark that point to his indifference, if not hostility, to Jesus' Davidic background. In 2:23–27, where Jesus defends himself against Pharisaic objections to his disciples' rupture of the Sabbath law, Jesus cites David as a precedent for such behavior. The obvious statement, however, that a descendant of David should be permitted the same latitude as his forebear is not made. Had Mark, or the tradition, been intent on showing Jesus' Davidic ancestry, this would have been an excellent place to make that point. Again, in 6:1–3, there is a pejorative discussion of Jesus' parentage, with no hint of the idea that Jesus' descent was in any way significant. In fact, the point is just the opposite: it is just his descent that proves him unimportant.[47] At the very least, Mark has passed up opportunities to point to the Davidic descent of Jesus in these two places.

The usual way to wrest a positive meaning from 12:35–37 is to argue that its intention is not to deny Davidic sonship to the messiah, but to say that one must affirm more than that he is Davidic. One must also affirm that he is son of God.[48] Support is gathered for such a view

---

45. E.g., Klostermann, *Markusevangelium*, 144; Hahn, *Hoheitstitel*, 113. There has been considerable discussion about whether or not the event is historical (e.g., Lohmeyer, *Markus*, 263–64; Grundmann, *Markus*, 254) or the construction of the community (e.g., Bultmann, *Geschichte*, 145–46 = *History*, 136–37; Schweizer, *Markus*, 145 = *Mark*, 254, who argues it came from a Greek, not an Aramaic community; Burger, *Jesus als Davidssohn*, 57); but since we are concerned with the intention of Mark, we may leave that question aside.

46. Burger, *Jesus als Davidssohn*, 58, 166, where he argues that this was at least its original intention; Schweizer, *Markus*, 146 = *Mark*, 256, who observes that such an understanding "wäre sicher das nächstliegende Verständnis des Satzes"; Cullmann, *Christology*, 151; Kelber, *Kingdom*, 96, whose confirmation of the thesis I am here representing I did not discover until I had already formulated it. That Jesus was of Davidic descent is also denied in the *Ep. Barn.* 12:10–11. Burger, *Jesus als Davidssohn*, 176, claims there is also a polemic against Jesus' Davidic sonship in "den Pseudoclementinen (18,3)" with no further identification, but I have been unable to confirm this.

47. See Burger, *Jesus als Davidssohn*, 58.

48. E.g., ibid., 64, 66; Hahn, *Hoheitstitel*, 261; Gibbs, "Purpose," 460; Klostermann, *Markusevangelium*, 145; Robbins, "Healing," 242.

from Rom 1:3–4, where Jesus as son of David κατὰ σάρκα ("according to the flesh") is contrasted to Jesus as son of God,[49] and from the parallel passage in Matt 22:41–45, where its use in a gospel that, by its genealogy, clearly proved that this passage could be interpreted in other than a negative sense, is seen as significant.[50] Yet the major christological title in Mark is not son of God, but rather as I have sought to show elsewhere,[51] son of Man (cf. the programmatic statement in 10:45, which Mark has placed as a kind of title over his account of the passion). Furthermore, the changes Matthew has made in the introduction to this story show clearly enough the difficulty he had in finding a positive meaning in Mark's account.[52]

A more subtle way to find this "son of David but more" intention in Mark 12:35–37 is to point to the change in interrogative particles with which the question is introduced the first (v. 35) and second (v. 37) times. In v. 35, the question is introduced with πῶς ("how"); in v. 37 it is changed to πόθεν ("in what sense"). Hahn and others have argued strongly that this change is the key to the pericope, since the second question now intends to ask, not "how" can the Christ be David's son, the meaning of v. 35, but rather, "in what sense" can the Christ be thought of as David's son. The answer is then "not exclusively," since he is also the *kyrios* and the son of God.[53] If in fact, however, it is correct that πόθεν means not "how" but rather "in what sense" or "to what extent," and the answer is "only partially," since the messiah is also, or even more importantly, son of God or even son of Man, then Jesus is summoning the scribes to debate, with the intention of getting them to concede a point, even as Jesus has conceded a point to them (i.e., Messiah is admittedly son of David, but he is also more). In that case, the silence of the scribes is a contemptuous refusal to debate, not the sullen silence of the defeated.

49. E.g., Burkill, "Strain," 34 n. 8; Burger, *Jesus als Davidssohn*, 166–67.

50. Gibbs, "Purpose," 461; Kingsbury, "Son of David," 596.

51. Achtemeier, *Mark*, ch. 5, "The Christology of Mark."

52. This is most marked in the changed question. In Matthew, Jesus asks about the Christ's sonship, and can then correct the Pharisees who say "David"; in Mark, Jesus directly questions the Davidic sonship. Matthew has thus created the situation he found lacking in Mark, viz, one in which "David's son but more" would be appropriate.

53. Hahn, *Hoheitstitel*, 261; Schweizer, *Markus*, 146 = *Mark*, 256.

Yet the context in which Mark has placed this pericope argues decisively against such an interpretation. If πόθεν retains its more obvious meaning of "how," (a meaning the parallel question in v. 35, with its πῶς, makes most obvious), then Jesus is confounding the scribes, as he confounded chief priests, elders, Pharisees and Sadducees in the preceding narrative (11:27–12:27). He is telling the scribes, as he told the Sadducees, that they are unable to understand Scripture (cf. 12:24). That Mark understood Jesus' intention as hostile, not as an invitation to debate, is clearly indicated by the contrast Mark draws between the acceptance of Jesus by the crowds and that accorded him by the authorities (12:37b), and still more clearly, by the hostile sayings against scribes that Mark places immediately following this pericope. The point is that both their theology (understanding of Scripture, 12:35–37) as well as their actions (hypocrisy, 12:38b–40a) will earn them condemnation (12:40b). In that context, it is unlikely Mark thought of Jesus as engaged in widening the scribes' comprehension of Scripture by conceding a point to win a point.

In sum, it is only by over-subtle interpretation (i.e., the πῶς / πόθεν differentiation), or by drawing on other NT evidence, that a positive statement regarding Jesus as son of David in Mark's theology can be drawn. Shorn of the support of Matthew, or the tradition in Rom 1:3–4, the point of 12:35–37 is the one most often recognized, if not acknowledged: Mark does not think the Messiah, and for him that means Jesus, is of Davidic descent.

With that understanding of 12:35–37, 11:9–10 now appear in a clearer light as well. Whatever the origin of these verses, they are notable not for the clarity with which they affirm Jesus' Davidic sonship, but rather for the unusual ambiguity with which they refer to any such relationship between Jesus and David.[54] Again, Matthew is frequently used as, if not the overt, at least the covert aid to the interpretation. Yet it is precisely the comparison with Matthew that shows how simple it was to turn the Markan form of the story into an acclamation of Jesus

---

54. Again, because we are interested in Mark's intention, not the possible historicity of this event, we will leave out of consideration the debate on whether the Markan acclamation is Hellenistic or Palestinian in origin, or whether the people intended to acclaim Jesus as messiah, or simply chant the usual pilgrim songs as they approach Jerusalem; cf. Burger, *Jesus als Davidssohn*, 48–52, 167; Räisänen, *Messiasgeheimnis*, 152, for examples of this discussion.

as son of David. By the simple expedient of adding the title "son of David" and omitting the ambiguous reference to the "coming kingdom of our father David," Matthew has transformed the passage into a statement about Jesus' Davidic sonship.[55] Had it in fact been Mark's intention to call attention to Jesus' Davidic sonship with this tradition, he would surely have followed the procedure of Matthew, who did pursue such an intention. That Mark did not introduce such changes indicates clearly that such was not his intention. Seen in the light of the negative tone Mark set on the messiah's Davidic sonship in 12:35–37, the ambiguity in 11:9–10 concerning Jesus as son of David becomes all the clearer. Rather than finding in 11:9–10 a further step toward a climax of Jesus as son of David, these verses point, if anywhere, in the opposite direction. Through their ambiguity, they prepare the way for the negative judgment in 12:35–37.

In view of the negative trajectory on Jesus' Davidic sonship we have seen in Mark 11 and 12, new light is now also cast on 10:46–52. It now becomes clear that Mark will not have inserted that story at this point in his narrative because of any desire to begin a climactic development of the idea of Jesus as son of David. Quite the contrary, the title is nowhere so clearly used of Jesus as it is in 10:47–48, and since from that point on Mark seems to want to de-emphasize, if indeed not discredit it entirely, two conclusions may be drawn. First, it is unlikely that Mark inserted the title into this story, since he obviously did not intend to make further positive use of it. One has the opposite impression: because it was already in the story, which Mark for other reasons wanted to use here, Mark included it, but thereafter arranged his material in such a way that its negative valence becomes clear.[56] Secondly, such a perspective now enables us to see more clearly the relative insignificance the title plays in the story of blind Bartimaeus itself. While it may be over-subtle to point out that Bartimaeus was still blind when he called Jesus "son of David,"[57] it is nevertheless clear that the title is not the point of the story. The title is changed at the crucial

55. Burger, *Jesus als Davidssohn*, 52, who acknowledges that these verses represent at best "eine indirekte Erwähnung seiner Davidssohnschaft"; cf. Hahn, *Hoheitstitle*, 265. Roloff (*Kerygma*, 125) denies it can be construed as a christological confession.

56. I am arguing here contra Robbins ("Healing," esp. 234) and in accord with Kelber (*Kingdom*, 96).

57. Johnson, *Mark*, 182; Kelber simply mentions it in passing (*Kingdom*, 95).

moment (to ῥαββουνί in v. 51). That leads to a further confirmation that the point of v. 52, with its reference to Bartimaeus' faith, points not to the title he used, at least not to "son of David," which he abandoned at the critical instant, but rather to his persistence in refusing to be kept from Jesus (cf. 7:26–30).[58]

If, then, Mark did not place the story of blind Bartimaeus where he did because of any desire to use it as a vehicle for christological affirmations about Jesus, either by title added or already present, how are we to account for its appearance here? Some have found the clue in the double reference to its locus, Jericho. Located there, the incident represents an event in the course of Jesus' journey from Galilee to Jerusalem, and hence is meant to serve as a transition to events in that city.[59] I think that unlikely for two reasons. First, scholars who urge such a reason for the present locus of the story in Mark must also urge that the transition is, for Mark, understood in christological terms, i.e., the movement is from the title "son of David" in the Bartimaeus story to an account of the entry of David's son into Jerusalem, and on to his passion. As we have seen, however, such an interpretation places more weight on the christological freight of references to David in both the Bartimaeus story and the account of the entry than either of them is capable of bearing.[60]

Second, and more importantly, I would want to urge that the story of Bartimaeus plays a much larger role in the plan of Mark's gospel than simply that of transition, or introduction to a subsequent section of that work. Rather, the story of blind Bartimaeus, along with the story of the healing of the blind man in 8:22–26, forms an *inclusio* to set off a major section of Mark's gospel: the instruction to the disciples into Jesus' fate and their necessary response to it. In that sense, both the story in ch. 8, as well as the story of Bartimaeus, serve as transitional pericopes, but their meaning is far from exhausted in that respect. They include between themselves a section containing traditions related to discipleship, and marked by a thrice repeated pattern of passion pre-

---

58. Räisänen, *Messiasgeheimnis*, 150; Taylor, *Mark*, 449; Nineham, *Mark*, 283; Schweizer, *Markus*, 128 = *Mark*, 225.

59. E.g., Roloff, *Kerygma*, 121, 125; Räisänen, 151; Burger, *Jesus als Davidssohn*, 63.

60. This point is made by Räisänen (*Messiasgeheimnis*, 151) and is demonstrated by the conclusions of Burger (*Jesus als Davidssohn*, e.g., 63) and Robbins ("Healing," e.g., 241).

diction, misunderstanding by disciples, and words from Jesus on true discipleship. The story of Bartimaeus thus stands as the climax of the central section of Mark's gospel in which the nature of true discipleship is discussed.[61]

If, as I suggested earlier, we have in the account of Bartimaeus a story that originally functioned as an account of the calling of a disciple, we may have the clue as to why Mark felt this was an appropriate location for it. What more appropriate way to conclude a section on discipleship than with the story of the way one man became a disciple? I would suggest that that was the reason that made this pericope seem appropriate to Mark to put at just this place in his narrative: its healing of blind Bartimaeus made it useful as the conclusion of a section begun with the healing of a blind man (an appropriate symbol for opening the minds of disciples by means of the teachings included between the two stories), and its emphasis on discipleship made it all the more appropriate for its present context. In that way, Mark showed Jesus seeking to open the blind eyes of his followers to the true significance of following him.

One question remains unanswered: why would Mark not have thought this appropriate as the story of the calling of a disciple? That Bartimaeus did not appear in the list of the twelve is not sufficient reason. Levi is also absent from the list, but the story of his call found its proper place in Mark's narrative. To answer our question, we must turn to an investigation of Mark's understanding of discipleship, and of miracle.

MIRACLES, FAITH, AND DISCIPLESHIP

I want to propose that when Mark used the story of blind Bartimaeus as he did, he acted in accordance with his overall understanding both of discipleship and of miracles. A brief comparison with the attitude of Luke to these two items will help bring into bold relief Mark's understanding of the relationship between the two.[62] In the following dis-

61. I have discussed this order at greater length in Mark, ch. 4, "The Structure of Mark," and I refer the reader to those pages for more detail. Burkill ("Strain," 32) and Kelber (*Kingdom,* 95) see the same significance for the two stories of healing the blind in Mark, as does Kertelge (*Wunder,* 181).

62. I am summarizing here the results of ch. 2: "The Lukan Perspective" above, and again I refer the reader to those pages for fuller discussion.

cussion, two points of comparison will be drawn: the attitude toward miracles and faith, and toward miracles and discipleship.

Luke's positive attitude on the relationship between faith and miracles can be plainly seen in those accounts in Acts where a wondrous deed performed by a follower of Jesus awakens faith in those who experience or observe it (e.g., Acts 9:35, 42; 13:12; 16:30, 33; 19:17). The repeated references to "signs and wonders" that the disciples do in the course of their missionary work (2:43; 5:12; 6:8; 8:6; 14:3; 15:12) also points to a positive relationship between the two. The same phenomena can be observed in the Gospel. More than any other evangelist, Luke appends to miracle stories references to the fact that those who had observed the miracles, or who had benefited from them, give praise to God (e.g., 5:25; 7:16; 9:43; 13:13; 17:15; 18:43), an attitude that belongs to the Lukan understanding of faith (cf. Acts 1:13; 2:22–23, 36; 4:27; 10:38). The emphasis on "seeing" in Luke, less prominent in the other gospels, also points to the significance of miracles for faith in Jesus (compare with their parallels, Luke 10:23–24; 19:37), and Luke's use of the story of the ten lepers (17:11–19) in the context of a discussion of the meaning of faith (17:1–10) shows further the significance of this connection.

Contrasted to the kind of understanding of the relationship between miracles and faith found in the Lukan writings, the attitude toward miracles in Mark comes into sharp relief. When faith is mentioned or implied in miracle stories, it seems to be regarded as in effect prior to, not as a result of, the miracle (cf. 2:3–5; 5:23, 34; 7:29), or the story is shaped to describe the absence of faith in those who have observed and anticipate miracles from Jesus (9:14–29). When something like faith does result, it is made public contrary to Jesus' wishes (1:44–45; 7:36–37), or the person who proclaims it nevertheless does so in contrast to Jesus' instructions (contrast 5:19, "how much the *Lord* has done," with 5:20, "how much *Jesus* had done"). Mark apparently has less confidence than Luke in the ability of Jesus' mighty acts to awaken useful faith in Jesus.

Closely related to this, and more important for our immediate consideration, is the relationship between miracles and discipleship. For Luke, miracles constitute a clearly legitimate basis for discipleship. Jesus' ability to perform wondrous deeds is announced (4:18–21, 23) and demonstrated (4:31–41) before any account of calling disciples, and the call of Peter, interwoven with a miracle, leaves little question that the mighty act has motivated Peter to his acknowledgment of Christ as master. Luke is so intent on this that he even placed the story of the healing of Peter's mother-in-law before Peter's call. Again, the calling of Levi is made to follow directly on the report of a miracle that is identified as such by a technical term (παράδοξα, 5:26–27). Luke further identifies the women who followed Jesus as ones from whom he had expelled demons (8:2–3); Mary Magdalene is among them. Even the missionary journey of the twelve is situated in such a way by Luke that it follows directly the accounts of four miracles (8:22—9:6).

Once more, the contrast with Mark is striking. The only event other than the material about John the Baptist that precedes the calling of the first disciples in Mark is the summary of Jesus' preaching of the Kingdom of God (1:14–15). Only after they have followed (1:16–20) are any miracles reported, and then the first exorcism is framed in such a way that the emphasis lies not on the act of power, but on the power inherent in Jesus' teaching (1:21–28). The call of Levi (2:14) is preceded by a reference to Jesus' activity as teacher (2:13), and the missionary journey of the twelve is prefaced not by miracles, but by an account of Jesus' failure as miracle-worker (6:5). Nowhere in Mark is there any hint that miracles are adequate grounds for discipleship. The only adequate grounds for Mark is readiness for martyrdom (8:34; Luke weakens this with his addition of the words καθ᾽ ἡμέραν [daily] in 9:23), something for which, in Mark's view, it would seem, knowledge of miracles is inadequate preparation.

In light of such a contrast, it is not hard to see why Mark would want to deal as he did with a story that related a miracle to the point at which Bartimaeus became a disciple of Jesus. What was clearly possible for Luke (cf. 5:1–11) is just as clearly impossible for Mark. Yet the story of blind Bartimaeus did understand faith in a way Mark found useful (cf. 10:52 with 5:34), and the symbolism of physical blindness for the disciples' inability to understand (compare 10:46–52 with 8:22–33) was also something Mark apparently wished to employ.[63] If Luke shows that it was clearly possible within the early Christian tradition to relate in a positive way discipleship and miracles, a point also made in the

63. While I agree that symbolism lies within Mark's intention, I do not think it can be carried to the extent that Schweizer, *Markus*, 127–28= *Mark*, 254–55, does; there it becomes almost allegorical.

story of Bartimaeus, Mark shows that it was clearly possible to reject such a view, a point made by the Markan treatment of that story.

CONCLUSION

In summary, all that we have seen of the way Mark relates miracles to faith and discipleship comports with the suggested origin and current placement in Mark of the story of blind Bartimaeus. The anomalies within the story can perhaps best be explained on the theory that it originated as the story of how a disciple of Jesus came to become that, and the way Mark has used it is surely in line with his understanding of the place of miracles in relation to discipleship. Mark clearly thinks of discipleship primarily in relation to the passion of Jesus (cf. 8:34–35), a point made clear by the repeated predictions of the passion precisely within the section dealing most clearly with the nature of discipleship (8:22—10:52). That same point may be indicated by the placing of the story of Bartimaeus just before the beginning of the events in Jerusalem that culminated in the passion. In that way, the proximity to those events, a proximity emphasized by the Markan addition of ἐν τῇ ὁδῷ ("in the way") in 10:52, a clear reminder of the "way" of Jesus to the cross—that proximity also aids in detaching the story from its original connection of discipleship with miracle and attaching it to the passion. Discipleship now means: following Jesus in the way of the cross.[64] In dealing with the story of Bartimaeus as he does, Mark has continued to use his sources in the service of his major task: to take captive the Jesus traditions in the service of his hermeneutical desire to subordinate them to the story of Jesus who died and rose again.[65]

---

64. This way of dealing with a miracle tradition would be analogous to the way I earlier suggested Mark dealt with two catenae of miracle stories that had been related to the eucharist; Mark detached the eucharist from the miracles, particularly those of the feeding, and related it to the passion (cf. 14:22–25), while preserving the miracles in another, for him theologically more benign, context: that of Jesus' earthly career. See ch. 4: "Isolation"; and ch. 5: "Origin and Function."

65. See Koch, *Bedeutung,* 131; cf. also Luz, "Geheimnismotiv," 30.

Jesus *and the* Disciples *as* Miracle-Workers *in the* Apocryphal New Testament

8

¶ IT IS OF COURSE IMPOSSIBLE TO CHARACTERIZE IN ANY COMPLETE or unified way the widely disparate writings that could be contained under the rubric "apocryphal New Testament." Those writings cover a range of some five or six centuries, and include everything from fragments of sayings to long, novel-like literary pieces. To gain a perspective on this material, we will lay our main emphasis on the mid-second to mid-third centuries, using other materials to indicate continuity where that seems advisable.

Our title will also guide the way we approach the world out of which our material grew and to which it spoke. Because our problem concerns Jesus and the disciples, we must remind ourselves of the canonical roots of our topic.

We shall therefore survey, very briefly, the roots of the understanding of Jesus and his followers as miracle-workers in the canonical NT writings. To gain further perspective, we will look, again briefly and selectively, at the way in which the non-Christian world of the second and third centuries viewed miracles, miracle-workers, and magic. The third component in our attempt to lay a groundwork for our study of this problem in the second and third century apocryphal NT writings will involve, again very briefly and selectively, an account of the developing line of Christian apologetic with regard to miracles and miracle-workers. We will limit ourselves here to Justin, Irenaeus, and Origen. Only against such a background will we be in a position to grapple with the problems involved in our topic, and the final part of our study will be devoted directly to that.

THE NEW TESTAMENT AND GRECO-ROMAN
LITERATURE AS BACKGROUND

It is hardly necessary to point out that the canonical gospels are filled with traditions about the mighty acts of Jesus. The healings, exorcisms, and prodigies (i.e., non-healing miracles) he performed are there amply recorded.

There is much that can be said about them: the history of the development of these stories in the pre-canonical period, the use to which the evangelists put them, the various and changing emphases they are given, and the historical problem they present to an age of scientific historiography, but we shall have to forego discussion of such problems here. It is sufficient to recall that Jesus was remembered as one who devoted an important amount of his time to such deeds.

More important for our purposes, as will become increasingly evident, is the fact that the canonical traditions recall that such power was also given to the followers of Jesus. Both at the time of the commissioning and the sending out of the Twelve (Mark 6:7; par. Matt 10:1, 8; par. Luke 9:1–2; Mark 3:14–15) and of the Seventy (Luke 10:9), the power to heal and cast out demons is given.[1] A comparison of Matt 10:8 and Luke 9:1–2 with Mark 6:7 and 3:15 indicates a growing tradition about the power granted to the disciples. In both instances there is an expansion of the Markan commission to cast out evil spirits. The further synoptic traditions about the success of the disciples in these matters (Mark 6:12–13; par. Luke 9:6; 10:17), along with some other evidence of miracles done, or expected to be done, by Jesus' followers (Mark 9:28–29, 38–39) point in the same direction.

Corroborative evidence from the same period as the pre-canonical synoptic traditions can be found in Paul. It is clear from his letters that followers of Christ, especially apostles, would perform mighty acts (e.g., Rom 15:18–19). In fact, Paul apparently thought there were no true apostles who could not and did not do miracles. Such activity was one of the signs of the true apostle (2 Cor 12:12; in light of that passage, cf. 1 Cor 2:4–5; 2 Cor 6:7). One has the further impression that such things could be expected in the normal course of the life of the local

---

1. This tradition is limited to the synoptic gospels. John lacks any tradition comparable to the synoptic representation of Jesus choosing the twelve, or any indication they were given power to work miracles. The one exception may be John 14:12, although this does not have to refer to miraculous deeds; cf. Brown, *John*, ad loc.; Bernard, *St. John*, ad loc.

church (1 Cor 12:10; Gal. 3:5); so much so that their presence would be necessary for any who wanted to imitate it (cf. 2 Thess 2:9).

The many miracles recorded of the apostles in Acts (in addition to those of Peter and Paul, miracles are reported of Stephen, 6:8; Phillip, 8:6; the apostles as a group, 2:43; 5:12; and of Paul and Barnabas, 14:3; 15:12), and the references to such events in Heb 2:3b–4 are further indication of the pervasiveness of this tradition within the canonical materials. It is interesting to note, along this line, that the only mention of possible miracles in the Coptic *Gospel of Thomas* concerns the healing activity of the disciples (logion 14).

The problem of the attribution of such acts to magical practices also surfaces in the canonical traditions, a fact that is less surprising when we note that already in the first century, the name of Jesus was understood to have a power of its own (e.g., Mark 9:38; Acts 3:6; 16:8; in a negative context, Matt 7:22–23; Acts 19:15). Given the tenor of the times, it is further hardly surprising that the author of Acts, on several occasions, gives a negative judgment on magic in relation to the Christian faith (8:18–24; 13:8–12; 19:19; with 19:13–16, cf. Mark 9:38–40).[2]

From such a cursory examination of the evidence in the canonical NT, it is clear that mighty acts were a part of the Christian traditions from the earliest stages, that not only was Jesus remembered to have done them, but that such acts were done, indeed expected, by those who followed Jesus. It should not be surprising, therefore, if later, non-canonical traditions share those views.

The second element of our survey of the background against which the apocryphal NT, and its view of Jesus and the disciples as miracle-workers, must be understood concerns the secular (i.e., non-Christian) world within which those writings had to make their way. As will quickly become apparent, forces were at work within that world which would have encouraged the development of traditions about Jesus and his disciples as wonder-workers, even apart from the canonical roots we have seen. The Hellenistic world of the second and third centuries

2. The use of περίεργα ("magic") in Acts 19:19 to designate incantations and spells may mean that one of the difficulties young widows got themselves into according to 1 Tim 5:13 was magical practices (περίεργοι) perhaps to lure another husband for themselves. Love potions and incantations made up a large share of the common magical practices of this period. A long incantation to induce love, apparently from a Jewish background, is given in Ludwig Blau, *Zauberwesen*, 97–99.

as earlier and later, was enormously interested in wonders and those who did them. Magic was a universal element within that world.

That such interest extended to, and pervaded, the interests of the Jewish population of that world is not to be doubted.[3] Although the more Hellenized Jews living outside the land of Palestine may have been more devoted to magic and allied arts than those of the Jewish homeland in Palestine, there is ample evidence for the fact that these latter also believed in and practiced magic, despite the direct commands to the contrary from Scripture and rabbis.[4] The Talmud, in addition to reporting events assuming widespread magical practices, e.g., the hanging of eighty witches at one time,[5] and numerous accounts of rabbis who practiced necromancy,[6] stipulates that no one could be a member of the Sanhedrin unless he had "a knowledge of sorcery."[7] While this last point of course does not mean its practice was required, it does indicate that such practices were so widespread, and charges regarding them so frequent, that anyone who aspired to judge the people had to be familiar with them.

With interest in the wondrous and the magical so widespread, it is not surprising that beliefs and practices knew no national or ethnic boundaries. That saliva, for example, was effective in cures, especially of the eyes, was widely believed, and the saliva of a fasting man is of greater power.[8] The evil eye was universally feared,[9] iron was universally thought to remain uninfluenced by, even provide protection against demons;[10] the name of the Hebrew God was universally thought to be

3. For the sake of convenience, we will on occasion distinguish between Jewish and Hellenistic (i.e., non-Jewish) elements within the Hellenistic world, but that in no way indicates, as we shall see clearly enough, any far-reaching difference in belief or practice along these lines.

4. E.g., *m. Sota* 9, 13; *b. 'Erub.* 64b; see also Blau, *Zauberwesen*, 27, 64, 97.

5. *b. Sanh.* 45b; see the note in the Soncino translation, ad loc. I use this edition when quoting from the Talmud. Cf. also *b. Sanh.* 91a.

6. *b. Shabb.*152b; *b. B. Meṣ'ia* 107b.

7. This prescription, attributed to R. Johanan, is found in *b. Sanh.* 17a; *b. Menaḥ.* 65a.

8. For curative power, cf. Suetonius, *Lives* 7.2–3; on the same event, cf. Tacitus, *Histories* 4:81; for the uses of saliva in general, see Pliny, *Nat.* 28.7.35–39); that the saliva of a fasting person is more effective, see Pliny, *Nat.* 28.7.35); the Talmud, *b. Shabb.* 108b; *b. Sanh.* 49b; *b. Zebaḥ.* 95b; see also Blau, *Zauberwesen*, 162–63.

9. E.g., *b. B. Meṣ'ia* 107b; Pliny, *Nat.* 7:13ff; 28:30.

10. E.g., *b. Shabb.* 67a; Lucian, *Philops.* 15, 17; Blau, *Zauberwesen*, 69; Hopfner,

especially powerful;[11] bits of bone stuck in the throat could be helped by putting bits of the same bone on one's head;[12] such a list could be extended almost indefinitely.[13]

That such universality also contained elements of mutual influence is clear enough from the evidence. We have already mentioned the power imputed to the Hebrew God,[14] and if Hellenistic practices and beliefs influenced Jews both in and outside of Palestine, it is also clear that Jews enjoyed a certain reputation among Gentiles as particularly given to magical practices.[15] It is a further corollary of such universality of belief and practice that one is hard put to maintain the uniqueness of one's own system of belief and practice. A common device to that end was to attribute one's own acts to the Deity, those of one's opponents to magic. Such accusations were common among Jews,[16] and while Gentiles were for the most part oblivious to the religious force of monotheism that made such accusations natural, even necessary, to the Jews, they nevertheless leveled, as one of their most serious charges, the accusation of "magician" at their enemies, great and small alike.[17]

There are some other elements, common to the magical beliefs and practices of the Hellenistic world, which bear more direct relevance to the attempt to illumine the background of the apocryphal

---

"Mageia" 326.

11. In addition to the many occurrences of forms of the personal name of the Hebrew God (Ια, Ιαω, etc.) in the magical papyri, see Blau, *Zauberwesen,* 123; Origen (*Cels.* 4.33) says that "almost all who deal in magic and spells" use the name of the God of the Jews, especially in spells against demons (quoted from the translation of Chadwick).

12. b. *Shabb.* 67a; Pliny *Nat.* 18.49. Blau finds evidence that the Greek origin of this particular practice was known to the rabbis (*Zauberwesen,* 76).

13. Many others will be found in Blau, *Zauberwesen,* 35–36 and passim.

14. See, in addition, esp. Blau, *Zauberwesen,* 129–35.

15. E.g., Juvenal, *Satire* 6.11.542–47; Pliny, *Nat.* 30.2.11, where a whole branch of magic is attributed to "the Jews"; Solomon was also known as a great magician, see *Testament of Solomon,* passim; Josephus, *Ant.* 8.42–59.

16. What Egyptians do by magic, Aaron does by God in Exod 7:8–12; God's superiority is demonstrated when Aaron's "rod" swallows the others. Guttman ("Significance," 365) points to the same phenomena. Cf. also b. *'Abod. Zar.* 55a, against cures in the temples of idols; b. *Ber.* 59a, against a certain necromancer. See also Blau, *Zauberwesen,* 30–31, for other examples from the Talmud.

17. E.g., Apollonius of Tyana (see Philostratus, *Life* 8.7.2) and Apuleius (see his *Apologia*). Hopfner, "Mageia," 383–87 gives many other examples.

NT writings, and to those elements we must now direct our attention. The first of these is the power that was believed to accrue to those who know the name of a deity. Pliny reports that one of the methods used by the Romans when laying siege was to summon the deity of the invested town, and promise that deity superior worship in Rome. For that reason, Pliny continue, the name of the tutelary deity of Rome was kept a carefully guarded secret.[18] Lucian of Samosata refers to the belief that curses can be accomplished by means of "holy names";[19] and Origen has an interesting discussion on the need to use the indigenous language when using such divine cognomens.[20] Incantations also frequently accompanied such names, in the belief that this made the invocation more powerful,[21] and if that incantation could be in a foreign language, it would be proportionately more powerful.[22]

It is not surprising that the Jews also regarded the name of God as powerful;[23] it may be more surprising to note that the Jews used that divine name in the same way the Gentiles did in their magic. The Talmud contains instructions for the cure of one bitten by a mad dog; one of the steps is to prepare an amulet bearing the sacred tetragrammaton.[24] The source of Solomon's power over demons consisted of a ring on which was engraved the divine name,[25] and Solomon in turn was so powerful that demons could be driven out in his name.[26] Much later tradition ascribed Jesus' power, understood as magic, to his knowledge

18. Pliny, *Nat.* 28.4.18; it is supposed the name, in Greek, was ἔρως, which has the Latin equivalent *amor*, or *Roma* spelled backwards.

19. Lucian, *Philops.* 10.

20. Origen, *Cel.* 1.24.

21. E.g., Lucian, *Philops.* 11, 35; Plotinus says some nasty things about such practices (*Enneads* 14).

22. E.g., Lucian, *Philops.* 31; cf. Origen, *Cel.* 25, who rationalizes this by saying demons must be summoned forth in their native language.

23. E.g., *Midrash Rabbah Exodus* 1.29, where Moses slew the Egyptian by pronouncing God's name against him. While he who used the name ought only to use it for moral purposes, it was powerful enough even to effect immorality and murder (so Blau, *Zauberwesen*, 138–39).

24. *b. Yoma* 84a; cf. Blau, *Zauberwesen*, 102, who also reports that forms of the tetragrammaton were especially used in amulet formulae found in the magical papyri (103).

25. *b. Gi.* 68a, b; this is also the way Solomon controlled the various demons he summons before him in the *Testament of Solomon*.

26. E.g., Josephus, *Ant.* 8.47–48.

of the secret divine name.[27] Incantations were also known and used by the Jews, some of which were intelligible,[28] some of which consisted of non-sense syllables,[29] and some of which the contents were not given, merely mentioned.[30] It is worth noting in passing that demons, against whom incantations are normally directed, played a large part in the Jewish beliefs recorded in the Talmud.[31]

A second element to be considered is the great power attributed to the use of herbs and other materials in wondrous and magical acts. An Egyptian raises a corpse to life by, among other things, placing an herb on its mouth three times, and another on its chest.[32] Diogenes Laertius reports that Empedocles knew "drugs" that would do everything from retarding age and curing ills to altering the weather,[33] and Pliny knows endless tales of the uses of all sorts of materials for all sorts of purposes, many obviously magical in intent.[34] Typically, Lucian of Samosata caricatures such beliefs and practices by carrying them to absurd extreme.[35] The Talmud, too, knows endless ways to use the strangest materials, from the afterbirth of a black she-cat[36] to the heart of speckled swine (!).[37] The rabbis also knew how to distinguish between magical practices, and acceptable customs, e.g., ways to make a pot boil quickly.[38] Josephus knows of roots that will expel demons

27. E.g., in the *Toledoth Yeshu* (translation in Goldstein, *Jesus*).

28. E.g., *b. Pesah.* 110a-b.

29. E.g., *b. Pesah.* 111a–112b; cf. also Blau, *Zauberwesen*, 84–85.

30. E.g., *b. Sanh.* 68a, where R. Eliezer plants and harvests a field of cucumbers with a "statement," the content of which is not given.

31. E.g., *b. Ber.* 6a: they are numberless; *Pesah.* 111b: each tree has it own demon; for accounts of individual demons, cf. *b. Pesah.* 112b; *Git.* 70a, *Qidd.* 29b, and *Me'il.* 17b, where a demon, ben Temalion, helps the Jews outwit the Romans.

32. Apuleius, *Metam.* 2.28–29. For the theory behind this kind of practice, i.e., the "sympathy" existing between various elements within the world, cf. Hopfner, "Mageia," 311–27, esp. 312–14.

33. Empedocles, 8.9.

34. Pliny, *Nat.* 28, as an example.

35. Lucian, *Philops.* 7; this may be absurd for us, but perhaps not so strange for Pliny, or a Jew who knew Talmudic traditions (see n. 37 below).

36. *b. Ber.* 6a.

37. *b. Shabb.* 110b; for other such practices, see *b. Shab.* 67a; *Gittin* 68b–70a.

38. *b. Shabb.* 67b; to urinate in front of it is "Amorite practice," i.e., magic; to put a mulberry chip and broken pieces of glass is permitted. Cf. also *Sanh.* 67b.

if they are merely applied to the sufferer,[39] and gives an example of another universal practice when he describes the special way the root must be procured.[40]

Another element common to Hellenistic magical beliefs was the power of a magician to turn himself or herself, or someone else, into another form, i.e., metamorphosis. Known to the Greeks since the time of Homer, where the gods repeatedly turn themselves into other forms, or appear in the guise of someone else, and do the same to mortals, belief in such metamorphoses continued into the Hellenistic period unabated. It was of course the subject of Ovid's work by that name, and constituted the major theme of Apuleius' story of Lucius and his adventures in altered form.[41] While it did not capture the Jewish imagination to the extent that some other items from the Hellenistic world did, the Talmud also has a few accounts of metamorphoses, in one case, interestingly enough, of an ass that is transformed, although the story bears no resemblance to that of Lucius.[42]

The final element common in the Hellenistic world to which we want to call attention concerns the fact that Egypt was the origin and home of wonders and of magic. Greek magic books were known as "Egyptian books," apparently because of their point of origin,[43] and time and again, in popular literature, Egyptians appear as magicians,

39. Josephus, *Ant.* 8.46–48; *War* 7.185; cf. Tobit 6:7–8.

40. *War* 7.178–84; cf. Hopfner, "Mageia," 322–24, on ways to gather various plants and herbs, so their power is not lost. On the magical uses of plants and herbs generally, see 319–26.

41. Ovid's opening line announces the theme: "In nova fert animus mutatas dicere formas corpora." In Apuleius, *Metamorphoses*, Pamphile the sorceress changes herself, by means of salves, into an owl (3.21); secretly watching this performance, Lucius decides to duplicate it but, getting the wrong salve, he changes into an ass (3.24). The goddess Isis then brings about his retransformation (11.13). Lucian of Samosota has what I think is a shorter, more original version ("Lucius, or the Ass"), which Apuleius then lengthened into a religious tract for the religion of Isis, but this is no more than a conjecture on my part at this point. Many scholars take Lucian's version to be a compend of Apuleius' longer story.

42. *b. Sanh.* 67b; in one story an ass becomes a "landing board"; in the other, a sorceress becomes an ass that Jannai then rides into town.

43. So Blau, *Zauberwesen*, 42–42, citing Dieterich, *Abraxas*, 155 n. 1. He asserts Egypt was known as the home of magic from Homer to late Hellenism (42). Cf. also the first lines of Pseudo-Callisthenes, *The Life of Alexander of Macedon* (1.1). Strangely, Pliny insists that Persia was the home of magic (= Magi), and cites many "authorities"; *Nat.* 30.2.3–6.

or magical phrases are most powerful when they can be recited in the "Egyptian language."[44] Celsus shares this belief, and then uses it in his anti-Christian polemic by maintaining that Jesus learned his ability to do wondrous acts in Egypt. Because of such acts, Celsus says, he then called himself God.[45]

The Talmud also reflects this belief concerning the origin of magic. Nine-tenths of the world's witchcraft descended on Egypt,[46] and the Midrash on Exodus knows that even children of four or five could duplicate the wonder Aaron performed with his staff (Exod 7:10).[47] Only a fool is not careful when buying anything in Egypt, lest it have a spell upon it,[48] and the demon driven out by Tobit's magic flees to its home, the "farthest parts of upper Egypt" (8:3). Like Celsus, the Talmud also has the tradition that Jesus (= ben Stada) learned his witchcraft in Egypt,[49] and the growing influence of the Christian faith, with its traditions of the miracles of Jesus and of his disciples, appears to have considerably lessened the traditions of wonders and magic done by rabbis, both in number and significance.[50] Although folk-traditions of magic appear to have continued, miracles, after about the year AD 90, play a less significant role in the learned traditions and debates of the rabbis.[51] As far as miracle traditions and wondrous acts are concerned, the Christians appear to have won the religious competition with the Jews.[52]

---

44. Arignotus, for example, has many Egyptian books on magic and exorcises a demon from a house using an imprecation in the Egyptian language (Lucian, *Philops.* 31).

45. Origen, *Cel.* 1.68; cf. also 1.38, 46.

46. *b. Qidd.* 49b; cf. also Blau, *Zauberwesen*, 38.

47. *Midrash Rabbah Exodus* 11.6.

48. *b. Sanh.* 67b.

49. *b. Shabb.* 104b

50. So Guttmann, "Significance," 402–5.

51. Ibid., 384–85. Guttmann attributes the refusal to allow a *Bat Qol* (=voice from heaven) to influence doctrinal decisions to the growing anti-Christian polemic that developed between AD 90 and 100, and mentions that R. Eliezer, who was sympathetic to Christians, called upon it to confirm his legal interpretations (384–86; for the dispute, cf. *B. Meṣ'ia* 59b).

52. For this view, it was better for a faithful Jew to let a person die than to be healed by a Christian; cf. *b. 'Abod. Zar.* 27b, where a rabbi who does just that is called "blessed."

JUSTIN, IRENAEUS, AND ORIGEN

The third element in our survey of the background against which to understand the apocryphal NT writings of the mid-second to mid-third centuries is the growing apologetic trends as they affect the way wondrous deeds are reported and understood. As was true of the previous reviews, this will also be highly selective. We will limit our treatment to the writings of Justin Martyr and Irenaeus, and to the *Contra Celsum* of Origen.

Perhaps the most striking fact is the relative absence of references to the miracles of Jesus. Whereas the Apostolic Fathers had virtually ignored such acts of the Lord, the apologists do mention them, but as a rule limit such treatment to summaries. There is no evidence either of a growing tradition of miracles of Jesus, nor are any miracles ascribed to him that were not already reported in the synoptic gospels.[53] That does not mean a corresponding loss of interest in miracles as such, however, nor in their importance. It is quite clear that at the time the apologists wrote, wondrous activity was still very much a part of contemporary church life. When Irenaeus lists the activities then current in the church, he includes exorcisms, foreknowledge (through visions), healing the sick and raising the dead.[54] It is further clear that such acts are done through the power of Jesus. This is commonly expressed by pointing to miracles done by his followers as being done "in his name." Justin refers to the "mighty deeds even now done through his name,"[55] and Origen, while not always having as his point of emphasis the power of Jesus' name, nevertheless regularly points to contemporary Christian miracles done in that name.[56]

In addition to general healing activity on the part of contemporary Christians, it is apparent that the exorcism of demons still plays a large part in the miracles reported. Justin speaks of the "numberless demoniacs" who have been healed by Christians in the name of Jesus,[57] and makes it clear to Trypho that "to this day" demons are be-

---

53. For further evidence on this point, see ch. 3: "Gospel Miracle Tradition," 47, esp. the notes.

54. Irenaeus, *Haer.* 2.32.4

55. Justin, *Dial.* 35.

56. Origen, *Cel.* 1.67; 2.33; 3.24, 28.

57. Justin, *2 Apol.* 6.

ing exorcised by that name.[58] Origen similarly mentions the "countless demons" that Christians have expelled in Jesus' name.[59] Such activity point to "Jesus' divinity," although not as the primary evidence; that remains, for Origen, the existence of the Church itself.[60] Origen also speaks of the "spiritual miracles" of Christians, i.e., opening the eyes of those blind in soul, the ears of those deaf to talk of virtue, etc., and refers to them as the "greater works" Jesus promised his followers (John 14:12),[61] but there is little question Origen also intends to report "physical" miracles. In all of this, it is clear that such wondrous activity can be 'traced in a direct line from contemporary Christians, through the disciples, back to Jesus himself. Clearly, Irenaeus thinks the wonders done in his day are the same kind as Jesus performed.[62]

If, then, miracles are still a lively issue, what are the apologetic themes that emerge when miracles are discussed by the three Fathers under consideration? One such theme centers around the idea that miracles awaken faith in Christ, and awaken it legitimately. Justin, in fact, argued that it was by such deeds that Jesus compelled his contemporaries to recognize him.[63] Irenaeus points out that being cured from demon possession has frequently led that person to faith in Jesus,[64] and his allegorical treatment of Jesus' use of clay to heal the blind man (John 9:6) leads to the point that such acts were performed so that those who saw them should be restored to the "fold of life."[65] Origen also points out that miracles were necessary for the faith of those who by custom asked for "signs and wonders,"[66] but he qualifies the point

---

58. Justin, *Dial.* 30, 76.

59. Origen, *Cel.* 1.25.

60. Ibid., 3.33.

61. Ibid., 2.48.

62. E.g., Irenaeus, *Haer.* 2.31.2.

63. Justin, *Dial.* 69. This is not so foreign to the NT perspective as has on occasion been argued. Faith based on miracles is regularly reported in Acts (8:9–11; 9:35, 42; 13:12; cf. also 16:30; 19:17), and Paul apparently thought it not only likely, but legitimate, that signs and wonders should lead people to faith in Christ (1 Cor 2:4; cf. Rom 15:18–20, where it appears such wondrous acts are part and parcel of "preaching the gospel"). Although the total picture in John is ambiguous, that gospel also implied that faith can be based on mighty acts (e.g., 2:11; 4:53; 6:14; 11:15).

64. Irenaeus, *Haer.* 2.32.4.

65. Ibid., 5.11.2; cf. 3.11.5.

66. Origen, *Cel.* 2.52.

by urging a) that miracles were more necessary earlier on before man had progressed in intelligence to the point where such things were no longer so necessary;[67] b) that while the masses need miracles, the elite are better served by teaching;[68] and c) that it is wrong to deduce from the miracles only that Jesus was divine, without recognizing also his humanity.[69]

Despite such qualifications, however, Origen is prepared to argue that without miracles, the disciples' preaching would not have met with success, and that the miracles of Jesus did in fact lead many to the "wonderful teaching of the gospel."[70]

A second theme, allied to the first, consists in the argument that Christian miracles are credible because they are the fulfillment of prophecy. This theme is particularly characteristic of Justin, who uses it to defend Christ against pejorative comparison with healers of classical antiquity,[71] to give added weight to the credibility of the reports of Jesus' miracles,[72] or to defend those acts against claims that they were done by magic.[73] Irenaeus calls upon prophecy to lend credence to the reality of Jesus' miracles; they were more than mere appearances.[74] Origen calls upon prophecy to refute Celsus' claim that Jesus' miracles were mere sorcery.[75]

A third theme that emerges in the discussion of Jesus' mighty acts has already been hinted at, namely, the need to defend Jesus against the charge of having performed his mighty works by means of sorcery. The apologists were intent on showing that there was a difference between Christian miracles and pagan magic. Justin recognizes that there are contemporaries who appear to be doing the kind of thing Jesus did and his followers do, e.g., Simon, and his disciple, Menander,

---

67. Ibid., 4.80.

68. Ibid., 3.21.

69. Ibid., 3.28.

70. Ibid., 1.46.

71. Justin, *1 Apol.* 22–22, 54; *Dial.* 69.

72. Justin, *1 Apology* 48.

73. Ibid., 30.

74. Irenaeus, *Haer.* 2.32.4.

75. Origen, *Cel.* 2.48; 8.9. A similar appeal to prophecy to bolster the legitimacy and uniqueness of Jesus' miracles is found in the *Recog. Clem.* 1.41; 3.60. It was probably a more widespread device than our brief treatment has indicated.

both from Samaria,[76] but they did their mighty acts by magic, a claim that is totally false when leveled against Jesus.[77] Irenaeus also knows of magicians, both former and contemporary, who appear to have done things similar to those miracles done by Jesus,[78] but he points out two ways in which such magicians differ from Christ and from those who perform miracles as his followers. In the first place, their goal is self-aggrandizement through deceit, and they glorify themselves, charging fees for their deeds and "doing more harm than good."[79] In the second place, their deeds are not permanent, they really do not have the power to heal, and any demons they cast out they have previously sent into the person.[80] The fact that Jesus rose from the dead, while these magicians have not, is proof for Irenaeus that Jesus is not to be compared with them.[81]

Origen, interestingly enough, argues for the reality of magic, linking it to his argument for the reality of the power of names,[82] but he never tires of refuting the claim that Jesus performed his miracles by magic or as a sorcerer. Celsus misrepresents Jesus when he levels such claims,[83] for Jesus was neither a boaster nor a sorcerer.[84] The death he met bore no resemblance, as Celsus claimed, to those put to death for sorcery,[85] and Origen calls upon the difference between the deeds of Moses (divine) and the Egyptians (trickery) to point to and characterize the difference between Jesus and the "Antichrists."[86] Far from working by means of demonic powers, or servant demons, Jesus brought an end to the power of the demons;[87] indeed, it was when the magi sensed that their (demonic) power was weakened that they set out to

76. Justin, *1 Apol.* 26, 56.

77. Justin, *Dial.* 69.

78. Simon and Carpocrates; Irenaeus, *Haer.* 3.31.2; Marcus, a contemporary, it appears, *Haer.* 1.13.1–2.

79. Ibid., 2.31.2; 3.32.3.

80. Ibid., 2.31.2; cf. the account of the demon ben Tamalion, *b. Me'il.* 17b.

81. Irenaeus, *Haer.* 2.32.3.

82. Origen, *Cel.* 1.24.

83. Ibid., 2.48; cf. 50.

84. Ibid., 2.32; cf. 1.71.

85. Ibid., 2.44.

86. Ibid., 2.50.

87. Ibid., 4.32.

find the cause, and made the journey to Palestine.[88] But Origen's basic argument against magic in the Christian context centers on the kind of men who perform miracles in Jesus' name, and the kind of deeds they do. No magician calls men to moral reformation by means of his tricks, as disciples do by their miracles, and no sorcerer is concerned, as were Jesus and his disciples, with proclaiming the will of God and his final judgment.[89] It is therefore the lives and moral character of those who do wondrous acts that shows the difference between sorcery and Christian miracle.[90] Indeed, the disciples risked their lives to proclaim a teaching that itself forbids magic.[91]

A fourth theme, a corollary of the third, concerns the ways in which wondrous deeds are done. We have already seen, from the positive side, that Christian miracles are done in the name of Jesus. But the apologists also felt it necessary to defend Christians against the charges of magic and sorcery by pointing out, in a negative way, the differences between them. Justin points out that while Christians exorcise demons in the name of Jesus alone, both Jews and Gentiles are forced to use incantations, drugs, and incense.[92] Irenaeus in similar language points to the miracles of the church as happening without incantations or any other "wicked, curious art."[93] Origen refutes the charge of Celsus that Christians get their wondrous power by means of the names of demons or incantations,[94] and brands as a lie Celsus' claim that Christian writings contain names of demons and magical formulas.[95] Whereas magi work their wonders by means of the formulas they use to invoke demons to do their bidding, Christ's coming has weakened such power.[96] In fact, the most potent invocation seems to be the name of Jesus, which Origen concedes has been used effectively even by "bad men" to drive out demons,[97] but any hint of sorcery involved in such

88. Ibid., 1.60.

89. Ibid., 1.68.

90. Ibid., 2.51.

91. Ibid., 1.38.

92. Justin, 2 Apol. 6; Dial. 85.

93. Irenaeus, Haer. 2.32.5

94. Origen, Cel. 1.6.

95. Ibid., 6.40.

96. Ibid., 1.60.

97. Ibid., 1.6.

use is eliminated, Origen argues, by the fact that Christ predicted such things would happen. In fact, such activity proves the "divine power" of Jesus.[98]

NEW TESTAMENT APOCRYPHA

With the completion of the rapid survey of the New Testament roots of Jesus and the disciples as miracle-workers, the view of miracles and magic in the secular world, and the emerging themes of the Christian apologists in the discussion of miracles and magic, we are now ready to turn our attention to the NT apocryphal writings of the mid-second to mid-third centuries, and discern the way in which they present Jesus and the disciples as miracle-workers. As the discussion proceeds, the combination of secular elements and apologetic themes effected in these apocryphal writings will become increasingly clear.

The picture of Jesus as miracle-worker in the apocryphal NT writings is remarkable for its absence. To be sure, Jesus is still remembered in such terms. When, in a letter quoted by Eusebius, Irenaeus recalls his contacts with Polycarp, and the latter's conversations with the apostle (?) John, the two things recalled from John's reports are the teachings and the miracles of Jesus.[99] There are also scattered, if remarkably rare, summaries of the miracles of Jesus to be found in these apocryphal writings, a state of affairs duplicated in the remaining Christian corpus, including the Fathers, of this period.[100]

Unfortunately, we do not possess in any degree of completeness the apocryphal gospels from this period. Of those we do possess, in part or complete, I am aware of only three references to miracles of the mature Jesus.[101] Only in a much later writing do we find further

---

98. Ibid., 2.50.

99. Eusebius, *Hist. eccl.* 5.20.6. In the translation by Lake (Loeb Classical Library series), those miracles are unaccountably reported as "their miracles" and "their teachings," i.e., as those of the apostles (αὐτοῦ is translated as though the text read αὐτῶν). For the correct translation, cf. Lawlor and Oulton, eds., *Eusebius,* vol. 1, ad loc.

100. For a list of such summaries, see ch. 3: "Gospel Miracle Tradition" above; Bauer, *Das Leben Jesu* 364. To those lists may be added the summary found in the *Ep. Apos.* 5; cf. *NTA* vol. 1.

101. The *Gospel of the Nazaraeans* (cited by Jerome in his Commentary on Matthew, Matt 12:13; cf. *NTA* 1:148), where the man with the withered had identifies himself as a mason, and asks to be cured; *The Gospel of Philip,* p. 111, §54 (see Wilson, *Philip,* 39), where Jesus throws 72 colors into the vat in Levi's dye-works, and takes

miracles reported of the mature Jesus that are completely new and different from those in our canonical gospels,[102] and even then in very limited number.

The situation is quite different in the case of the infancy gospels, where new and unique miracles of the infant and youthful Jesus abound. The remarkable point here, however, is the kind of miracle reported of Jesus. In the second century *Infancy Gospel of Thomas*,[103] there are only three healing miracles, and one of those concerns Jesus' lifting the curse on those he had earlier blinded. By contrast, there are four punitive miracles, in each instance performed by Jesus against those who have irritated or insulted him. There are also six prodigies, ranging in subject matter from reading Hebrew by the power of the Holy Spirit (in contrast to the normal learning process) to stretching a board in his father's carpenter shop. The remaining three miracles concern Jesus' raising the dead. Later variations on the infancy gospel theme restrict themselves almost entirely to prodigies.[104]

The basic tendency, then, of the traditions about miracles of the mature Jesus in the second century and beyond, including the material subsumed under the general heading "apocryphal NT," is to ignore Jesus as miracle-worker. The reason for this is obscure, and the consequences intriguing.[105] We will have some further comments on this puzzle at the conclusion of this study.

---

them all out white (a miracle similar to this is found in the *Arabic Infancy Gospel*; cf. *NTA* 1:400); and in the *Gos. Thom.* 14, where the charge to the disciples to heal is not necessarily to be interpreted as miraculous power, but in the tradition is probably so to be understood. Perhaps one ought also to reckon here the "longer" ending of Mark (16:17–18), although all but one of the types of miracles there are reflected in the NT (casting out demons: Mark 9:38; Luke 10:17; glossolalia: Acts 2:4, 11; 10:46; 19:6; picking up serpents: Luke 10:17–20; healing: Acts 9:17; 28:8). Only drinking poison unharmed is not reflected in the canonical NT; but cf. Eusebius, *Hist. eccl.* 3.39.9.

102. *Acts of Andrew and Matthias*, perhaps as late as the sixth century. Here we learn that during his life, Jesus made stone sphinxes walk and talk, who summoned the three patriarchs from Mamre to speak to the high priests, all in an unsuccessful effort to convince them of Jesus' importance. Other miracles for the same purpose performed in private before the same group are not detailed. For a translation, see ANF 8:517–25.

103. For a translation, see *NTA* 1:392–99.

104. For translations, see idem, 399–417; ANF 8:395–415.

105. If the trend is in the direction of the disappearance of the miracle story about the mature Jesus, can we continue to assume, as Bultmann did, that the miracles are a late addition to the canonical gospel traditions, and that the trend was toward increas-

When we turn from the figure of Jesus, and the apocryphal gospels, to the apostles, and the apocryphal acts, the situation is reversed. We have many such accounts of Jesus' disciples, and they are replete with miracles entirely independent of those told in the canonical Acts of the Apostles.

In order to gain a perspective on these apocryphal acts, and to understand something of the milieu out of which they came, and to which they intended to speak, it is necessary to consider them from the standpoint of the history of literary forms.

One of the contributions of the later Hellenistic period to Greek literature was the novel (= romance).[106] The genre is hard to define, but it had certain characteristics, among them the theme of a couple separated from one another, yet remaining true despite great pressures against such a course of action. This theme, completely foreign to the canonical Acts, appears in adapted form, with startling regularity in the second and third century acts. In this adapted form, a woman, often highborn, withdraws from marriage with her husband due to an apostle's preaching, and lives an ascetic life, despite the persecution and torture instigated by the irate husband (or lover) against both the woman and the apostle. Peter is persecuted by Albinus, Caesar's friend, when Albinus' wife Xanthippe follows Peter (*Actus Ver.* §§314ff).[107] Paul is persecuted by Thamyris when his betrothed, Thecla, leaves him to follow Paul (*Acts Paul* §§7–24—the theme of separation and reunion is also carried out with Paul and Thecla in §§21–24, and then again in §§26–40). Andrew is persecuted by Aegaetes because his wife, Maximilla, has left him to follow Andrew (*Acts Andr.* §§4ff). Thomas is persecuted by Charisius because his wife Mygdonia leaves him to

---

ing emphasis on the miracles of Jesus? Changes from Mark to Matthew and Luke, with respect to miracle stories, may be due as much to the intentions of the respective evangelists as to any traditional trajectory. Development of this point, however, must await a later time.

106. A convenient, brief summary of this kind of literature, and some of its representatives, can be found in Wright, *History,* 292–308. There are of course many other such accounts. For a study more directly related to this topic, see Söder, *Apostelgeschichten.*

107. Some idea of the pressure on this unknown author to include this motif is indicated by the fact that this becomes the motive for Peter's martyrdom at the hands of Caesar, after Peter had won the approval of the whole of Rome through his prodigy-laden victory over Simon. Peter's death from faithfulness to Christ becomes here his death due to a jealous husband.

follow Thomas (*Acts Thom.* §§82ff), and by King Misdaeus when his
wife Tertia leaves him to follow Thomas (§§134ff). In the acts of John,
improper advances to Drusiana, wife of Andronicus, lead to that faithful woman's death (*Acts John* §§63–86).[108] Obviously, in none of these
instances are the apostle and the lady pictured as lovers, yet it is equally
clear that the commendable faithfulness of the woman is to the apostle
and his teaching, not to the husband. In that way, apostle and woman
become the "devoted couple" who remain true (to the doctrines taught
by the apostle) despite all the temptations and pressures to the contrary. The repeated theme of "love at first sight" (i.e., the woman is
totally taken with the apostle and his teaching from the moment she
first encounters them, and exhibits symptoms that the distraught husband or lover interpret as infatuation) is further indication that we are
dealing with motifs adapted from the Hellenistic romance.

Other elements that figure in the novelistic literature of this
period—accounts of travel, occasionally including visits to distant
and unknown lands; accounts of prodigies, including bizarre events,
strange people and stranger customs; accounts of miracles, done and
observed by the hero or other characters; trips to Hades to learn various secrets, including future events; wondrous interventions by the
gods, especially to lighten and hasten sea travel[109]—are also found in
the apocryphal acts. Although some of these elements also appear in
the canonical gospels and Acts—i.e., accounts of journeys, wondrous
deliverance from dangers, miracles—the shape they assume in the
apocryphal acts indicates the closer relationship of this latter literature
to the novelistic literature of the Hellenistic world. A simple reading of,
say, the canonical Acts and the apocryphal *Acts of Thomas* will clearly
demonstrate the differences between canonical and apocryphal literature on this score.

If it is true, therefore, as seems to be the case, that the authors of
the apocryphal acts have adapted literary conventions of the Hellenistic
world in the composition and structure of their narratives, and if, as
seems equally to be the case, those elements make the acts more "en-

108. The novelistic nature of this last instance is heightened by the merely peripheral involvement of the apostle John in this episode. The erotic elements, present in
most of the apocryphal acts, are here carried to rather bizarre lengths.

109. These are some of the major motifs Söder finds in her analysis of novelistic
literature. Most of them go all the way back to the *Odyssey*.

tertaining," and thus more likely to be read, then it would also seem to be the case that the authors had some kind of apologetic and/or missionary intention underlying their work. They appear to have wanted to gain readers for their works, and were willing to cast those works in a form currently popular. To that extent, they adapted their understanding of the Christian message to the literary tastes of the second and third centuries.[110]

We must now turn to a consideration of the way in which the apostles were pictured as miracle-workers in the apocryphal acts. We shall devote major attention to three compositions that appear to originate in the late second century: the *Acts of Andrew* (*ANT*, 245–67), *Acts of Paul* (*ANT*, 350–88), and *Acts of Peter* (*ANT*, 390–426), and to two that appear to originate in the third century: *Acts of John* (*ANT*, 303–47) and *Acts of Thomas* (*ANT*, 439–511).[111]

An indication of the direction in which these apocryphal acts are moving in their portrayal of the disciples lies in the fact that while the healing miracles reported of them are not numerous, accounts of people being raised from the dead, both by the disciples and by those temporarily empowered by the disciples to do it, are much more numerous. John has only one episode of healing reported of him (he cures a group of aged women of their diseases: §37);[112] Andrew's only healing was the casting out of a demon (Papyrus Coptic Utrecht p. 14); Paul, although he recites the healing miracles of Jesus (PHeid. pp. 7–8), heals only one blind man upon whom he lays his hands (PHeid. p. 33). More

110. Any author, of course, writes to be read. But the continuing and unresolved debate over the possible genre of the canonical gospels indicates that such adaptation to current Hellenistic literary tastes was not so great an element in their formation, as in that of the apocryphal acts. The same is true of the canonical Acts, if in somewhat modified degree. Cf. Plümacher (*Lukas*, 139), who sees Luke as dependent on Hellenistic historiography for his model, but never using elements drawn from it to arouse interest or decorate his narrative to make it palatable to Hellenistic tastes. It is just this, it seems to me, that the authors of the apocryphal acts are doing.

111. For a discussion of possible dates, cf. *NTA* 2 ad loc. The remaining acts, e.g., the *Acts of Philip* (see *ANT*, 515–18), *Acts of Barnabas* (as told by John Mark), *Acts of Pilate* (see *ANT*, 164–85), *Acts of the Holy Apostles Peter and Paul, Acts of Andrew and Matthias in the City of the Maneaters* (see *ANT* 283–99), and the *Martyrdom of the Holy and Glorious Apostle Bartholomew*, appear to date from the fourth century and later, and will be referred to only rarely.

112. Paragraph numbers refer to the acts of the respective apostles. The *Acts of Peter* (called *Actus Vercellenses*) are hereafter cited as "*Actus Ver.*"

are recited of Peter, and of Thomas, but only four in each case.[113] In addition, Thomas is recognized as the unknown young man who cured an old woman (§154), and dust from Thomas' grave heals a king's son (§170).[114] Healing miracles occur with even less frequency in the later apocryphal acts.

Stories of people being raised from the dead, on the other hand, are much more numerous. John raises to life four people (§§23, 51, 75, 80) and empowers, on three other occasions, another person to do the same (§§24, 47, 82–83). Thomas raises two (§33, when a serpent at Thomas' command withdraws its poison from a man, who then returns to life; §81), and empowers a youth to raise a girl the youth had murdered in a fit of jealous passion (§§53–54). Peter raises three (§§27, 28, and a girl whom he had previously caused to die, Ps.-Titus, *de disp. sanct.*, pp. 83ff; for the latter, see *NTA* 2:278–79), and empowers a man to raise a youngster (§26). Paul raises a young girl (P. Heid. p. 42) and a young man (P. Heid. pp. 53–58). Of Andrew, interestingly enough, none are reported.

There are of course many other miracles reported in these acts in addition to those of healing and raising the dead. During a prayer of John, the altar and temple of Artemis in Ephesus are shattered, killing the priest (§42), and at John's word bedbugs abandon the bed upon which he intends to sleep, and then again at his word, return to it the next morning (§§60–61). An adulteress is paralyzed at Paul's approach (*Actus Ver.* §2) and his prayer causes rain and hail to quench the fire meant to burn Thecla (*Acts Paul* §§22–23). At Peter's bidding a dog announces a challenge to Simon (§§9, 12), and a baby speaks with the voice of a man (§15). When a demon, leaving on Peter's command, shatters a statue, Peter instructs another on how to cause the statue to restore itself immediately (§11), and to show his power, Peter makes a smoked fish swim and eat (§13). Thomas causes a serpent to tell its story after its bite has killed a man (§§31–32), causes a wild ass to speak

113. Cf. Peter, two healings and a restoration of sight (Berlin Coptic Papyrus 8502, pp. 128–32, 135-41; *NTA* 2:276–78), and a general healing (*Actus Ver.* §31); of Thomas, two general healings (§§20, 59), expulsion of a demon (§§42–47) and restoration of withered hands (§52).

114. The Apostle Thaddaeus heals King Abgar in an account that may have been written in the second or third century, although it is not recorded until later in Eusebius, *Hist. eccl.* 1.13.17, where a general reference to Thaddaeus' healing "every disease and infirmity" is also included (1.13.12).

(§§39–40) and summons four wild asses to draw his wagon (§70; at his summons the whole herd appears, but Thomas dismisses them after choosing the four largest), and sends one of them into a city to summon forth a demoniac (§74).

Punitive miracles are also recorded, though not in great abundance. An unworthy woman was paralyzed when she received the eucharist at Paul's hands (*Actus Ver.* §2), and an unworthy lad's hands withered when he took the elements from Thomas (§51). As a result of slapping Thomas, a man dies, as Thomas had predicted he would (§8). Simon is struck dumb when a baby speaks to him with a man's voice, and Simon kills a boy by whispering in his ear (*Actus Ver.* §§15, 25). At Peter's prayer, the flying Simon falls and breaks his leg in three places (§32).

A further indication of the nature of this material consists in the things that happen to the apostles, most often for their benefit, which they are not responsible for producing. Water welled up from the ground to cool the heated metal Thomas was to be forced to walk on, and disappeared just before it threatened to flood the city (§§140–41). Thecla, Paul's companion, is repeatedly saved from martyrdom by prodigies: a lioness befriends her in the arena and holds off the other animals to the point of its own death (§33); she is saved from the seals in the pool into which she has dived by a lightning flash and a cloud of fire (§34); she is saved from wild beasts in the arena when they fall asleep, and from being torn apart by wild bulls when the ropes tying her to the beasts are wondrously burned through (§35). Paul himself is saved from death by a lion when the lion speaks to Paul, and acknowledges he is the same one whom Paul had earlier baptized, and Paul is then saved from other beasts when hail falling from a clear sky kills them (§7). Thomas is reminded of his duty to preach the gospel by a homilitizing wild ass (§§78–79). and John is blinded for two years for wanting to marry (§113). Paul, at his prayer, is freed from prison fetters by a youth appearing from heaven (§7), and Thomas has prison doors open for his freedom three times (§§122, 154, 162) as well as having fetters wondrously removed (§119).

Visions are regularly reported, both by the apostles and others, which foretell the future (*Acts Thom.* §91; *Actus Ver.* §17), give instructions (*Actus Ver.* §1; *Acts Thom.* §29; *Acts John* §§18, 48), and allow the recipient to see Jesus (*Acts Paul* §10; *Acts John* §§92, 97; *Actus Ver.* §§5,

30, 32; *Acts Thom.* §§1, 29; *Acts Andr.* §8, Vat. 808), or to see someone else (a mother her dead daughter, *Acts Paul* §28; one blind sees
light, hears a voice, Berlin Copt. Pap. 8502, pp. 136f; an innkeeper sees
Paul, *Actus Ver.* §6; demons appear, *Actus Ver.* §22). Heavenly voices
are heard (*Actus Ver.* §§1, 5; *Acts Thom.* §§121, 158; *Acts John* §18),
another's thoughts are discerned (*Acts John* §56), and foreknowledge is
a regular occurrence (*Acts John* §46, 86; *Acts Andr.*, Vat. 808 §17; *Actus
Ver.* §§1, 4, 5, 16–17, 22, 32; *Acts Thom.* §§6, 91; *Acts Paul* §11).

Another regular feature of this literature is accounts of metamorphoses, especially of Jesus appearing in another's form. He appears to
a group of widows as an old man, a youth, and a boy, each form to a
different portion of the group (*Actus Ver.* §21). He appears to Thecla
in the form of Paul (*Acts Paul* §21) and to Maximilla in the form of
Andrew (*Acts Andr.* Vat. 808 §14). To Drusiana he appears in the form
of John, and of a young man (*Acts John* §87), to John he appears as
an old man, to James, who was with John, as a youth (*Acts John* §89),
and to a young married couple on their wedding night he appears as
Thomas (*Acts Thom.* §11).

The world of the apocryphal acts, in sum, is a world of miracles
and prodigies, of dreams, foreknowledge and visions, of metamorphoses and voices from heaven. It is a world of wondrous rescues and
miraculous punishments, a world in which men return from the dead,
having learned secrets of the future, and having seen the torments of
the damned while there (*Acts Thom.* §§22ff., 55), a world in which
demons not only possess people (*Acts Andr.* Pap. Copt. Utr. I, p. 14;
Acts Thom. §§46, 75; *Actus Ver.* §11), but are seen and described (*Acts
Thom.* §§43, 46, 64; *Acts Andr.* P. Copt. Ut. p. 10; *Actus Ver.* §22). It is,
in many ways, the Hellenistic world in which magic and sorcery were
quite at home.

It is no wonder, therefore, that accusations of sorcery are raised,
both against Christ's followers, and by them against others. The same
rule seems to apply that we observed earlier, viz, one's own deeds are
by God's power, those of others by magic. A praetor in Ephesus ac-
cuses John of sorcery by means of magical devices, and a magical name
(§31); Paul is denounced as a sorcerer by the crowds (*Acts Paul* §§15,
20; *Actus Ver.* §4); and Thomas is regularly called a sorcerer (§§16, 98,
99, 101, 102, 114, 116, 117, 128, 130, 134, 138, 162, 163) and a magician
(§§20, 89, 96, 104, 106). Thomas is accused of having used a potion to

lure the king's wife away, and he is asked by another to teach him his magic (§§134, 139).

Similarly, the opponents of the disciples are accused of practicing magic and sorcery. John calls all non-Christian worship sorcery (§43), and the demon whom Andrew cast out from a young girl had been conjured up by a sorcerer for the purpose of winning the girl for himself (Pap. Copt. Utr. I, p. 14). But the great opponent of the Christian faith is Simon, and he comes to represent, as it were, the incorporation of the evil powers of magic and sorcery arrayed against the Christian faith. Jesus in a vision to Peter identifies Simon as a sorcerer (*Actus Ver.* §5) and as a magician (§17), and all that Simon really can do is deal in appearances and illusions. His attempt to restore a Roman senator (or lad; the story is confused) to life results in slight movements of the corpse, and the mere illusion of life (§28), and all of his apparent healings and raisings from the dead are magical tricks (§31).

Almost as if to disprove any charge against the apostles as sorcerers or magicians, the apocryphal acts never describe their miracles in such a way as even to hint at the use of herbs or incantations, or magical devices.[115] John is commanded to perform a miracle, appearing naked in the public theater, so that he may hide nothing, and is forbidden to hold anything in his hands or use a "magical name," and, apparently, even under such conditions, he heals the sick who had been brought there for that purpose (§§31–37). While this is the most obvious example of anti-magical polemic in the way a miracle is performed, the intention is symptomatic of the other accounts of miracles done by the followers of Jesus. Miracles are regularly performed either by prayer, or in the name of Jesus (occasionally both), when any method of performance is mentioned at all. There is no predictability, however, about the mode in which miracles are performed, or reported. Some are done by prayer. Thus, Paul through prayer restores a man's sight (§4), Peter raises a widow's son (§27), Thomas raises two women (§§80–81), and John does many miracles (§106), to cite a very few. Some, on the other hand, are done by the power of the name of Jesus, mentioned by way of command. John thus commands Cleopatra to rise by the name of Him "whom every ruler fears" (§23), and instructs her to raise her husband

115. King Abgar is impressed by the fact that both Jesus and Thaddaeus heal without drugs and herbs, an observation that could stand as a motto for the way the disciples perform miracles in these Acts; cf. Eusebius, *Hist. eccl.* 1.13.6 and 18.

by the name of God (§24). Peter casts out a demon in the name of
Jesus (§11) as does Thomas (§75), who later expressly affirms that his
power is from Jesus, not achieved by magic (§140). Combinations of
these two elements may be used, i.e., prayer and Jesus' name, and the
command by the disciple that the desired end be accomplished may
also be added. Thus, John raised Drusiana by prayer and command
(§80), Paul restored a man's sight by prayer and the laying on of hands
(§4), Peter raised a senator (or a boy) by means of prayer, command
and touch (§27), and a youth raised a murdered girl after prayer and
in the name of Jesus, both at the instruction of Thomas (§§53–54).
The disciple's power is thus not limited to himself. At his command,
and in his presence, others are able to do what the disciple desires, as
Marcellus, at Peter's instructions, restored a shattered statue (§11). In
fact, the apostle's command at times is able, by itself, to cause another
to perform a miracle. At John's command, a young man raises a priest
of Artemis, killed when the temple collapsed upon him, with neither
prayer nor the name of Jesus being mentioned (§§47). Or the apostle
may himself perform a miracle without prayer or the name of Jesus, as
Peter does when he simply commands a dog to speak (§§9, 12).

In the great majority of cases, however, it is clearly by the power of
Jesus that the disciples are able to perform their miracles. That would
appear to be the manifest intention of the accounts of miracles performed by the disciples, as they are told in the apocryphal acts. Yet on
occasion, stories are told that point simply to the apostle as wonder-
worker, able to do mighty things by his own word of command, or
to empower others by instructing them in what to do, as Peter does
when he tells Marcellus to pray, sprinkle water on the broken statue,
and command the statue in Jesus' name to be restored (§11). Given
the magical potency of water, one is tempted to see here an invasion of
magic into the narrative. Yet clearly the empowering act is the prayer
to, and the name of, Jesus. An apostle is thus a mighty man of wonders,
but withal he remains the apostle of Christ, indeed, his slave, as the
opening narrative of the *Acts of Thomas* make clear.[116]

There are at least two other points made by the miracle stories
in these apocryphal acts, to which we must give some attention. The

---

116. In §§1–3, Thomas, having refused the assignment to evangelize India, which
was his by lot, is sold by Jesus to a merchant from India. Jesus says to the merchant: "I
have a slave who is a carpenter, and I wish to sell him" (*NTA* 2:443).

most important of those is the emphasis on the miracles as capable of awakening faith. Indeed, they seem to be indispensable to making the Christian message believable. Perhaps at this point, the apologetic intention of the acts to a Hellenistic world saturated with magic, and belief in the potency of sorcerers and magicians, comes clearest. These men, not themselves magicians, nevertheless outdo the most celebrated sorcerers and magicians. Therefore they deserve to be believed.

That such belief not only can, but must be based on miracles, is made explicit repeatedly in these apocryphal acts. John, brought into the theater in Ephesus, affirms he will "convict even your praetor's disbelief" by healing the ill women John has commanded to be brought to the theater for the purpose of his display.[117] He tells the miracles of Jesus to encourage faith in Jesus (§93), and chides the Ephesians for their unbelief despite the miracles they have witnessed (§39; cf. Matt 10:20–23). Those same Ephesians are then converted when a temple collapses, and they cry to God "We are converted, now that we have seen thy marvellous works."[118] Those who are healed by Thomas believe in Jesus (§59),[119] a crowd confesses God is One when Paul raises a dead girl (§8), and Tryphaena believes in the resurrection as a result of the prodigies that save Thecla from death in the arena (*Acts Paul* §39). Andrew claims the people have seen signs that will not let them disbelieve (*Acts Andr.*, Vatic. 808, §16). The writing in which this point is most explicitly and repeatedly made, however, is the *Actus Vercellenses*, which recounts the deeds of Peter. Marcellus, who had been perverted in his faith by Simon, renews his faith in Christ when he hears a dog speak at Peter's command (§10), and it is further strengthened when, at Peter's instructions, he miraculously restores a shattered statue (§11). In response to a popular request for another sign, so the people can believe in God, since "Simon too did many signs in our presence, and therefore we followed him," Peter causes the smoked fish to swim and eat (§§12–13).[120] Peter, in contest with Simon, annunciates the principle that "We must put no faith in words, but in actions and deeds" (§17),[121]

117. §33; *NTA* 2:223.

118. §42; *NTA* 2:237.

119. Oddly, despite the large number of miracles and prodigies in the *Acts of Thomas*, this is the only instance where faith results from such events.

120. *NTA* 2:295.

121. *NTA* 2:299.

a principle then validated when Peter's purpose in raising a widow's dead son is achieved: the people believe in Jesus (§§26–27). As a result, Peter was venerated as a god, which appears to have been quite proper. Neither he nor anyone else repudiates it (§29; cf. Acts 10:25–26!). It is thus, in this one case at least, clear that the line is not always clearly drawn between the apostle working solely by God's power, as indicated by the presence of prayer and the name of Jesus as empowering devices, and working by his own inherent power, as indicated in those instances where he performs the miracle simply by his own command. The apostle has taken something of the divine power into himself.

The second point, closely allied to the first, viz. that miracles are necessary to make the Christian faith credible, is the emphasis on the ability of the apostle to win contests of miraculous power. If, as seems evident, the crowds follow the one who performs the greatest wonders, then the way to establish the truth of faith claims is to see who can do just that. Such a view, close to the surface at any time where miracles are understood as a potent argument for the credibility of faith-claims, as is the case in these second and third century acts, becomes explicit in the Acts of Peter. Indeed, the core of this writing seems to concern the contest between Peter and Simon in Rome. Simon, driven out of Palestine at an earlier time by Peter, has now captivated Rome, having arrived, apparently, in a flying cloud (§4), and Peter has been summoned to combat the enormous influence Simon has won through his wonders. After some preliminary sparring, in which Peter's miracles begin to win back the once-faithful, Simon calleges Peter to a contest of miracles (§11), and it is agreed that the winner will be believed (§23). All of official Rome gathers to witness the contest. Simon kills a lad by whispering in his ear (§25), and Peter raises him (§26—this was the first contest, its contents proposed by a Roman official). The mother of a dead senator then proposes to both that they raise her son. Simon is able to restore only a semblance of life, but Peter restores him fully (§28). Simon, at this point in the contest admittedly enfeebled, proposes as a final test that he will fly "up to my Father" to prove the truth of his claims (§32). This he does, but Peter's prayer to Jesus, in which he warns that if Simon is successful, "all who have believed on thee shall now be overthrown, and the signs and wonders which thou gavest them through me shall be disbelieved," asks that Simon fall and break his leg in three places, which then happens. The onlookers react appropriately. "They (the crowd) stoned (Simon) and went to their own homes; but from that time they all believed in Peter."[122] It only remains for a former follower of Simon to pronounce the theological rationale of such a contest: "Simon, if the Power of God is broken, shall not the God himself, whose power you are, be proved an illusion?" He then says to Peter, the winner, "I too desire to be one of those that believe in Christ."[123] Thus Simon, the sorcerer, who performed his wonders by tricks and incantations, was defeated by Peter, the apostle of Christ, who overcomes Simon by prayer, and the name of Jesus.

APOLOGETIC AND APOCRYPHAL MOTIFS

We have now completed our brief survey of the view of Jesus and the disciples as miracle-workers contained in the NT apocrypha of the second and third centuries. Let us, in conclusion, examine the inter-relationship of secular and Christian worlds, and of apologetic and apocryphal motifs.

We noted that the world of the second and third centuries is a world in which magic plays a large role. Magic evidently occupied, in one way or another, people from all ranks of social life and intellectual endeavor. From the philosopher or the writer who must defend himself against the charge of magic, to the humblest love-sick swain seeking to bend the amorous interest of some maiden toward himself, magic was part of the cultural milieu in which all shared. This world is reflected in the apocryphal acts we have examined, and is reflected in the writings of the three apologists, at which we cast a quick glance. The frequency with which metamorphoses are narrated in the apocryphal acts, along with numerous astonishing prodigies, seem to indicate that the Hellenistic view of magic has been taken over less critically there than by the apologists. Yet both apologists and apocryphal traditions attempt to separate themselves from magic, primarily, it would seem, by denying that Christian miracles involve the usual techniques of magic, e.g., drugs, herbs, and incantations, and by affirming that they do involve solely the power of God or of Jesus, applied by prayer, or by using the name of Jesus. In this regard, we appear to catch sight of an

122. *NTA* 2:316.
123. §32; *NTA* 2:316.

emerging Christian consensus on the way in which Christian wonders are to be separated from non-Christian magic.

In a similar vein, the view that followers of Jesus continue to be capable of performing wonders, a view found in the apologists, is carried forward as a major emphasis in the bulk of apocryphal writings preserved for our examination. The apostles, however much their power may be attributed to Christ, nevertheless occupy center stage in the drama, and references to miracles of the mature Jesus are as rare in the apologetic as in the apocryphal literature. If it could be assumed that interest in the church loomed as large in the thinking of those who composed and transmitted the traditions contained in the apocryphal acts[124] as it did in the thinking of the apologists, then we could perhaps see here the growth of the idea that the Church is the major miracle, representing God and his power on earth. But, given the gnostic flavor of the apocryphal acts,[125] and the paucity of our knowledge about the conditions of their origin and composition, such an assumption is

---

124. It seems appropriate to speak of "traditions" because of indications, contained in the apocryphal acts, of literary compilation and editing. This is indicated, in addition to the episodic nature of the works, and the patent insertions, e.g., the "Hymn of the Pearl" into the *Acts of Thomas* (§§108–113), by the confusion of geography and characters within some narratives, rather clear indication of combination of traditions, or later literary additions. Such indications are: confusion of characters within a story (*Acts of Andrew*, Vat. 808, §§8, 10; an attempt to repair the confusion, §14; *Acts of John* §§63–73; *Actus Ver.* §28); confusion of detail, with events already narrated forgotten (*Actus Ver.* §32) or changed within the story (*Acts of John* §§71–76). There appears to be the insertion of a wisdom discourse in the *Acts of Andrew*, Vat. 808, §9, within another story, §§8, 104.

125. Phrases that reflect gnostic cosmology and beliefs occur with some regularity within the apocryphal acts we have examined, e.g., John reports that Jesus sometimes had a material, sometimes an immaterial body, and left no footprints when he walked (§93); a youth cannot praise God because it is not in his "nature" (§84); when one understands himself, he understands all (*Acts. Andr.* §6); Paul's opponents affirm that the resurrection of the Christian has already occured (§14); a person must recognize what he was, is now, and that he is to become again what he was (*Acts Thom.* §15); those who realize that the true meaning of Christ's passion and cross is something other than that which is visible, and who withdraw from the material world, will learn the "whole secret" of their salvation (*Actus Ver.* §37, *NTA* 2:319). Such instances could be multiplied many-fold. Along with this is a strong ascetic strain present in all the apocryphal acts here examined, and aimed primarily against sexual intercourse, to the point that a lion, baptized by Paul, refuses to yield himself to the blandishments of a lioness (from a yet-unpublished Coptic papyrus; *NTA* 2:189). A thorough examination of these motifs lies beyond the scope of our present study.

questionable at best. But for whatever reason, the apostles and followers of Jesus emerged in the late second and early third centuries as the
chief workers of miracles.

The assumption, already evident in the apologists, that faith can
be awakened and strengthened on the basis of miracles, bursts into full
flower in the apocryphal acts, and becomes most explicit in the *Acts
of Peter*. The corollary idea, viz. that the competition among wonder
workers to prove whose faith-claims are valid, while appearing with
some regularity, at least in implied form, in the apocryphal acts, seems
not to have been used by the apologists in relation to the miracles of
the apostles and followers of Jesus. Yet the existence of the Church,
for Origen the greatest of miracles, seems to play a similar role in
the apologists' thought. The triumph of the gospel, rather than of the
miracle-working followers of Christ, seems to hold priority of place.

The appeal to prophecy, appearing in the apologists as evidence
for the credibility of Christian miracles, appears only once in the apocryphal acts we have examined, and then in somewhat different application. To Simon's sneering charge that the true God can neither be born
nor crucified, Peter replies that such things fulfill prophecy (*Actus Ver.*
§§23–24). Such an appeal, however, apparently did not commend itself
to the authors of apocryphal tradition as an important way to defend
and differentiate Christian wonders from pagan magic.

There is, finally, an enigma associated with the apocryphal NT
literature, namely the virtually total absence of new miracle stories told
of the mature Jesus. That is true right through the sixth century. Only
the *Gospel of Philip* and the later *Acts of Andrew and Matthias* report
miracles of Jesus not contained in the synoptic accounts, and they total only three. Miracles reported of the apostles, on the other hand,
abound, as we have seen. So do miracles of the period in Jesus' life not
covered in the canonical gospels, viz. his childhood. It has been argued
that this is an indication of the towering importance of the original,
canonical traditions.[126] But this must be quickly modified, since Peter
and Paul, whose activities are covered in the canonical Acts, figure
prominently in the apocryphal traditions. To say the apocryphal acts
fill out gaps in the canonical tradition is less than entirely accurate;

---

126. So Schlingensiepen, *Wunder,* 7–8. Although I did not come upon this study
until I was far along in my own research, I gladly note the similarity of approach and
conclusion in other areas of common investigation.

for example, the *Acts of Peter* tell mostly of Peter in Rome, activity not mentioned, or even hinted at in the canonical Acts, and the *Acts of Paul* give no indication they were understood to take place after his imprisonment in Rome, reported in Acts 28.

Again, to argue that the canonical gospels exercised a greater restraining force on the developing tradition than did the canonical Acts, and that for that reason, no additional miracles are told of the mature Jesus, faces one with the problem that the canonical traditions of Jesus exercised no such restraining force on the sayings of Jesus. But why such selective restraint on the part of the canonical traditions? To argue that the sayings of Jesus were multiplied by gnostics, who cared little for miracle accounts, is rendered less than convincing by the gnostic flavor of the apocryphal acts, where miracle accounts abound. Nor is there any indication in the canonical Gospels that while Jesus said things not there recorded, all of his wondrous acts had been set down.

In fact, the situation is quite the opposite. John 20:30 is an open invitation to the later tradition, an invitation of the kind rarely passed up,[127] to develop additional miracle stories of Jesus, something one would surely have expected if the earlier form critics were correct in their estimate of the origin and direction of the miracle stories in the canonical gospels.[128]

If John 21 be considered the acceptance of the invitation contained in John 20:30 (a miracle is reported in John 21:4–8), one has still to reckon with the same invitation re-extended in John 21:25a. Obviously the author of chapter 21 did not feel he had in any way exhausted that implied invitation. Surely, these two passages in John represent an impulse to tell more stories about the miracles of the mature Jesus. That that "invitation" was not accepted by the framers of apocryphal tradition remains a mystery within the development of Christian tradition in the second and third centuries.

---

127. For example, the time of the presence of the risen Lord on earth could be extended to allow for new teaching, as in the *Pistis Sophia*, where the period covers eleven years. An amusing example of such pretexts for expanding the tradition is to be found in a writing entitled *The Acts of Peter and Andrew*, where Jesus' saying about a camel passing through the eye of a needle (Matt 19:24) becomes an actual miracle Peter is forced to perform to pacify an enraged rich man to whom Peter had quoted that saying.

128. See the comments in n. 105, p. 178 above.

Miracles *in the* New Testament *and the* Greco-Roman World 9

INTRODUCTION

Definition

¶ In a general sense, the word "miracle" can be used to designate any surprising occurrence that defies normal explanation. An
unexpected rescue from dangerous circumstances, or a sudden unan-
ticipated solution to some problem can be termed "miraculous." In a
narrower sense, the word is reserved to designate an event that cannot
be accounted for within the framework of the regularly observed occurrences of the physical world. In this sense, the philosopher Hume
defined miracle as a "transgression of a law of nature."[1] Although the
modern discovery of the statistical character of "laws of nature" means
that such a "transgression" may simply be a statistically highly probable
event,[2] the point at issue remains events that normally do not occur.
For such an event to have religious significance, a further qualification
must be added, namely that the event must be attributable to a deity, and must conform to some purpose the deity has for the world.
Hence, one can differentiate between "wonder" as an "exteriorly veri-
fiable phenomenon" due to "the extraordinary intervention of some
intelligent cause other than man,"[3] and "miracle" as a wonder attributable to the "intervention of a God who is unique and distinct from
the world."[4] It is this latter character of divine purpose that dominates
the understanding of miracles in the Jewish and Christian religious

1. Quoted in Swinburne, *Concept*, 11.
2. For a discussion of this point, see ibid., 2–4.
3. Tonquédec, *Miracles*, 1.
4. Ibid., 3; cf. Swinburne, *Concept*, 6.

literature of the Hellenistic world. Hence, an event that is perceived to set forth God's purposes in a striking way can be termed a "miracle" even if it is performed through some human agency.[5] The key category is thus not the fracture of some "law of nature," however such laws be conceived, but the purpose for which the event, admittedly "beyond" if not "contrary to" nature, occurs.[6] Ordinary events, whatever their results, cannot thus be understood within the category of "miracle," but neither can all extraordinary events be indiscriminately so understood. A "miracle" is therefore some extraordinary event whose origin, even if mediately, can be attributed to a deity, and in which the religious purposes of that deity can be discerned.[7]

Miracles and Magic

The point of origin of the extraordinary event is of primary significance, since many extraordinary events were reported in the ancient world whose origin was not divine but human. Such events were attributed in the Hellenistic world to magical practices, and some consideration of those practices is necessary if we are to form a clear understanding of the way that world understood the nature of magic, so that some differentiation from miracle may be achieved.[8]

Although the period of the highest flowering of the magical arts did not occur until the third to fifth centuries AD, and hence long after the canonical Biblical literature had been produced,[9] there can be no question that magical procedures were known and practiced already in remotest antiquity. Our sources reveal, however, that a clear differentiation between events that are magical in origin, and those that can

5. This is a general point of Talmudic theology; cf. Guttmann, "Significance," 365. Herodotus also seems to have thought of such events as occurring through natural conditions influenced by divine power; cf. McDonald, "Herodotus," 89.

6. See for example Tillich, *Systematic Theology*, 1:114–18.

7. This appears to have been the way Josephus understood "miracle"; cf. MacRae, "Josephus," 136. On this basis, as Guttmann observes ("Significance," 366), revelation would be the most important type of miracle for the biblical times.

8. Some such differentiation was necessary, since the effect achieved by witchcraft or magic could be the same as that achieved by a genuine miracle; cf. Exodus 7:10–12; Guttmann, "Significance," 365.

9. See Hopfner, "λιθικά," 767; Hull, *Hellenistic Magic*, 26–27. For a study of Greco-Egyptian magic, cf. Hopfner, *Griechisch-egyptischer Offenbarungszauber*, 1921; for a study of Jewish magic, cf. Blau, *Zauberwesen*.

properly be called miracles, is difficult to achieve.[10] Neither Homer nor the traditions about Pythagoras show any clear attempt to differentiate between wondrous events that are miraculous in origin, and those that are clearly the result of magical practices.[11] For Lucian of Samosata, many centuries later, there was no distinction at all.[12] Although the Acts of the Apostles in the New Testament clearly oppose magical practices (e.g., Acts 19:18–20), the description of some miracles done by the Apostle Paul show traces of magical elements (19:11–12).[13] This kind of confusion of magic and miracles led the early church fathers to attempts to differentiate the miracles of Jesus, and the acts of others. Irenaeus, though acknowledging the similarity of acts, claims two differences: magicians perform their wonders to glorify themselves, and what they do is not permanent.[14] Justin Martyr argues that while magicians use incantations and various magical herbs, Jesus did not.[15] Origen pointed to the moral reformation brought about by Jesus and his followers, and affirmed that no magician called to similar reformation by means of what he did.[16] Irenaeus added that the miracles of Jesus, unlike the deeds of magicians, fulfill prophecy.[17]

All of this indicates the need to come to clarity on a working differentiation between magic and miracles. Unlike miracles, which are the result of divine activity, and hence inexplicable, magic represents the manipulation of various elements that have known effects on supernatural powers. Magic enables the performer to compel the deity or demon to work the performer's will. It "overcomes and enslaves the divine power to human intention."[18] Underlying the belief that such activity is possible are two fundamental assertions: that the world is full of divine and quasi-divine beings (gods and demons), and that reality

10. On this point, see Hull, *Hellenistic Magic*, 54–61.

11. For a discussion, see ibid., 48, 52.

12. Ibid., 49.

13. Cf. Schüssler Fiorenza, "Miracles, Mission, and Apologetics," 13.

14. Irenaeus, *Haer.* 2.31.2; 3.32.3 on the first point; 2.31.2 on the second.

15. *2 Apol.* 6; *Dial.* 85. This point is also taken up in the apocryphal NT literature; cf. above, "Jesus and the Disciples," 168–69, 177.

16. Origen, *Cel.* 1.68; 2.51.

17. Justin, *1 Apol.* 22–23, 30, 48; *Dial.* 69.

18. Hippocrates, ΠΕΡΙ ΙΕΡΗΣ ΝΟΥΣΟΥ 4.15–16; cf. also Tarn, *Hellenistic Civilization*, 352.

is so constituted that every element in the world has some positive or negative relationship to such divine beings (sympathy/antipathy).[19] If every stone, metal, plant, and animal stand in some sort of positive or negative relationship to the divine being who stands at the head of such a "chain of being," the knowledge of which elements are related to which divinity enables one to attract or repel that deity, and hence to compel it to do one's will.[20] Magic thus consists in such knowledge, and the resulting manipulation of the appropriate elements. If, for example, one wants to compel the god Seth to do one's will, some part of a donkey (skin, hair, milk, blood) will be useful, since that animal stands in the chain of being to which Seth also belongs, and hence can exert a power over him.[21] Similarly, the image of the divinity carved in a stone belonging to that chain of being will render the stone more effective.[22]

For magic to be effective, therefore, one had first to call upon the appropriate divinity within whose range of capability the desired action lay. The next step was to compel the assent of that divinity through placating offerings, and through the manipulation of elements bound to it in sympathetic relationship. Highly important was the final step, in which the divinity was dismissed, lest having performed the act it was compelled to do, it then turn upon the magician.[23] It was for the performance of such acts that the great variety of bizarre and obscure items were necessary, and which are associated with magic down to the present time. The great popularity of astrology in the ancient world was also linked to this understanding of magic, since every planet, understood as a god, ruled not only its own chain of being, but also specific times, right down to the hours of the day, each of which was under the sway of a different divinity.[24]

---

19. Haufe, "Volksfrömmigkeit," 77.

20. For a complete discussion of the role of sympathy/antipathy in Hellenistic magic, see Hopfner, "Mageia," 311–27. For a Hellenistic statement, cf. Eusebius, *Praep. evang.* 4.1.131c–132a (I owe this reference to Hull, *Hellenistic Magic*, 152 n. 84). See further Haufe, "Volksfrömmigkeit," 78–79; Hopfner, "λιθικά," 751–52.

21. Haufe, "Volksfrömmigkeit," 78.

22. Hopfner, "λιθικά," 760

23. See Haufe, "Volksfrömmigkeit," 81

24. Hopfner, "Mageia," 353–357; see also Haufe, "Volksfrömmigkeit," 82ff.; MacMullen, *Enemies*, 139–41.

The roots of Hellenistic magical beliefs and practices are ancient and varied, and reflect the syncretistic outlook that dominated the mentality of that period. The theory of sympathy/antipathy probably originated with the Persians, as did the rudiments of astrology. Their chief religious figure, Zoroaster, had the reputation as their greatest magician, and the Persian language contributed the name to the art ("magi," which meant seer, is the root of the word "magic").[25] A second root lies in Egyptian practices. Unlike most other magic, Egyptian practices were not purely apotropaic, but also sought, in a more positive sense, to compel divine powers to work human desires.[26] To them, Hellenistic magic also owes the idea of the power of words, secret, often meaningless, yet to be repeated over and over if they were to work their compulsion on the divinity who heard them.[27] A third root lies in Jewish practices. Noah reportedly had had a book listing the magical properties of herbs, and Solomon had purportedly written books about the magical properties of all elements.[28] Yet the major contribution of the Jews to Hellenistic magic was the all-powerful name of their deity. Again and again, "Iao," "Sabaoth," and "Adonai" appear in incantations in the magical papyri.[29]

That the Hellenistic world did to some extent strive to achieve a differentiation between miracles and magic is apparent from the vocabulary used in their respective descriptions. Some words were used almost without exception to describe magic and its practitioners, and they carried a negative connotation; γόης, ἀγύρτης, *magicus, ariolus*.[30] There was also an attempt by the Neoplatonic philosophers to differentiate between γοητεία as concerning itself with the lower ranks of demons and θεουργία as being concerned with the higher ranks and the divinity itself.[31] Similarly, the phrase τὰ περίεργα πράσσειν was the

---

25. Hull, *Hellenistic Magic*, 29–30. That the Persians took over the idea of sympathy/antipathy from the Babylonians, see Hopfner, "λιθικά," 749.

26. Hull, *Hellenistic Magic*, 27. The Hellenistic world thought of Egypt as the source of all magic; cf. above, ch. 8: "Jesus and His Disciples," 170–71.

27. Hull, *Hellenistic Magic*, 28.

28. Cf. ibid. 47; Hull draws on *Jub.* 10:12–13. For Solomon, see Josephus, *Ant.* 8.42–59; cf. also Gager, *Moses*, passim.

29. Cf. Blau, *Zauberwesen*, 117–46; Gager, *Moses*, 142–43.

30. MacMullen, *Enemies*, 110.

31. Haufe, "Volksfrömmigkeit," 81.

technical term for deeds of magic.[32] Other, more general words that describe a general, miraculous occurrence—παράδοξος, σημεῖον, τέρας, ἐπιφάνεια—tended to resist inclusion in the vocabulary of magic. Lack of any clear distinctions, however, is indicated by the ease with which "magician" could be used as a pejorative epithet for a wonder-worker whom one opposed, while the deeds of those whom one favored could be attributed to his wisdom or holiness. It was no easier in the Hellenistic world than it is now to draw hard and fast distinctions between miracles and magic, but we may say that if a wondrous event has as its cause the desire of the performer, that it occurs whenever certain rituals are exactly carried out, and that the cause-effect relationship between ritual and event are understood in terms of the sympathy existing within the various chains of being, one has to do with magic.[33]

Forms of the Miracle Story

Healings

While the accounts of wondrous healings told in the Hellenistic world are capable of almost endless variations, three elements belong to this genre, and are present in the overwhelming majority of cases.[34] First, the problem is recited, often in considerable detail, and with emphasis on its difficulty, to which the miracle-worker gives his attention.[35] The problem is frequently accompanied by a request for help, either by the suppliant or his or her companions.[36] Second, the solution by which the problem is resolved is indicated, and may include gestures as well as words on the part of the miracle-worker.[37] Third, proof that the solution has in fact resolved the problem is given, frequently in the form

32. See, e.g., Acts 19:19; cf. Hull, *Hellenistic Magic*, 17.

33. For a similar definition, see Hull, *Hellenistic Magic*, 54.

34. The following description is based on elements described by Bultmann (*Geschichte*, 236–41 = *History*, 218–26), although some elements have been modified. For a recent attempt at a different kind of analysis of New Testament miracle stories, see Theissen, *Wundergeschichten* = *Miracle Stories*.

35. E.g., Mark 5:25–27; 5:2–5; Philostratus *Life* 4.20, 25; Epidauros Stele A: 3, 5, 6 (see Herzog, "Wunderheilungen," 9–11).

36. E.g., Mark 5:23b; 7:32b; 8:22b; Philostratus, *Life* 11108; Epidauros Stele A: 1, 4, 9.

37. E.g., Mark 8:23–25a; John 9:6–7; Philostratus, *Life* 6.27; Epidauros Stele A: 8, 12, 14.

of an action that prior to the solution was impossible: one who was lame now dances, one who was dumb now speaks, one who was dead now walks about and eats, and the like.[38] An element that occasionally accompanies such proof is a reaction on the part of bystanders, confirming that the problem has indeed been successfully resolved.[39] This formal structure is not limited to healings; other kinds of wondrous deeds are also told in this way. Yet this form is most evident in stories of wondrous healings, and for that reason has been included here.

Exorcisms

Accounts of the exorcism of demons form a sub-class of their own. While exorcisms were known already in the thirteenth century BC,[40] further reports of them remain scarce until the Christian era.[41] Virtually absent in Greek literature, they do occur in Jewish writings. In addition to the story of Tobit, who exorcises the demon Asmodius, Josephus tells of one Eleazar who drew demons out through the nose of the victims with a ring containing a root "prescribed by Solomon," who was regarded by Josephus as the originator of the art of exorcising.[42] A further account tells of how Abraham exorcised Pharaoh after Pharaoh had taken Sarah into his harem,[43] but that nearly exhausts the stock of exorcisms prior to the time the gospels were written.

After the first century of the Common Era, however, such accounts proliferate rapidly. The world was filled with demons, and they represented a clear and present danger to all human beings.[44] Since they were arranged in hierarchic importance, it was necessary for the

38. E.g., Mark 5:15; 5:42a; Philostratus, *Life* 4.10; 6.43; Epidauros Stele A: 10, 15, 19.

39. E.g., Mark 7:37; 8:8; Luke 7:16; Philostratus, *Life* 4.20.

40. It concerned the expulsion of a demon by the god Khonsu in the form of his statue; for a discussion, see Hull, *Hellenistic Magic*, 62. For an account of the development of the idea of demons beginning with the time of Homer, see Waser, "Daimon," 2010–12, and the additional article by the same title in Supplementband 3, beginning with col. 267.

41. Hull, *Hellenistic Magic*, 63.

42. Josephus, *Ant.* 8.42–47.

43. Genesis Apocryphon, 20:28–29.

44. See "Daimon" in *PWSB*, 271–77. Even seeing a demon placed one in danger (col. 276, lines 60–61). Demons were also perceived by Jews to be a danger; see Goldin, "Magic," 131 et passim.

exorcist to know the rank of demon possessing the victim, and which demons were more powerful than others. It was generally conceded that demons ranked lower than the gods, but higher than heroes or ordinary humans in power.[45]

A regular form of exorcisms was developed, which has left its mark on New Testament stories of similar activity. The demon was forced to speak, and to give its name; countermeasures were often initiated by the demon.[46] Regular formulae developed by means of which the exorcists commanded the demon to leave (ἀποπομπή).[47] Sometimes the demon simply transferred to another habitat (ἐπιπομπή).[48] Care had to be taken at the time of the exit of the demon, since the victim was in great danger as the demon left,[49] and the exorcist was in danger lest the demon enter him. In all this, control was exercised over demons by the use of certain potent herbs and roots, as well as by the power of certain words and incantations.[50] The names of the more powerful deities were effective, as were phrases in foreign tongues, especially Egyptian, since Egypt was regarded as the natural abode of many demons.[51] Foreign languages were effective, so the rationalization went, since the demon needed to be addressed in its own language.[52] The border between miracle and magic is here all but eliminated in favor of magic, yet the New Testament exorcisms are characterized by a complete lack of the use of any means for exorcisim—drugs, herbs, rings—other than

45. See Hull, *Hellenistic Magic*, 39; Waser, "Daimon," 2011.

46. E.g., Mark 5:9; 1:24; Theissen, *Wundergeschichte* 97 nn. 20, 21; Hull, *Hellenistic Magic*, 69.

47. E.g., the "οἶδα formula"; cf. Bauernfeind, *Worte*, 13–18; Hull, *Hellenistic Magic*, 67–68; Haufe, "Volksfrömmigkeit," 79–80; cf. Mark 1:244. For a command to depart, see Mark 1:25; 9:25; cf. also Pfister, "Dämonologie," 753–58. Departing demons often gave some sign of their departure: cf. Mark 1:26; 9:26; Philostratus, *Life* 4.20; Lucian, *Philops.* 16; Josephus, *Ant.* 8.48.

48. E.g., Mark 5:10–13a.

49. E.g., Mark 1:26; 9:26.

50. Josephus, *Ant.* 8.47; he gives advice on how to extract such roots in *War* 7.180–85; cf. Apuleius, *Metam.* 2.28–29; Lucian, *Philops.* 7.

51. Tobit 8:3; Lucian, *Philops.* 31; Origen, *Cel.* 1.68; 1.38, 46; see also Blau, *Zauberwesen*, 42–43; Pseudo-Calisthenes, *Life* 1.1; *b. Qidd.* 49b; *Midrash Rabbah Exodus* 11.6; *b. Sanh.* 67b; *Shabb.* 104b.

52. Cf. Origen, *Cel.* 1.24; such foreign phrases also occur in miracles of Jesus: e.g., Mark 5:41; 7:31.

words. If one can call the New Testament exorcisms "miracles" instead of "magic," it will be primarily on that basis.

Prodigies

A third kind of miracle, in addition to healings and exorcisms, involved natural forces or substances.[53] The term "prodigy" is perhaps to be preferred to "nature miracles," in part because the latter term has carried the connotation of pejorative judgment on the value of the miracle, in part because such events as in healings and exorcisms, it is not nature, but people who benefit or suffer from the acts. Such events as rescue from perilous seas,[54] wondrous provision of bread,[55] and even the stretching of timbers,[56] reported across the Hellenistic world, occur for the benefit of the people involved, and that is true in the New Testament as well. Again, the absence of such magical practices as incantations or the use of various devices or materials is all that distinguishes such stories in the New Testament from magical practices.

MIRACLES IN THE GRECO-ROMAN WORLD

In order to form a conception of the background against which miracles in the New Testament are to be understood, it is useful to survey the Hellenistic world in which the New Testament was born and for which it was written. We will need to investigate not only the kinds of stories that were told, but also the attitudes, official and popular, toward them. Such a survey will help in placing New Testament miracle stories into a Hellenistic, rather than an anachronistic modern perspective.

Place of Miracles in the Greco-Roman World

The syncretistic tenor of the times combined with the universal Hellenistic culture to ensure than no ethnic boundaries were observed in the telling of magical and miraculous events. Popular stories show up in different times and different places, and while the characters change,

53. Such events were also characteristic of the claims of magicians; cf. Hippocrates 4.

54. E.g., Mark 4:35–41; on Asclepius, see Pietschmann, "Askiepios," 1655; Weinreich, *Heilungswunder*, 14; on Serapis, see Kertelge, *Wunder*, 97 n. 353.

55. Mark 8:1–9; *b. Taʾan.* 24b–25a.

56. *b. Taʾan.* 25a; *Inf. Gos. Thom.* 13 (Latin text, 11).

the plot does not.[57] Common motifs occur and recur, leaving little doubt that belief in, or at least wonder at, miraculous events was universal in the Greco-Roman world.

Universal Scope

Belief in wondrous acts knew no cultural boundaries. Nor is such belief the sole province of the lower classes. If there was some skepticism about such events in the first centuries BC and AD, it gradually faded until in the latter years of the Hellenistic period, doubt had all but disappeared.[58] Plutarch was convinced that because the gods can do great and powerful things, belief in oracles was not only proper but rational.[59] If he rationalized portents from statues,[60] he nevertheless accepted and believed in divination. Pliny the Elder, Nero, and Hadrian all believed in the reality of wondrous events.[61] Josephus, himself one who was credited with miraculous events,[62] tells a story that indicates the extent to which belief passed into gullibility. One Mundus, who desired a high born woman named Paulina, and whose attempt to buy her favors had been spurned, bribed a priest of Isis to tell Paulina that the God Anubis desired to have her in the temple of Isis. Her husband

---

57. E.g., miraculous survival of the bite of a poisonous serpent: *b. Ber.* 33a; Acts 28:3–6; *Inf. Gos. Thom.* 16 (Latin text, 14); Lucian, *Philops.* 11; *Acts Thom.* 33; *(Arab.) Gos. Inf.* 42; an ill man dreams of his own stay of execution, awakes cured, and learns his neighbor died in the night: Lucian, *Philops.* 25; Augustine, *De Cura pro Mortuis Gerenda* 12.15, along with many other versions; see Reitzenstein, *Hellenistische Wundererzählungen*, 4–6 (I owe this reference to Hull, *Hellenistic Magic,* 154 n. 22). The universal belief in astrology provides another example (cf. the discussion of astrology in Haufe, "Volksfrömmigkeit," beginning on 82).

58. Hippocrates denied disease was due to the action of a divinity (4.48–53) and took a generally jaundiced view of wonder-workers of any stripe (2.1–10). Lucian showed his inviolable skepticism again and again (cf. esp. *Philopseudes, Alexander the False Prophet,* and *The Death of Peregrinus*). On the general trend, see MacMullen, *Enemies,* 120–21.

59. Cf. MacKay, "Plutarch," 104 (the reference is to *Coriolanus* 38). Plutarch remained skeptical of freelance diviners, however, 101 (*De Pythiae Oraculis* 407C).

60. MacKay, "Plutarch," 103, 101 (*Coriolanus* 38).

61. See MacMullen, *Enemies,* 120–21. Hadrian was particularly taken by the magician Pachrates, and doubled his salary after a particularly impressive demonstration of power; see MacMullen, *Enemies,* 101.

62. For a good discussion of Josephus' own attitude toward the miraculous, see MacRae, "Josephus," esp. 132–33, 140–41.

agreed, knowing her devotion to Isis and her reputation for chastity, and she spent the night with Mundus who posed as Anubis. The affair had an unhappy outcome. When Tiberius learned of it, he had the priest of Isis crucified, Mundus exiled, the temple razed, and the statue of Isis cast into the Tiber.[63]

Official Attitudes

If belief in miracles was widespread, as was belief in magic (and at times it is difficult to the point of impossibility to differentiate between them), the official attitude of Rome remained nevertheless opposed. Anti-magic legislation, whose foundation was laid by Sulla,[64] reaches back to the Twelve Tables, where some forms of magic (incantations, tampering with a neighbor's fields) were already proscribed.[65] In the Hellenistic period, the official Roman attitude toward magic concerned itself in large measure with those forms of magic that pursued some political intent (e.g., forecasting the date of an emperor's death).[66] Augustus, for example, not only sought to bring divination under control, but attempted as well to forbid prophecy, confiscating books on that subject, and prohibiting their private ownership.[67] Tiberius put a check on the Sibylline oracles,[68] and such attitudes continued through Caracalla and Constantine.[69] Italy was regularly cleared of all persons suspected of performing any sort of occult practices in the period between 33 BC and AD 93,[70] and succeeding emperors regularly renewed the ban on astrologers, which was inaugurated in 138 BC.[71] In such an atmosphere, there was little chance that any fine distinctions between

63. Josephus, *Ant.* 18.65–80.

64. MacMullen, *Enemies*, 125.

65. Cf. the *New Encyclopaedia Britannica, Macropaedia*, 15:1060. It is not clear what form of magic in relation to a neighbor's field was proscribed, whether to bring his crops to ones own field (so Rose, *Roman Religion*, 117), or to destroy the neighbor's crops (MacMullen, *Enemies*, 12L), or to transfer the fertility of the neighbor's field to one's own (Bailey, *Phases*, 14).

66. Haufe, "Volksfrömmigkeit," 82.

67. MacMullen, *Enemies*, 130.

68. Ibid., 126, 125.

69. Ibid., 126, 125.

70. Ibid., 132.

71. Haufe, "Volksfrömmigkeit," 85.

magic and miracles would be drawn. Indeed, for some at least, not only the practice but even belief in such things was to be condemned, since such practices, so it was held, either denied the gods' existence, or were effected by compelling the gods to follow human volition.[72]

A second factor causing the line between miracle and magic to be blurred lay in the practice of accusing one's opponent of magic while affirming miracles on the part of those whom one favored. This occurred on the part of both proponents and opponents of Christianity, for example.[73] Closely allied with that is the attempt to discredit a foe by accusing him or her of practicing magic, since the official attitude toward magic was almost uniformly negative. As a result, accusations abounded against people, prominent and humble, which sought to brand them as practitioners of magical arts. Apuleius stood branded as a magician, accused of having used devious arts in the wooing of Pudentilla, his wife, and was forced to make a long defense.[74] Apollonius of Tyana, of whom many wondrous deeds were reported, was branded a magician, and put on trial for his life on that charge. One purpose at least that motivated Philostratus to compose his life of Apollonius was to defend the latter against the charge that he was a "wizard."[75] While Apuleius would hardly have been termed a miracle-worker even by his friends, the followers of Apollonius may well have made such claims about him. That of course was no defense against accusations of being a magician. Similarly, in the Talmud there are charges that what Jewish heroes did by the power of God, their opponents did by magic.[76] The prohibition against any kind of miracles, even the Bat Qol (voice from heaven), seems to have increased as the power of Christianity grew, until after about AD 90 the general rule was laid down that in matters

---

72. E.g., Hippocrates 4.8–16.

73. E.g., Justin, 2 *Apol.* 6; *Dial.* 85; Irenaeus, *Haer.* 2.32.5; Origen, *Cel.* 1.6, 60; 2.50; 6.40. It is continued in the apocryphal Acts of the Apostles; cf. above, ch. 8: "Jesus and the Disciples," 172–75.

74. See his *Apology*, esp. 2, 42, 90, for the accusations.

75. In 1.2, Philostratus asserts Apollonius' wondrous deeds were due not to magical arts but to his wisdom; cf. also 5.12; 8.7.2. Books 7–8 concern Apollonius' trial and his defense. Hopfner, "Mageia," 383–87 gives many other examples of people hailed into court on the charge of magic.

76. E.g., *b. 'Abod. Zar.* 55a; *Ber.* 59a; cf. Blau, *Zauberwesen,* 30–31 for further examples.

of halakic controversy, no miracle could be cited as evidence.[77] A rabbi whose opinions were confirmed by a heavenly voice was put under a ban, and expelled from the community.[78]

Yet despite such official and unofficial attitudes toward miracles and magic, and their practitioners, belief in both forms of wondrous activity only increased during the Hellenistic period.[79] It is instructive to survey some of the more important sources of miracle stories in the Greco-Roman world.

Miracle Stories in the Hellenistic World[80]

Asclepius

Information about Asclepius is scattered throughout the literature of the Greco-Roman world.[81] The son of a human mother by the god Apollo, Asclepius was raised by the centaur Chiron, from whom he learned the healing arts.[82] Famed for his miraculous cures during his life (he cured blindness, insanity, and a hip wound suffered by Hercules), he was killed by a Jovian thunderbolt when, at Diana's request, he raised Hippolytus from the dead.[83] His fame in the Greco-Roman world of the Hellenistic period was centered on the temple at Epidauros. There were temples at other locations, among them Pergamum and Cos,[84] but

---

77. Guttmann, "Significance."

78. Rabbi Eliezer; see ibid., 386–88.

79. Among the most frequent claimants for miraculous activity were the various apologists for the Christian faith. That is true both of the Fathers as well as of non-canonical Christian literature; on this whole matter, see above, ch. 8: "Jesus and the Disciples."

80. I use the term "Hellenistic" here in the narrow sense of "gentile" or "non-Jewish." Jews of the Greco-Roman world were enormously influenced by outside forces, and can rightly be understood as part of Hellenistic culture at this time. I use the labels "Hellenistic" and "Jewish" for convenience only.

81. This information has been collected by Edelstein and Edelstein, *Asclepius*; cf. also Herzog.

82. Apollodorus, *Bibliotheca* 3.10.3,5—4,1; Scholia in Pindarum, *Ad Pythias* 3.9; material collected in Edelstein and Edelstein, *Asclepius*, 1:3, 54.

83. On his healing acts, cf., e.g., Xenophon, *Cynegeticus* 1.1–6 (Edelstein and Edelstein, *Asclepius*, 1:9, 56); Pietschmann, "Asklepios," 1:7–9, 33 (§3, 54).

84. See Haufe, "Volksfrömmigkeit," 70; the locus at Cos had no miracles associated with it. Pliny describes the kind of material associated with Asclepius at Cos in almost prescription-like form: *Nat.* 20.24.264.

the most famous was undoubtedly at Epidauros. At its height, this area included the temple, dormitories and other outbuildings, and a series of stone steles, recording the wondrous healings that occurred within the temple precincts. Of these steles, three, and parts of a fourth, have been recovered.[85] The steles were of approximately the same size, and the form of the letters, and the regularity of language and content indicate that the material engraved on the steles had undergone some sort of unified recasting.[86] As the first story on stele "A" shows, some at least of these stories were taken from the votive plaques that were left by those who had been healed to commemorate the event and honor the god.[87]

The stories normally tell of the suppliant's coming to the temple, his undergoing the rite of incubation (sleeping within the holy precincts) during which in a dream the healing is foretold or actually occurs, and finally his paying a votive offering. There are exceptions: not all stories concern healings, not all report incubation periods, and not all report votive offerings, but the majority have this form. The purpose of the stories is not simply historical, nor is it merely to awaken amazement at the deeds of Asclepius. The purpose is to give advice to those seeking help: skepticism is out of place, since nothing is beyond help to those who believe;[88] the suppliant should do what the god advises in the dream, when it has occurred; they should pay the proper votive offering when the cure is effected.[89] Other reports of such miracles done by Asclepius are recited in the writings of Aristides, a devoted follower.[90] So famous was Asclepius, in fact, that early Christian authors felt themselves forced to cast aspersions on him, lest by comparison the stories told of Jesus of Nazareth seem repetitious, if not inferior.[91] As late as the fifth century AD, a prayer to Asclepius reportedly healed a young girl over whom physicians had despaired.[92]

---

85. When Pausanius visited Epidauros in AD 165, six still remained; see 2.27.3.

86. So Herzog, "Wunderheilungen," 2.

87. Ibid., 56–57.

88. So ibid., 3, 4, 9.

89. See ibid., 9; some stories do not follow the normal routine, showing that anything happening within the temple area was regarded as a cure by Asclepius, e.g., 8, 16.

90. See, e.g., *Oration* 39.1–18; 42.1–15.

91. E.g., Justin, *1 Apol.* 21, 54; *Dial.* 69; Origen, *Cel.* 111.25.

92. Marinus, *Vita Procli*, ch. 29; Edelstein and Edelstein, *Ascleipus*, 1:322–24.

Apollonius of Tyana

The basic source of our information on Apollonius is the account composed sometime in the early third century AD at the behest of the Empress Julia. Charged with presenting the story of Apollonius' life in a more elegant form than had hitherto been accomplished (I, 3),[93] Philostratus, drawing on earlier accounts,[94] presented a narrative containing stories of Apollonius' travels, his wisdom, his various activities, wondrous and otherwise, and his trial on charges of magic. Since Philostratus is writing with the express purpose of showing that Apollonius' deeds were due to his wisdom rather than to magic (I, 2), we would expect the miraculous elements to be played down. Nevertheless, the picture that emerges of the first-century AD Neopythagorean sage[95] is replete with wondrous acts. Apollonius demonstrates wondrous foreknowledge (IV, 6, 24; V, 13, 18, 24; VI, 32, 39; VIII, 26), is wondrously transported from one region to another (IV, 10; VIII, 10), heals (III, 39; VI, 43), expels demons (III, 38; IV, 20; cf. II, 4), drives away a vampire (IV, 25) and a satyr (VI, 27), recognizes and causes to be stoned a plague-demon in the form of a beggar at Ephesus (IV, 10), raises to life a young girl (IV, 45), and frees, then returns, his leg to its fetters while in prison (VII, 38). He is, in addition, capable of understanding foreign languages, and can speak with animals. To what extent such acts were understood by Philostratus or others to be miracles is no longer recoverable from Philostratus' account. That Apollonius was accused of magic does not prove he so understood himself, or was so understood by his followers. Apollonius' acts, as Philostratus describes them, would probably qualify Apollonius for the title of miracle-worker, given the relative absence of incantations, charms, and other paraphernalia of the full-blown magician.[96]

---

93. All references are to Philostratus, *Life of Apollonius of Tyana*.

94. Written sources: Danis, Maximus, the will of Apollonius; he warns against the books of Moerangenes, which he says are ill-informed (1.3). Philostratus claims also to have visited cities and temples with which Apollonius was associated (1.2).

95. He is reported to have written a biography of Pythagoras; cf. Hempel, "Apollonius," 476. See also Petzke, *Traditionen*.

96. So, at least, Philostratus seems to have thought; cf. 5.11, where Apollonius' foreknowledge was attributed to "a divine impulse" (δαιμονίᾳ) and to "things the gods revealed" (προέγιγνωσκε . . . ἐξ ὧν οἱ θεοὶ ἔφαινον).

Lucian of Samosata

That not all people of the Greco-Roman world accepted or believed wondrous tales is amply demonstrated by the writings of Lucian. He was a tireless debunker of tall tales, and much of his writing is concerned with poking fun at such tales and at those who told and believed them. His "Lover of Lies" (*Philopseudes*) is filled with tales of wondrous deeds, which one of the characters, Tychiades, never tires of questioning with sarcastic remarks and flippant humor. His "A True Story" is a parody of stories of adventures in exotic lands with incredible prodigies, a *genre* that reaches back to the *Odyssey* itself. Indeed, Lucian spares neither Homer nor Herodotus from his acid pen.[97] Whether ancient or contemporary, none are spared Lucian's vituperative attacks on what he sees as the credulity of his age.[98] Yet in his own perverse way, Lucian does throw considerable light on the kinds of stories that circulated, and claimed belief, among so many of his contemporaries. In his "Lover of Lies" we learn of the expulsion of demons (§§16, 31), of a cure effected by the use of divine names (10), of statues that walk by night (§§19, 21), of trips to Hades where the future is learned (§25), of a viper bite cured by incantation and a fragment from a dead virgin's headstone (§11), of ghosts (§§15, 29) and further incantations (§§31, 35), to mention only a few from one of his writings. Despite his own intention, Lucian is a valuable source for the kind of wondrous tales that circulated and found acceptance in the Greco-Roman world.[99]

Apuleius

The most important work of Apuleius for wondrous tales is his Metamorphoses, or The Golden Ass, in which the author has taken the framework of an older plot (cf. Lucian of Samosata, "Lucius, or the Ass") and filled it out with an abundance of tales and anecdotes, many of which display the popular beliefs in magic and wondrous deeds. A dead man is raised (II, 29), a magician's arts are described (III, 16–21), oracular dreams occur (VIII, 8–9), fortunes are told (IX, 8), spirits of the dead appear (IX, 31), prodigies occur that are portents of the future

97. Lucian, *Philops.* §2.

98. E.g., *Dialogues of the Gods, Alexander the False Prophet, Philosophies for Sale,* and *The Death of Peregrinus.*

99. For a discussion of miracle stories in Lucian, see Betz, *Lukian.*

(IX, 34) and there is of course the double metamorphosis of Lucius into an ass, and then into his former self.

Pythagoras

Although Pythagoras pre-dates the Hellenistic period by some centuries, the account of his life by Iambliches does belong to it, and Pythagoras himself enjoyed a widespread reputation as wonder-worker in the Greco-Roman world. Philostratus pictures Apollonius of Tyana as a latter day follower of Pythagoras, a trait that may well be authentic to the historical self-understanding of Apollonius. Pythagoras, as Iamblichus portrays him, displays wondrous foreknowledge (chs. 15, 17, 28, 32), predicts the number of fish in a catch (ch. 8), tames a wild bear and speaks with an ox (ch. 13), experiences a wondrous translocation, expels pestilence, ends rain, calms the seas and remains unharmed by a poisonous serpent (all in ch. 28), and knows incantations that could cure diseases (chs. 29, 34). Whether Iamblichus understood such activity as miraculous or magical is not clear, since he records Phythagoras' ability to cure by ointments (ch. 34), other medicines (ch. 15), and even by music (ch. 15, 25), in the same way as he records healings by incantations. The net effect, however, clearly places Pythagoras in the ranks of wonder-workers admired in the Greco-Roman world.

Others

A number of other writings also contain reports of wondrous deeds and magic formulae, such as the *Natural Histories* of Pliny, and the writings of Plutarch. Large numbers of wondrous stories were brought together in the so-called apocryphal NT writings, particularly the various accounts of the activities of the disciples of Jesus. These Acts, modeled on the Hellenistic "romance," portray the disciples as wonder-workers par excellence, with the ability to perform any and all of the wondrous deeds told of any other person in the Greco-Roman world.[100]

---

100. See above, ch. 8: "Jesus and the Disciples"; the Acts of our period are probably the *Acts of Andrew, Acts of Paul and Thecla, Acts of Peter, Acts of John,* and *Acts of Thomas*. For a general treatment of wondrous acts in this period of the Greco-Roman world, see Haufe, "Volksfrömmigkeit," the section "Heilgötter und Wundermänner."

Miracle Stories in the Jewish World

As in the Hellenistic world, it is often difficult to separate miracles from magic in stories of Jewish wonder-workers. That magical practices were common among Jews in the Hellenistic period is evident from the space devoted to them in the Talmud.[101] Jews also enjoyed a wide reputation in the Greco-Roman world as skilled practitioners of magic.[102] Small wonder that the Talmud stipulates in one passage that no one may be a member of the Sanhedrin unless he had a knowledge of sorcery, not so that he could practice it, but so that he could recognize those who did, and mete out their just punishment.[103] There is a recognizable trend, however, to downplay the miracles of contemporary Jewish wonder-workers that set in about AD 90. Apparently at this time, the polemical activity of the rabbis against Christianity began in full force, and because of the Christian emphasis on miracle, the rabbis undertook to suppress accounts of miracles in their own time.[104] Thus, Torah miracles were held superior to those of Talmudic times, and rather than tell of contemporary wonders, Biblical miracles were expanded.[105] Similarly, miracles are told more frequently of early Talmudic teachers than of later ones.[106] The upshot of this movement was the establishment of the rule that in matters of *halakah*, no miracle could be involved in deciding a dispute.[107]

Unlike miracle stories in Hellenistic sources, the miracles reported in the Jewish tradition were effected by means of prayer. Even in those stories where prayer is not expressly mentioned, the comment on the stories indicates it was presumed to be present.[108] Again, these stories were frequently told for their didactic value, to the extent that on oc-

---

101. E.g., *b. Shabb.* 109b–110b; *Pesahim,* passim; *Git.,* 68a–70a; *Sanh.* 67b–68a; see also Blau, *Zauberwesen,* 27, 64, 97.

102. Cf. Origen, *Cel.* 1.26; Justin, *Dial.* 85; Pliny, *Nat.* 30.11; Juvenal, *Satire* 6.542–47.

103. *b. Sanh.* 17a; *Menah.* 65a; for actions against magic, see *b. Shabb.* 152b; *B. Mes'ia* 107b.

104. See Haight, *Pseudo-Calisthenes,* esp. the discussion beginning on 384.

105. So Guttmann, "Significance," 402, 406.

106. Ibid., 404.

107. Ibid., 392, 405.

108. E.g., *b. Ta'an.* 23a–23b, 25a; *Pesah.* 112b.

casion we do not learn the result of a prayer for a wondrous deed.[109] Obviously, the content of the prayer was the important element.

Whatever differences there may be in the form of the stories of Hellenistic and Jewish miracles, there can be no doubt that like the rest of the Hellenistic world, the Jews too had their famous wonder-workers. It is instructive to examine the stories told of some of them.

Ḥanina ben Dosa

A Galilean of the first century AD, Ḥanina was the subject of a number of miracle stories. At the request of friends, his prayer on two occasions healed those who were ill, in the first instance in the exact moment in which he announced his prayer had been successful.[110] He wondrously foresaw the rescue (by an old man leading a ram) of a young girl from a cistern,[111] and he stopped then restarted rain with his prayers.[112] Bitten by a lizard, he was unaffected, although the lizard promptly died,[113] and he permitted a night demon he met to roam the nights of Sabbaths and Wednesdays, instead of banning her altogether.[114] In a cycle of five stories, Ḥanina's wife had bread miraculously provided in her oven although she was too poor to buy dough; he provided for himself a golden table leg to alleviate his poverty, but when he learned that in the future life while other pious men ate at three-legged tables, his would have but two, he returned it; although his daughter accidentally mixed vinegar with the oil for the Sabbath light, the mixture burned as Ḥanina had said it would; informed that his goats were doing damage, he said that if true, bears should devour them, but if not, the goats should return with bears on their horns, and the latter was the case; when a neighbor building a house discovered the beams to be too short, Ḥanina lengthened them.[115] Typically for rabbinic miracle stories, in each instance

109. *b. Taʿan.* 23b.

110. *b. Ber.* 34b; Ḥanina knew his prayer for healing was answered if it was fluent in his mouth; if it was not, it went unanswered.

111. *b. B. Qam.* 50a; it is also found in *Yebam.* 121b.

112. *b. Taʿan.* 24b; in this instance, the first prayer was motivated by the personal comfort of Ḥanina: when he was outside, he halted the rain. The second prayer was for the good of the world: once he was inside, the rain which benefited others resumed.

113. *b. Ber.* 33a.

114. *b. Pesaḥ.* 112b; this is very similar to the epipompè in exorcisms.

115. *Taʿan.* 24b–25a; the story of the goats is also referred to in *B. Meṣʿia* 106a. For

the effectual agent of the miracle was the holy man's prayer, where not expressed then implied by the comment in the Talmud. It is further clear that many of the stories were told for the teaching to be drawn from them, rather than simply to glorify a miracle-worker. Finally, it is noteworthy that despite his miracle working powers, Ḥanina lived a life of poverty, clearly eschewing self-enrichment through the performance of such acts.

Ḥoni the Circle Drawer

A rabbi from the first century BC, Ḥoni was famous primarily for his successful prayer for rain in a period of drought. Asked to pray for rain, Ḥoni did so unsuccessfully. He then drew a circle around himself and told God he would not move from it until rain came. When the ensuing rain was too little Ḥoni prayed for more, and when that prayer resulted in too much, he prayed a third time and rain fell normally. His later prayer, accompanied by a bullock as sacrifice, caused the rain to cease.[116] Although he is also reported to have slept for seventy years, no further miracle stories are told of him.[117] During the dispute between Aristobulus II and Hyrcanus II, Ḥoni was asked to pray for the success of the forces of the latter. When he refused, he was killed by the mob.[118] One may again note that like Ḥanina, Ḥoni performed his miracle with prayer, but that he refused to pray when he thought the cause unjust.

Other Miracle Working Rabbis

Most of the other miracles told of the rabbis in the Talmud concern successful prayers for rain and their wondrous fulfillment,[119] although some other stories are also recounted. R. Isaac b. Elishab caused the in-laws of R. Mani, at the latter's request, to become poor and then rich, and he caused R. Mani's wife to become beautiful, and then to become

---

a discussion of Ḥanina ben Dosa as miracle-worker, see Vermes, "Ḥanina ben Dosa."

116. *b. Taʿan.* 19a; the story is expanded in *Taʿan.* 23a.

117. *b. Taʿan.* 23a.

118. Josephus, *Ant.* 14.22.

119. E.g., Ḥiyya ben Luliani, *b. Taʿan.* 25a; R. Yonah, *Taʿan.* 23b; R. Ḥanan ha-Nehba, the grandson of Ḥoni the Circle Drawer, *Taʿan.* 23b; Abba Ḥilqiah, also a grandson of Ḥoni, *Taʿan.* 23a–23b; R. Jose caused a fig-tree to produce fruit before it normally would have, *Taʿan.* 24a; for still others, see *Taʿan.* 25a.

ugly once again.[120] R. Mani, annoyed at the persecution he suffered at the hands of certain people, caused the knees of their horses to become stiff as they passed the grave of Mani's father where Mani was praying, and they remained so until the persecutions ceased.[121] The latter part of the Hellenistic age saw the disappearance of such stories told of contemporary rabbis, perhaps, as suggested above, in direct ratio to the number of miracle stories told of the disciples of Jesus of Nazareth.

Moses

Although Moses was of course not a figure of the Hellenistic period, his reputation as a wonder-worker was widely known during that time. Pliny knew of him as a magician (though in his estimate later than and inferior to Zoroaster), as did Apuleius.[122] His reputation rested on two incidents reported in the OT: his connection with the plagues in Egypt, and the revelation to him of the divine name. On the first rests his reputation as a magician,[123] on the second his usefulness to later ages who sought to duplicate his deeds.[124] By the Hellenistic period, he was known as a master magician, an alchemist, and the originator of magical formulae, and a number of writings that concerned magic were attributed to him.[125] His name appears frequently in the magical papyri, evidence of the widespread acquaintance with him and at least some events of his life.[126]

Solomon

The reputation of Solomon for magical arts and miraculous deeds was based in 1 Kgs 4:29–33, where his wisdom in proverbs, and his knowledge of "trees . . . beasts . . . birds . . . creeping things . . . fishes" were interpreted as knowledge of chains of being so familiar to the magical world view. Josephus makes clear that this was the way Solomon was

120. *b. Ta'an.* 23b.

121. Ibid.

122. Pliny, *Nat.* 30.2.11; Apuleius, *Apology* §§90–91; I owe these references to Gager, *Moses*, 138–39.

123. E.g., Josephus, *Ant.* 11.284–87; cf. Hull, *Hellenistic Magic*, 32–33.

124. E.g., Josephus, *Ant.* 11.275; cf. Gager, *Moses*, 144.

125. For an excellent discussion of these points, see Gager, *Moses*, 146–53.

126. For references, see Hull, *Hellenistic Magic*, 32; Gager, *Moses*, 143–44.

understood, and claims to have witnessed the expulsion of a demon by a man following the prescripts of Solomon (*Ant.* 8.42–48). His name also figures in the magical papyri[127] and a book called the "Testament of Solomon" tells how he was able to force demonic powers to aid him in the construction of the Temple, giving detailed descriptions of the various demons and their powers along the way.[128]

MIRACLES IN THE NEW TESTAMENT

Hellenistic Character

As is true in many other respects, the New Testament proves itself a Hellenistic book by the kind and number of miracles it records. The form of the miracle story found in the New Testament, particularly in the Synoptic Gospels,[129] is closer to the pagan than to the Jewish. Jesus is never recorded as having performed a miracle by means of prayer, and he is never remembered as having affected rainfall, a favorite activity of the wonder working rabbis. On the other hand, Jesus is not remembered to have used any kind of incantations, or magical metals or plants in the working of miracles. Yet there are common elements in the New Testament miracle stories and those of the Hellenistic world. Jesus uses saliva in the healing process,[130] his exorcisms contain elements familiar from the Hellenistic world,[131] and in two instances, reports contain reference to foreign phrases.[132] Many wondrous acts are also reported of his followers, and it is clear from them that the name of Jesus soon

127. For references, see Hull, *Hellenistic Magic,* 35.

128. For the Greek text, see McCown, *Testament of Solomon*; for a translation, see Conybeare, "The Testament of Solomon."

129. The "synoptic gospels" are Matthew, Mark, and Luke, so named because of similarities in content and outline. Mark was probably one of the sources used by the authors of both Matthew and Luke. The Gospel of John is different in content and to some extent in outlook from the other three.

130. Mark 7:33; 8:23; John 9:6; cf. Suetonius, *Lives* 7.2–3; Tacitus, *Hist.* 4.81; Pliny, *Nat.* 28.7; *b. Shabb.* 108b; *Sanh.* 49b; *Zebaḥ.* 95b; see also Blau, *Zauberwesen,* 162–63.

131. ἀποπομπή: Mark 1:25; 9:25; ἐπιπομπή: Mark 5:10–13; οἶδα-formula: Mark 1:24.

132. Mark 5:41; 7:31; this is true only of the account in Greek. Since Jesus presumably spoke Aramaic as his native language, Aramaic phrases in his mouth will not have had any magical intent such as that attributed to foreign phrases. Their inclusion does show the influence on these stories of general Hellenistic beliefs, however.

came to be regarded as having great power. It will be useful to look at some of the persons who figured prominently in early Christian records as miracle-workers, and at the stories told about them.

Miracle-Workers

Jesus of Nazareth

The absence of the marks of a magician—incantations, use of magical materials or devices—indicates that we can probably call these deeds miracles, although some of the acts he did were also reported of some magicians. He apparently saw these acts as signs of the inbreaking Kingdom of God that he announced (Luke 11:20; Matt 12:28), although his opponents classed him with magicians who were able to compel the demonic powers to do their will (Luke 11:5; Matt 12:24). This inherent ambiguity in the probative value of miracles makes it unlikely that the wondrous acts of Jesus were created only after the Christian movement confronted similar tales of Hellenistic miracle-workers. They probably belong to the earliest strata of traditions about Jesus. Formally, all but a very few of the miracle stories in the gospels have intrusive theological elements, indicating the need to adapt them to points other than the simple recitation of a miracle.[133] It is likely that the reputation of Jesus as miracle-worker, evident in the gospels, is rooted in the acts of Jesus himself.[134]

The range of miracle stories told of Jesus is great. He healed the paralyzed (Mark 2:1–12), the crippled (Mark 3:1–6; Luke 13:10–16), the blind (Mark 10:46–52; John 9:1–7), and the leprous (Mark 1:40–45; Luke 17:11–19); he healed children (Mark 7:25–30) and adults (Matt 9:20–24); he raised the dead (Mark 5:35–42; Luke 7:11–17; John 11:43–44) and exorcised demons (Mark 9:14–29; Luke 4:33–37; Matt 8:28–34); he wondrously provided bread (John 6:1–15) and wine (John 2:1–11); he killed a fig tree (Matt 21:18–22), stilled a storm (Mark 4:35–41) and walked on water (Mark 6:41–52).[135] Summaries of Jesus'

133. Those formally without theological intrusion are Mark 1:30–31; 8:22–25; for instances of theological intrusion into a miracle story, see Mark 2:1–12; 3:1–6. They are among those most easily recognized, but even such verses as Mark 4:40; 9:23; or Matt 9:29, to give but three examples, are also theological intrusions into the story.

134. On this point, cf. Vermes, *Jesus the Jew*.

135. Some thirty different miracles are reported of Jesus in the gospels. Of those,

activity make it clear that the authors of the gospels understood the stories they reported to be exemplary, not exhaustive (Mark 1:32–34; 3:10–12; 6:56; Matt 21:14; John 20:20). In volume of stories recounted, Jesus was the most prolific miracle-worker in the Greco-Roman world of the Hellenistic period.

The followers of Jesus also have wondrous acts reported of them. Jesus gave such power to his twelve disciples (Mark 3:14–15; 6:7) and to seventy of his followers (Luke 10:9), and the ability to work wonders became one of the identifying marks of a true apostle (2 Cor 12:12; Rom 15:18–19; Acts 2:43; 5:12). The name of Jesus was also early regarded as possessing peculiar power (Matt 7:22–23; Mark 9:38; Acts 3:6; 16:8) although its abuse could bring swift retribution (Acts 19:13–16). Of the followers of Jesus of whom miracles are reported in the New Testament (Stephen, Acts 6:8; Philip, Acts 8:6; Barnabas, Acts 14:3; 15:12), the two who are singled out most are Peter and Paul.

Peter

Although Peter fades from the scene in the later chapters of Acts, he is clearly the dominant figure in the first half of the book. In addition to his preaching and traveling, a number of miracles are attributed to him. He healed a lame man (3:2–10) and a paralytic (9:32–35), he raised a young woman from the dead (9:36–42), and at his curse two people died (5:1–10).[136] So potent was his wondrous power that even those whom his shadow crossed were healed (5:15–16). He was also the recipient of a vision (10:9–16), and twice he was released from prison by an angel (12:6–10; 5:17–20). While there are no trappings of magic in the form of incantations or special substances, the name of Jesus clearly was regarded as capable of causing wondrous events (3:6; 9:34), and the potency of Peter's shadow borders surely on the magical.[137]

---

ten appear in all three synoptics (one of them is also included in John), three are unique to Matthew and Luke; one is unique to Mark, one to Matthew, five to Luke, and four to John.

136. Punitive miracles against people are not reported of Jesus; the one act of this type was directed against a fig tree (Matt 21:18–19).

137. It is clear that, as far as the author of Acts is concerned, there is a great difference between magic and what the apostles do: see Acts 8:18–24; 19:13–16, 19, for evidences of opposition to magic in Acts.

Paul

If Peter dominates the first half of the book of Acts, Paul dominates the second half. He is no less capable as a miracle-worker than Peter. Paul cures a lame man (14:8–10) and casts out a demon from a slave girl (16:16–18), he restores a young man to life (20:9–12), and at his curse, a man becomes blind (13:8–11).[138] His miraculous-potency is demonstrated when kerchiefs that had come into contact with him were able to cure diseases (19:11–12), and others seek to use his name in performing wonders (19:13). He is further the recipient of three visions of Jesus (18:9–10; 22:17–21; 23:11; cf. 2 Cor 12:1) and one of an angel (27:24), and is released from prison with another apostle in a wondrous manner (16:25–26). In addition to these stories, which roughly parallel the stories told of Peter, Paul survived a viper bite (28:1–6), cured a man of fever and dysentery (28:8), and a number of others of various diseases (28:9). He was also capable of wondrous foreknowledge (27:10, 22, 34), something not recorded of Peter. In all of these activities, only one act is attributed specifically to the name of Jesus (16:16–18; cf. a possible second one, in 13:8–11, where "Lord" may be the equivalent of "Jesus"). Paul functions very much like a Hellenistic "divine man" in Acts 27:9—28:10, where he displays wondrous foreknowledge, survives a serpent's bite, and performs wondrous acts. More so than Jesus or Peter, Paul there appears to conform to the image of the Hellenistic wonder-worker.[139]

MIRACLES IN THE APOCRYPHAL NEW TESTAMENT WRITINGS[140]

Several tendencies make themselves felt in the apocryphal New Testament writings. Miracles reported of the mature Jesus virtually disappear from this literature. With very few exceptions, no new miracles are told of him.[141] Miracles reported of Jesus in the canonical gospels

138. That the blinded man was a magician (13:8) is further evidence of Acts' polemic against magic.

139. Other wondrous events in Acts include the foreknowledge of Agabus (11:28; 21:12), appearance of angels to Philip (8:26) and to Cornelius (10:4–7), Philip's healing and exorcisms (8:7) and his wondrous transportation to another area (8:39–40; Cf. Iamblichus, *Life of Pythagoras*, ch. 28); the restoration of Paul's sight (9:17).

140. "Apocryphal" in this instance means gospels, epistles, and accounts of the activities of various apostles that were not included in the NT canon.

141. See *Gos. Philip* §54; *Acts of Andrew and Matthias,* perhaps as late as the sixth

are occasionally summarized,[142] and references are made to him as miracle-worker,[143] but for the most part, new miracles told of Jesus are limited to the so-called "Infancy Gospels."[144] Here Hellenistic imagination ran wild, attributing to the child Jesus a variety of wondrous deeds, but no such imagination worked on the figure of the mature Jesus.

That is not the case with reports of wondrous acts done by Jesus' disciples, however. Both those of whom such events are reported in Acts, as well as those who do not figure in that way in that narrative, have such stories told of them. Peter, Paul, Andrew, John, and Thomas have such works written about them in the Hellenistic period, and while healings in which they participate are somewhat rare, they are frequently reported to have raised the dead.[145] In addition, a variety of other miracles, occasionally punitive, are told of them[146] along with a variety of prodigies[147] and metamorphoses.[148]

The form in which these accounts are cast was borrowed from the literary genre of the Hellenistic world known as the "novel" or "romance." Themes characteristic of this type of literature, unknown to the canonical Acts of the Apostles, are regular components of the apocryphal Acts. Travel to distant and unknown lands, with accounts of prodigies, bizarre events, strange people and their stranger customs, secrets learned via trips to Hades, divine intervention to lighten travel

century AD. For this latter, cf. *ANT,* 283–99.

142. Eusebius, *Hist. eccl.* 1.13.5 (the Agbar legend); *Acts Paul,* P. Heid., p. 79; *Acts Pil.* 1; *Recog. Clem.* 5.10; *Clem. Hom.* 1.6; 2.34; *Gos. Nic.* 4 (20), 10; Justin, *1 Apol.* 22; *Dial.* 69; *Ep. Apos.* 5; cf. Bauer, *Das Leben Jesu,* 364.

143. E.g., Eusebius, *Hist. eccl.* 5.20.6.

144. *Infancy Gospel of Thomas;* there are three healing miracles, four punitive miracles, three raisings from the dead, and six prodigies, including stretching a board otherwise too short. Later variations on this second-century AD work are limited almost entirely to prodigies; see *ANT,* 75–83.

145. *Acts John* §§23, 51, 75, 80, and he empowers another to do it, §§24, 47, 82–83; *Acts Thom.* §§33, 81, and he empowers another to do it, §§53–54; *Acts Pet.* ,§§27, 28, and he empower another to do it, §26; *Acts Paul and Thecla,* Coptic Papyrus no. 1 in Heidelberg, pp. 42, 53–58.

146. See *Actus Ver.* 2 (Paul), 15, 25, 32 (Peter); *Acts Thom.* §§8, 51.

147. See *Acts John* §§42, 60–61; *Actus Ver.* §§2, 22–23 (Paul); 9, 11, 12, 13, 15 (Peter); *Acts Thom.* §§31–32, 39–40, 70, 74; *Acts Paul* §§7, 33, 34 35; this list is by no means exhaustive.

148. These take the form of appearances of Jesus in the form of some other person, e.g., *Actus Ver.* §21; *Acts Paul* §21; *Acts John* §89; *Acts Thom.* §11.

by sea—all are elements present in these Acts.[149] The most striking characteristic, perhaps, is the theme of a couple separated from one another yet remaining true to each other despite great pressures to the contrary. Apostle and companion are united on a spiritual, rather than a physical, level, yet the theme of the woman disciple remaining true to the apostle—despite great pressure against it brought by her husband, lover, and/or family—is a regular theme of these accounts.[150] Clearly, these narratives of the apostles have been adapted to a popular contemporary literary form, with little influence exerted on them either by the form or the content of the canonical Acts, a situation apparently just the reverse of the case of the canonical Gospels and the later picture of Jesus.[151]

149. See Söder, *Die apokryphen Apostelgeschichten.*

150. See *Actus Ver.* 34–36 for Peter; *Acts Paul* §§7–24, 26–40 (Paul); *Acts Andr.* §§4–6; *Acts Thom.* §§82–84., 134–36; *Acts John* §§63–86.

151. For a fuller discussion of this literature, see above, ch. 8: "Jesus and the Disciples."

Acknowledgments

❡ ALL PREVIOUSLY PUBLISHED ESSAYS ARE USED WITH PERMISSION OF the original publishers. The author and publisher gratefully acknowledge these publishers for their permission and cooperation.

"Jesus and the Storm-Tossed Sea" was first published as "Person and Deed: Jesus and the Storm-Tossed Sea" in *Interpretation* 16 (1962) 169–76.

"The Lukan Perspective on the Miracles of Jesus" was first published as "The Lucan Perspective on the Miracles of Jesus: A Preliminary Sketch" in *Journal of Biblical Literature* 95 (1975) 547–62.

"Gospel Miracle Tradition and the Divine Man" was first published in *Interpretation* 26 (1972) 174–97.

"Toward the Isolation of Pre-Markan Miracle Catenae" was first published in *Journal of Biblical Literature* 89 (1970) 265–91.

"The Origin and Function of the Pre-Markan Miracle Catenae" was first published in *Journal of Biblical Literature* 91 (1972) 198–221.

"Miracles and the Historical Jesus" was first published as "Miracles and the Historical Jesus: A Study of Mark 9:14–29" in *Catholic Biblical Quarterly* 37 (1975) 471–91.

"Miracles and Discipleship" was first published as "'And He Followed Him': Miracles and Discipleship in Mark 10:46–52" in *Semeia* 11 (1978) 115–45.

"Jesus and the Disciples as Miracle-Workers in the Apocryphal New Testament" was first published in *Aspects of Religious Propaganda*, edited by Elisabeth Schüssler Fiorenza (Notre Dame, IN: University of Notre Dame Press, 1976) 149–86.

Bibliography

Achtemeier, Paul J. "'And He Followed Him': Miracles and Discipleship in Mark 10:46–52." *Semeia* 11 (1978) 115–45.

———. "Gospel Miracle Tradition and the Divine Man." *Int* 26 (1972) 174–97.

———. *Introduction to the New Hermeneutic.* Philadelphia: Westminster, 1969.

———. "Jesus and the Disciples as Miracle Workers in the Apocryphal New Testament." In *Aspects of Religious Propaganda,* edited by Elisabeth Schüssler Fiorenza, 149–86. Notre Dame, IN: University of Notre Dame Press, 1976.

———. "The Lucan Perspective on the Miracles of Jesus: A Preliminary Sketch." *JBL* 95 (1975) 547–62.

———. *Mark.* Proclamation Commentaries. Philadelphia: Fortress, 1975. 2d ed. Minneapolis: Fortress, 1986. Reprinted, Eugene, OR: Wipf & Stock, 2004.

———. "Miracles and the Historical Jesus: A Study of Mark 9:14–29." *CBQ* 37 (1975) 471–91.

———. "Person and Deed: Jesus and the Storm-Tossed Sea." *Int* 16 (1962) 169–76.

———. "The Origin and Function of the Pre-Markan Miracle Catanae." *JBL* 91 (1972) 198–221.

———. "Toward the Isolation of Pre-Markan Miracle Catanae." *JBL* 89 (1970) 265–91.

Apuleius. *The Golden Ass.* Translated by W. Adlington. LCL. Cambridge: Harvard University Press, 1947.

Bailey, Cyril. *Phases in the Religion of Ancient Rome.* Sather Classical Lectures 10. Berkeley: University of California Press, 1932.

Bammel, Ernst. "John Did No Miracle: John 10:41." In *Miracles: Cambridge Studies in Their Philosophy and History,* edited by C. F. D. Moule, 179–202. London: Mowbray, 1965.

Bauer, Walter. *Das Leben Jesu im Zeitalter der neutestamentlichen Apokryphen.* Tübingen: Mohr/Siebeck, 1909. Reprinted, Darmstadt: Wissenschaftliche Buchgesellschaft, 1967.

Bauernfeind, Otto. *Die Worte der Dämonen im Markusevangelium.* BWANT 44. Stuttgart: Kohlhammer, 1927.

Becker, Jürgen. "Wunder und Christologie." *NTS* 16 (1969–70) 130–48.

Bernard, J. H. *St. John.* Edited by A. H. McNeile. ICC. Edinburgh: T. & T. Clark, 1928.

Best, Ernest. *The Temptation and the Passion: The Markan Soteriology.* SNTSMS 2. Cambridge: Cambridge University Press, 1965. 2d ed., 1990.

Betz, Hans Dieter. *The Greek Magical Papyri in Translation, including the Demotic Spells.* Chicago: University of Chicago Press, 1986.

————. "Jesus as Divine Man." In *Jesus and the Historian: Written in Honor of Ernest Cadman Colwell,* edited by F. Thomas Trotter, 114–33. Philadelphia: Westminster, 1968.

————. *Lukian von Samosata and das Neue Testament: Religionsgeschichtliche und paränetische Parallelen. Ein Beitrag zum Corpus Hellenisticum Novi Testamenti.* TUGAL 76. Berlin: Akademie, 1961.

————. "Ursprung and Wesen christlichen Glaubens nach der Emmauslegende (Lk 24:13–32)." *ZTK* 66 (1969) 7–21.

Bieler, Ludwig. *ΘΕΙΟΣ ΑΝHP: Das Bild des "Goettlichen Menschen" in Spätantike und Frühchristentum.* 2 vols. Vienna: Höfels, 1935–36. Reprinted, Darmstadt: Wissenschaftliche Buchgesellschaft, 1967.

Blau, Ludwig. *Das altjüdische Zauberwesen.* 2d ed. Berlin: Lamm, 1914.

Böcher, Otto. *Dämonenfurcht und Dämonenabwehr: Ein Beitrag zur Vorgeschichte der christlichen Taufe.* BWANT 90. Stuttgart: Kohlhammer, 1970.

Bonner, Campbell. "Traces of Thaumaturgic Technique in the Miracles." *HTR* 20 (1927) 171–81.

Boobyer, G. H. "The Eucharistic Interpretation of the Miracles of the Loaves in St. Mark's Gospel." *JTS* 3 (1952) 161–71.

Branscomb, B. Harvie. *The Gospel of Mark.* Moffatt New Testament Commentary. New York: Harper, 1937.

Brown, Raymond E. *The Gospel according to John.* 2 vols. Anchor Bible 29, 29A. Garden City, NY: Doubleday, 1966–70.

————. "Jesus and Elisha." *Perspective* 12 (1971) 85–104.

Bultmann, Rudolf. *Die Geschichte der synoptischen Tradition.* 3d ed. FRLANT 29. Göttingen: Vandenhoeck & Ruprecht, 1958.

————. *The History of the Synoptic Tradition.* 2d ed. Translated by John Marsh. New York: Harper, 1968.

Burger, Christoph. *Jesus als Davidssohn: Ein traditionsgeschichtliche Untersuchung.* FRLANT 98. Göttingen: Vandenhoeck & Ruprecht, 1970.

Burkill, T. Alec. *Mysterious Revelation: An Examination of the Philosophy of St. Mark's Gospel.* Ithaca, NY: Cornell University Press, 1963.

————. "Strain on the Secret: An Examination of Mark 11:1—13:37." *ZNW* 51 (1960) 31–46.

Carlston, Charles E. "The Things that Defile (Mark VII. 14) and the Law in Matthew and Mark." *NTS* 15 (1968–69) 75–96.

Chadwick, Henry, translator. *Contra Celsum,* by Origen. Cambridge: Cambridge University Press, 1980.

Clavier, Henri. "La multiplication des pains dans le ministère de Jesus." *SE* 1 (1959) 441–57.

Conybeare, F. C., translator. *Philostratus: The Life of Apollonius of Tyana.* 2 vols. LCL. London: Heinemann, 1917.

————. "Testament of Solomon." *JQR* 11 (1898) 1–45.

Conzelmann, Hans. *Die Mitte der Zeit: Studien zur Theologie des Lukas.* BHT 17. Tübingen: Mohr/Siebeck, 1954.

————. *The Theology of St. Luke.* Translated by Geoffrey Buswell. New York: Harper, 1961.

Cranfield, C. E. B. "St. Mark 9:14–29." *SJT* 3 (1950) 57–67.

Cullmann, Oscar. *The Christology of the New Testament*. Rev. ed. Translated by Shirley C. Guthrie and Charles A. M. Hall. NTL. Philadelphia: Westminster, 1963.

———. "The Meaning of the Lord's Supper in Primitive Christianity." In *Essays on the Lord's Supper*, by Oscar Cullmann and F. J. Leenhardt, 5–23. Translated by J. G. Davies. Ecumenical Studies in Liturgy 1. Richmond: John Knox, 1958.

Delling, Gerhard. "Das Verständnis des Wunders im NT." *Zeitschrift für systematische Theologie* 24 (1955) 265ff.

Dibelius, Martin. *From Tradition to Gospel*. Translated by Bertram Lee Woolf. New York: Scribner, 1934. Reprinted, Greenwood, SC: Attic, 1982.

Dieterich, Albrecht. *Abraxas: Studien zur Religionsgeschichte des spätern Altertums*. Leipzig: Teubner, 1891.

Dillmann, A. *Genesis*. 2 vols. Translated by William B. Stevenson. Edinburgh: T. & T. Clark, 1897.

Duling, Dennis C. "Solomon, Exorcism, and the Son of David." *HTR* 68 (1975) 235–52.

Duprez, Antoine. "Guérisons païennes et guérisons évangéliques." *FoiVie* 69 (1970) 3–28.

Easton, B. S. "A Primitive Tradition in Mark." In *Studies in Early Christianity*, edited by Shirley Jackson Case, 83–101. New York: Century, 1928.

Edelstein, Emma J., and Ludwig Edelstein. *Asclepius: A Collection and Interpretation of the Testimonies*. 2 vols. Baltimore: Johns Hopkins University Press, 1945.

Edwards, Richard A. "The Eschatological Correlative as a Gattung in the New Testament." *ZNW* 60 (1969) 9–20.

Eitrem, S. "Heros." In PW 8:1111–45.

———. *Some Notes on the Demonology in the New Testament*. Symbolae Osloenses. Fasc. Supp. 20. 2d ed. Oslo: Oslo University Press, 1966.

Epstein, I., editor. *Babylonian Talmud*. London: Soncino, 1938.

Evans, C. F. *The Beginning of the Gospel: Four Lectures on St. Mark's Gospel*. London: SPCK, 1968.

Fenton, John. "The Order of the Miracles Performed by Peter and Paul in Acts." *ExpTim* 77 (1966) 381–83.

Ferguson, J. "Thoughts on Acts." *Congregational Quarterly* 35 (1957) 117–33.

Fisher, Loren R. "Can This Be the Son of David?" In *Jesus and the Historian: Written in Honor of Ernest Cadman Colwell*, edited by F. Thomas Trotter, 82–97. Philadelphia: Westminster, 1968.

———. "From Chaos to Creation." *Encounter* 26 (1965) 183–97.

Flammer, B. "Die Syrophoenizerin." *Theologische Quartalschrift* 148 (1968) 463–78.

Fortna, Robert Tomson. *The Gospel of Signs: A Reconstruction of the Narrative Source underlying the Fourth Gospel*. SNTSMS 11. London: Cambridge University Press, 1970.

Freyne, Sean. "Hanina ben Dosa." In *Galilee and Gospel: Collected Essays*, 132–59. WUNT 125. Tübingen: Mohr/Siebeck, 2000.

Friedrich, Gerhard. "Die beiden Erzählungen von der Speisung in Mark 6:31–44; 8:1, 9." *Theologische Zeitschrift* 20 (1964) 10–22.

Fuller, Reginald H. *Interpreting the Miracles*. Philadelphia: Westminster, 1963.

Gager, John G. *Moses in Greco-Roman Paganism*. SBLMS 16. Nashville: Abingdon, 1972.

Georgi, Dieter. *Die Gegner des Paulus im 2. Korintherbrief: Studien zur religiösen Propaganda in der Spätantike.* WMANT 11. Neukirchen-Vluyn: Neukirchener, 1964.

———. *The Opponents of Paul in Second Corinthians: A Study of Religious Propaganda in Late Antiquity.* Philadelphia: Fortress, 1986.

Gibbs, J. M. "Purpose and Pattern in Matthew's Use of the Title 'Son of David.'" *NTS* 10 (1964) 446–64.

Ginsburg, H. L., translator. "Ugaritic Myths, Epics, and Legends." In *ANET,* 129–58.

Ginzberg, Louis. *The Legends of the Jews.* 7 vols. Translated by Henrietta Szold and Paul Radin. Philadelphia: Jewish Publication Society, 1913–38.

Glasswell, M. E. "The Use of Miracles in the Markan Gospel." In *Miracles: Cambridge Studies in Their Philosophy and History,* edited by C. F. D. Moule, 149–63. London: Mowbray, 1965.

Goldin, Judah. "The Magic of Magic and Superstition." In *Aspects of Religious Propaganda,* edited by Elisabeth Schüssler Fiorenza, 115–47. Notre Dame, IN: University of Notre Dame Press, 1976.

Goldstein, Morris. *Jesus in the Jewish Tradition.* New York: Macmillan, 1950.

Gordon, Cyrus H. *Adventures in the Nearest East.* Fairlawn, NJ: Essential Books, 1957.

Grant, Frederick C. *Hellenistic Religions: The Age of Syncretism.* New York: Liberal Arts, 1953.

Grundmann, Walter. *Das Evangelium nach Markus.* 2d ed. THNT 2. Berlin: Evangelische Verlagsanstalt, 1959.

Gunkel, Hermann. *Creation and Chaos in the Primeval Era and the Eschaton: A Religiohistorical Study of Genesis 1 and Revelation 12.* Translated by K. William Whitney. Biblical Resource Series. Grand Rapids: Eerdmans, 2006. German ed., 1895.

———. *Genesis.* Translated by Mark E. Biddle. Mercer Library of Biblical Studies. Macon, GA: Mercer University Press, 1997. German ed., 1910.

Guttmann, Alexander. "The Significance of Miracles for Talmudic Judaism." *Hebrew Union College Annual* 20 (1947) 363–406.

Hadas, Moses, and Morton Smith. *Heroes and Gods: Spiritual Biographies in Antiquity.* London: Routledge & Kegan Paul, 1965.

Hahn, F. *Christologische Hoheitstitel.* 2d ed. Göttingen: Vandenhoeck & Ruprecht, 1964.

———. *The Titles of Jesus in Christology: Their History in Early Christianity.* Translated by Harold Knight and George Ogg. New York: World, 1969.

Haight, Elizabeth H., translator and editor. *The Life of Alexander of Macedon.* New York: Longmans, Green, 1955.

Harden, J. A., SJ. "The Miracle Narratives in the Acts of the Apostles." *CBQ* 16 (1954) 303–18.

Harmon, A. M., translator. *Lucian.* 8 vols. LCL. Cambridge: Cambridge University Press, 1947.

Hartmann, Gerhard, SJ. *Der Aufbau des Markusevangeliums.* NTAbh 17. Münster: Aschendorf, 1936.

Haufe, G. "Hellenistische Volksfrömmigkeit." In *Umwelt des Urhristentums,* edited by Johannes Leipoldt and Walter Grundmann, 1:68–100. 3 vols. Berlin: Evangelische Verlagsanstalt, 1965.

Heising, A. "Exegese und Theologie der alt- und neutestamentlichen Speisewunder." *ZKT* 86 (1964) 80–96.

Heitmüller, Wilhelm. "Abendmahl—I. im Neuen Testament." In *RGG*¹, 1:24–38.

Held, Heinz Joachim. "Matthew as Interpreter of the Miracle Stories." In *Tradition and Interpretation in Matthew,* Günther Bornkam et al., 165–299. Translated by Percy Scott. NTL. Philadelphia: Westminster, 1963.

Hempel, Johannes. "Apollonius von Tyana." In *RGG*³ 1:476.

Hennecke, Ernst, and Wilhelm Schneemelcher, editors. *New Testament Apocrypha.* 2 vols. Translated by R. McL. Wilson. Philadelphia: Westminster, 1963.

Herzog, Rudolph. "Die Wunderheilungen von Epidauros." *Philologus,* Supplementband 22.3 (1931) 9–11.

Hopfner, Theodor. *Griechisch-ägyptischer Offenbarungszauber.* Leipzig: Haessel, 1921.

———. "λιθικά." In PW 13:747–69.

———. "Mageia." In PW 27:301–93.

Hull, John M. *Hellenistic Magic and the Synoptic Tradition.* SBT 2/28. Naperville, IL: Allenson, 1974.

Iersel, Bas van. "Die wunderbare Speisung und das Abendmahl in der synoptischen Tradition." *NovT* 7 (1964–65) 167–94.

Jenkins, L. H. "A Markan Doublet: Mark 6:31—7:37, and 8:1–26." In *Studies in History and Religion: Presented to Dr. H. Wheeler Robinson,* edited by E. A. Payne, 87–111. London: Lutterworth, 1942.

Johnson, S. *A Commentary on the Gospel according to St. Mark.* Harper's New Testament Commentary. New York: Harper, 1960.

Keck, Leander E. "The Introduction to Mark's Gospel." *NTS* 12 (1965–66) 352–70.

———. "Mark 3:7–12 and Mark's Christology." *JBL* 84 (1965) 341–58

Kee, Howard Clark. *Miracle in the Early Christian World: A Study in Socio-historical Method.* New Haven: Yale University Press, 1983.

———. *Medicine, Miracle, and Magic in New Testament Times.* SNTSMS 55. Cambridge: Cambridge University Press, 1986.

Kelber, Werner H. *The Kingdom in Mark.* Philadelphia: Fortress, 1974.

Kertelge, Karl. *Die Wunder Jesu im Markusevangelium: Eine redaktionsgeschichtliche Untersuchung.* SANT 33. Munich: Kösel, 1970.

Kingsbury, Jack Dean. "The Title 'Son of David' in Matthew's Gospel." *JBL* 95 (1976) 591–602.

Klostermann, Erich. *Das Markusevangelium.* Handbuch zum Neuen Testament 3. Tübingen: Mohr/Siebeck, 1926.

Knigge, Heinz-Dieter. "The Meaning of Mark." *Int* 22 (1968) 53–76.

Knox, W. L. *The Sources of the Synoptic Gospels.* 2 vols. Edited by H. Chadwick. Cambridge: Cambridge University Press, 1953–57.

Koch, Dietrich-Alex. *Die Bedeutung der Wundererzählungen für die Christologie des Markusevangeliums.* BZNW 42. Berlin: de Gruyter, 1975.

Koester, Helmut. *Die synoptische Überlieferung bei den apostolischen Vätern.* TUGAL 65. Berlin: Akademi, 1957.

———. "One Jesus and Four Primitive Gospel." *HTR* 61 (1968) 203–47. Reprinted in James M. Robinson and Helmut Koester, *Trajectories through Early Christianity,* 158–204. Philadelphia: Fortress, 1971. Reprinted, Eugene, OR: Wipf & Stock, 2006.

Kretschmer, G. "Abendmahl—IV. Liturgiegeschichtlich." In *RGG*³, 1:40.

Lake, Kirsopp, translator. *The Ecclesiastical History* by Eusebius. 2 vols. LCL. Cambridge: Harvard University Press, 1964–65.

Lampe, G. W. H. "Miracles and Early Christian Apologetics." In *Miracles: Cambridge Studies in Their Philosophy and History,* edited by C. F. D. Moule, 203–18. London: Mowbray, 1965.

Lawlor, Hugh Jackson, and John E. L. Oulton, translators and editors. *The Ecclesiastical History and the Martyrs of Palestine.* London: SPCK, 1954.

Lietzmann, Hans. "Abendmahl: IV. Liturgiegeschichtlich." In *RGG²* 1:24–31.

———. *Mass and Lord's Supper: A Study in the History of Liturgy.* Translated by Dorthea H. G. Reeve. Leiden: Brill, 1953.

Linton, Olof. "The Demand for a Sign from Heaven (Mark 8:11–12 and par.)." *ST* 19 (1965) 112–29.

Lohmeyer, Ernst. "Das Abendmahl in der Urgemeinde." *JBL* 56 (1937) 217–52.

———. *Das Evangelium des Markus.* 15th ed. KEKNT 2. Göttingen: Vandenhoeck & Ruprecht, 1959.

———. "Vom urchristlichen Abendmahl." *ThRu* 9 (1937) 168–227, 273–312; 10 (1938) 81–99.

Loisy, Alfred Firmin. *Les évangiles synoptiques.* 2 vols. Paris: Nourry, 1907–1908.

Lucian of Samosota. *Philopseudes.*

Luz, Ulrich. "Das Geheimnismotiv und die markinische Christologie." *ZNW* 56 (1965) 9–30.

Mackay, B. S. "Plutarch and the Miraculous." In *Miracles: Cambridge Studies in Their Philosophy and History,* edited by C. F. D. Moule, 93–11. London: Mowbray, 1965.

MacMullen, Ramsay. *Enemies of the Roman Order: Treason, Unrest and Alienation in the Empire,* Cambridge: Harvard University Press, 1966.

MacRae, George, SJ. "Miracle in *The Antiquities* of Josephus." In *Miracles: Cambridge Studies in Their Philosophy and History,* edited by C. F. D. Moule, 127–47. London: Mowbray, 1965.

Malina, Bruce J. "Assessing the Historicity of Jesus' Walking on the Sea: Insights from Cross-Cultural Social Psychology." In *Authenticating the Activities of Jesus,* edited by Craig A. Evans and Bruce Chilton, 351–71. New Testament Tools and Studies 28.2. Leiden: Brill, 1999.

Marxsen, Willi. "Redaktionsgeschtliche Erklärung der sogennanten Parabel-Theorie des Markus." *ZTK* 52 (1955) 255–71.

Matera, Frank J. "Interpreting Mark—Some Recent Theories of Redaction Criticism." *LS* 2 (1968) 113–31.

McCasland, S. Vernon. *By the Finger of God: Demon Possession and Exorcism in Early Christianity in the Light of Modern Views of Mental Illness.* New York: Macmillan, 1951.

McCown, Chester Charlton, editor. *Testament of Solomon.* Untersuchung zum Neuen Testament 9. Leipzig: Hinrichs, 1922.

McDonald, A. H. "Herodotus on the Miraculous." In *Miracles: Cambridge Studies in Their Philosophy and History,* edited by C. F. D. Moule, 81–91. London: Mowbray, 1965.

Meeks, Wayne A. *The Prophet-King: Moses Traditions and the Johannine Christology.* NovTSup 14. Leiden: Brill, 1967.

Meye, Robert P. *Jesus and the Twelve: Discipleship and Revelation in Mark's Gospel.* Grand Rapids: Eerdmans, 1968.

Meyer, Arnold. "Die Entstehung des Markusevangeliums." In *Festgabe für Adolf Jülicher zum 70. Geburtstag, 26. Januar 1927*, 35–60. Tübingen: Mohr/Siebeck, 1927.

Miller, M. H. "The Character of Miracles in Luke–Acts." Ph.D. dissertation, Berkeley: Graduate Theological Union, 1971.

Montefiore, Hugh. "Revolt in the Desert?" *NTS* 8 (1961–62) 135–41.

Moule, C. F. D., editor. *Miracles: Cambridge Studies in Their Philosophy and History.* London: Mowbray, 1965.

Nineham, D. E. *The Gospel of St. Mark.* London: A. & C. Black, 1968.

Perrin, Norman. *Rediscovering the Teachings of Jesus.* New York: Harper & Row, 1967.

Pesch, Rudolf. *Jesu Ureigene Taten?* Quaestiones disputatae 52. Freiburg: Herder, 1970.

Petzke, Gerd. "Historizität und Bedeutsamkeit von Wunderberichten." In *Neues Testament und Christliche Existenz: Festschrift für Herbert Braun z. 70. Geburtstag am 4. Mai 1973*, edited by Hans Dieter Betz and Luise Schottroff, 367–85. Tübingen: Mohr/Siebeck, 1973.

———. *Die Traditionen über Apollonius von Tyana and das neue Testament.* Studia ad Corpus Hellenisticum Novi Testamenti 1. Leiden: Brill, 1970.

Pfister, Friedrich. "Zur Antiken Dämonologie und Zauberei." *Wochenschrift für kl. Philologie* 27 (1912) 753–58.

Philostratus. *The Life of Apollonius of Tyana.* Translated by C. P. Jones. Edited by G. W. Bowersock. Harmondsworth: Penguin, 1970.

Pietschmann, Richard. "Asklepios." In *PW* 2:1653–87.

Pilch, John J. *Healing in the New Testament: Insights from Medical and Mediterranean Anthropology.* Minneapolis: Fortress, 2000.

Plümacher, Eckhard. *Lukas als hellenistischer Schriftsteller: Studien zur Apostelgeschichte.* Studien zur Umwelt des Neuen Testaments 9. Göttingen: Vandenhoeck & Ruprecht, 1972.

Pseudo-Callisthenes. *The Life of Alexander of Macedon.* Translated by Elizabeth Hazelton Haight. New York: Longmans, Green, 1955.

Räisänen, Heikki. *Das Messiasgeheimnis im Markusevangelium: Ein Redaktionskritischer Versuch.* Schriften der Finnischen Exegetischen Gesellschaft 28. Helsinki, 1976.

———. *The 'Messianic Secret' in Mark.* Translated by Christopher Tuckett. Studies in the New Testament and Its World. Edinburgh: T. & T. Clark, 1990.

Reicke, Bo. *Diakonie: Festfreude and Zelos in Verbindung mit der altchristlichen Agapenfeier.* Uppsala Universitets Arsskrift 5. Uppsala: Acta Universitatis Upsaliensis, 1951.

Reitzenstein, Richard. *Hellenistische Wundererzählungen.* Leipzig: Teubner, 1906. Reprinted, Stuttgart: Teubner, 1963.

Robbins, Vernon K. "The Healing of Blind Bartimaeus (10:46–52) in the Marcan Theology." *JBL* 92 (1973) 224–43.

Robinson, James M. "The Johannine Trajectory." In *Trajectories*, 232–68.

———. "Kerygma and History in the New Testament." In *The Bible in Modern Scholarship*, edited by J. Philip Hyatt, 114–50. Nashville: Abingdon, 1965. Reprinted in *Trajectories*, 20–70.

———. "On the *Gattung* of Mark (and John)." In *Jesus and Man's Hope*, 1:99–129. Pittsburgh: Pittsburgh Theological Seminary, 1970.

———, and Helmut Koester. *Trajectories through Early Christianity.* Philadelphia: Fortress, 1971. Reprinted, Eugene, OR: Wipf & Stock, 2006.

Roloff, Jürgen. *Das Kerygma und der irdische Jesus.* Göttingen: Vandenhoeck & Ruprecht, 1970.

Rose, H. J. *Ancient Roman Religion.* London: Hutchinson's University Library, 1948.

———. "Herakles and the Gospels." *HTR* 31 (1938) 113–42.

Sahlin, Harald. "The New Exodus of Salvation according to St. Paul." In *The Root of the Vine: Essays in Biblical Theology,* edited by Anton Fridrichsen et al., 81–95. New York: Philosophical Library, 1953.

Schenk, Wolfgang. "Tradition und Redaktion in der Epileptiker-Pericope Mark 9:14–29." *ZNW* 63 (1972) 76–94.

Schille, Gottfried. *Die urchristliche Wundertradition: Ein Beitrag zur Frage nach dem irischen Jesus.* Arbeiten zur Theologie 29. Stuttgart: Calwer, 1967.

Schlingensiepen, Hermann. *Die Wunder des Neuen Testaments: Wege und Abwege ihrer Deutung in der alten Kirche bis zur Mitte des fünften Jahrhunderts.* Beiträge zur Förderung christlicher Theologie, 2. Reihe: Sammlung wissenschaftlicher Monographien 28. Gütersloh: Bertelsmann, 1933.

Schmidt, Karl Ludwig. "Abendmahl—I. im Neuen Testament." In *RGG*² 1:10–12.

———. *Der Rahmen der Geschichte Jesu: Literarkritische Untersuchungen zur ältesten Jesusüberlieferung.* Berlin: Trowitzsch, 1919. Reprinted, Darmstadt: Wissenschaftliche Buchgesellschaft, 1964.

Schmithals, Walter. *Wunder und Glaube: Eine Auslegung von Markus 4:35—6:6a.* BibSt 59. Neukirchen-Vluyn: Neukirchener, 1970.

Schneemelcher, Wilhelm. *New Testament Apocrypha.* Rev. ed. 2 vols. Translated by R. McL. Wilson. Philadelphia: Westminster, 1991–92.

Schulz, Siegfried. "Die Bedeutung des Markus für die Theologiegeschichte des Urchristentums." *TUGAL* 87 (1964) 135–45.

———. *Die Stunde der Botschaft: Einführung in die Theologie der vier Evangelisten.* 2d ed. Hamburge: Furche, 1967.

Schüssler Fiorenza, Elisabeth. "Miracles, Mission, and Apologetics: An Introduction." In *Aspects of Religious Propaganda,* 1–25.

———, editor. *Aspects of Religious Propaganda.* Notre Dame: University of Note Dame Press, 1976.

Schweizer, Eduard. "Das Abendmahl eine Vergegenwärtigung des Todes Jesu oder ein eschatologisches Freudenmahl?" *TZ* 2 (1946) 81–101.

———. "Abendmahl—I. im NT." In *RGG*³, 1:16.

———. *Das Evangelium nach Markus.* NTD. Göttingen: Vandenhoeck & Ruprecht, 1967.

———. *The Good News according to Mark.* Translated by Donald H. Madvig. Richmond: John Knox, 1970.

———. *Jesus.* Translated by David E. Green. Atlanta: John Knox, 1971.

———. *Jesus Christus: Im vielfältigen Zeugnis des Neuen Testaments.* Munich: Siebenstern Taschenbuch, 1968.

———. "Mark's Contribution to the Quest of the Historical Jesus." *NTS* 10 (1963–64) 421–32.

Smith, D. Moody. *The Composition and Order of the Fourth Gospel: Bultmann's Literary Theory.* Yale Publications in Religion 10. New Haven: Yale University Press, 1965.

Smith, Morton. "Prolegomena to a Discussion of Aretalogies, Divine Men, the Gospels and Jesus." *JBL* 90 (1971) 174–99.

Snoy, Th. "La Redaction marcienne de la marche sur les eaux (Mc. VI 45–52)." *ETL* 44 (1968) 205–41; 433–81.

Söder, Rosa. *Die apocryphen Apostelgeschichten und die romanhafte Literatur der Antike.* Würzburger Studien zur Altertumswissenschaft 3. Stuttgart: Kohlhammer, 1932. Reprinted, 1969.

Speiser, E. A., translator. "Akkadian Myths and Epics." In *ANET*, 60–119.

Spronk, Klaas. "Rahab." In *Dictionary of Deities and Demons in the Bible*, edited by Karel van der Toorn, 684–86. 2d ed. Leiden: Brill, 1999.

Stauffer, Ethelbert. "Antike Jesustradition and Jesuspolemik im mittelalterlichen Orient." *ZNW* 46 (1955) 2–30.

———. "Zum apokalyptischen Festmahl in Mc. 6:34ff." *ZNW* 46 (1955) 264–66.

Suhl, Alfred. *Die Funktion der alttestamentlichen Zitate und Anspielungen im Markusevangelium.* Gütersloh: Mohn, 1965.

Sundwall, Johannes. *Die Zusammensetzung des Markusevangeliums.* Acta Academiaae Aboensis. Humaniora 9.2. Abo: Abo Akademi, 1934.

Swinburne, Richard. *The Concept of Miracle.* New Studies in the Philosophy of Religion. New York: St. Martin's, 1970.

Tagawa, Kenzo. *Miracles et Evangile: La Pensee Personnelle de L'Evangeliste Marc.* Etudes d'Histoire et de Philosophie Religieuses 62. Paris: Presses Universitaires de France, 1966.

Tarn, W. W. *Hellenistic Civilization.* Revised with G. T. Griffith. 3d ed. London: Arnold, 1952.

Taylor, Vincent. *The Gospel according to St. Mark.* New York: St. Martin's, 1955. 2d ed., 1966.

Theissen, Gerd. *The Miracle Stories of the Early Christian Tradition.* Translated by Francis McDonagh. Philadelphia: Fortress, 1983.

———. *Urchristliche Wundergeschichten: Ein Beitrag zur formgeschichtlichen Erforschung der synoptischen Evangelien.* Studien zum Neuen Testament 8. Gütersloh: Mohn, 1974.

Thraede, Klaus. "Exorcismus." In *Reallexicon für Antike und Christentum* 7:44–117.

Tillich, Paul. *Systematic Theology.* Vol. 1. Chicago: University of Chicago Press, 1951.

Tonquédec, Joseph de, SJ. *Miracles.* Translated by F. M. Oppenheim, SJ. West Baden Springs, IN, 1955. Originally "Miracle," in *Dictionnaire Apologétique de la Foi Catholique*, 517–78. Paris: Beauchenese, 1926.

Uehlinger, Christoph. "Leviathan." In *Dictionary of Deities and Demons in the Bible*, edited by Karel van der Toorn, 511–15. 2d ed. Leiden: Brill, 1999.

Vermes, Geza. "Hanina ben Dosa." *JJS* 23 (1972) 28–50; 24 (1973) 51–64.

———. *Jesus the Jew: A Historian's Reading of the Gospel.* New York: Macmillan, 1974. Minneapolis: Fortress, 1981.

Waser, Otto. "Daimon." In *PW* 4.2:2010–12.

Weeden, T. J. "The Heresy that Necessitated Mark's Gospel." *ZNW* 59 (1968) 145–58.

Weinreich, Otto. *Antike Heilungswunder.* Religionsgeschichtliche Versuche und Vorarbeiten 8. Giessen: Töpelmann, 1909. Reprinted, Berlin: de Gruyter, 1969.

Weiss, Johannes. *Das älteste Evangelium: Ein Beitrag zum Verständnis des Markus-Evangeliums und der ältesten evangelischen Überlieferung.* Göttingen: Vandenhoeck & Ruprecht, 1903.

Wiegand, G. "Abendmahl: II. Dogmengeschichtlich." *RGG*² 1:15.

Wiles, M. F. "Miracles in the Early Church." In *Miracles: Cambridge Studies in Their Philosophy and History,* edited by C. F. D. Moule, 219–34. London: Mowbray, 1965.

Wilkinson, John. "The Case of the Epileptic Boy." *ExpTim* 79 (1967) 39–42.

Wilson, R. McL., translator. *The Gospel of Philip.* New York: Harper & Row, 1962.

Wrede, William. "Jesus als Davidssohn." In *Vorträge und Studien,* 147–77. Tübingen: Mohr/Siebeck, 1907.

Wright, F. A. *A History of Later Greek Literature from the Death of Alexander in 323 B.C. to the Death of Justinian in 565 A.D.* London: Routledge, 1932.

Wünsch, Richard. "Zur Geisterbannung im Altertum." In *Festschrift zur Jahrhundertfeier der Universität zu Breslau,* 9–32. Schlesische Gesellschaft für Volkskunde, Breslau, Mitteilungen 13–14. Breslau: Marcus, 1911.

Ziener, Georg. "Das Brotwunder im Markusevangelium." *Biblische Zeitschrift* 4 (1960) 282–85.

Index of Ancient Documents

∾

OLD TESTAMENT APOCRYPHA & PSEUDEPIGRAPHA

∾

~

RABBINIC LITERATURE

Mishnah

Babylonian Talmud

Midrash Rabbah
Exodus

Other

∾

GRECO-ROMAN
WRITINGS